'One of these dramas, is it?' asks Bartholo in *The Barber of Seville*. 'More modern rubbish!' The grasping, goatish old doctor can see little enough to admire in an era of 'free-thinking, magnetism, electricity, religious tolerance, inoculation, quinine, Diderot's *Encyclopaedia* and dramas'. But to men of the establishment the length and breadth of Europe, Beaumarchais' great comedy seemed on its first performance in 1775 to constitute the crowning offence of an outrageous age.

As for Figaro, he was a revolution all to himself. With a song in his heart and a quip for every occasion, Beaumarchais' lyrical barber still had a clear, sceptical eye for the abuse and hypocrisy of a corrupt regime. The willing servant of the Count's every whim, his street-smart wit showed plainly enough where the moral mastery lay. Radicals might inveigh as they liked against the evils of the existing order but Figaro was more dangerous by far. Their most savage denunciations bounced ineffectively off the aristocracy's armour of arrogance; his easy sharpness punctured the windy pomposities of power. Their complaints could never hope to penetrate the pride of the ruling class, but his hilarious humour spread the uncontainable sedition of laughter.

Large as life and twice as irreverent, Figaro returned to the stage in 1784, when *The Marriage of Figaro* was given its first performance. France's rulers were more scandalised than ever by his cheery impudence, and when five years later the storming of the Bastille heralded the regime's final collapse, there were many who blamed the barber for the cataclysm. Yet like his creator, Figaro was far too intelligent for dogmatism, far too perceptive to trust in politics for the solution of humanity's most fundamental problems. No dreamy Danton, neither was he capable of a Robespierre's fanaticism, and as the tumbrils rolled and jubilation gave way to terror, Figaro's mood darkened. His third and final appearance in
continued on back flap

continued on back flap

£20.00 in UK only

THE FIGARO PLAYS

BEAUMARCHAIS

THE FIGARO
PLAYS

Translated by
JOHN WELLS

Edited by
JOHN LEIGH
University of Cambridge

J. M. Dent London

First published in Great Britain in 1997
by J. M. Dent

© 1997 John Wells
The moral right of John Wells to be identified as the author
of this work has been asserted in accordance with
the Copyright, Designs and Patents Act of 1988

A CIP catalogue record for this book
is available from the British Library.

ISBN 0 460 87923 5

Consultant editor for this volume
Timothy Mathews
University College London

Typeset by SetSystems Ltd, Saffron Walden, Essex

Set in 10.5pt Sabon

Printed in Great Britain by
Butler & Tanner Ltd, Frome and London

J. M. Dent

Weidenfeld & Nicolson
The Orion Publishing Group Ltd
Orion House
5 Upper Saint Martin's Lane
London, WC2H 9EA

CONTENTS

NOTE ON THE AUTHOR

PIERRE-AUGUSTIN CARON DE BEAUMARCHAIS was born in Paris in 1732 as Pierre-Augustin Caron. He became an apprentice in his father's watchmaking workshop and, at the age of twenty-one, devised a new escapement. His invention was disputed but the Academy of Sciences found in his favour. In the first of three marriages, he wedded an aristocrat, taking the name of her property, Beaumarchais, and taught music to Louis XV's daughters at the court. He was embroiled in legal battles when he challenged the heir of his mentor, the financier Pâris-Duverney, and then accused the judge of the case, Goëzman, writing four *Mémoirs à consulter* in defiance. He travelled frequently to Europe on secretive diplomatic missions, making use of a trip to Spain to avenge his sister whom a Spaniard Clavigo had promised and failed to marry, an episode which was to become the subject of a play by Goethe.

Amid all these activities Beaumarchais began his own career as a playwright. The dramas *Eugénie* (1767) and *Les deux Amis, ou le négociant de Lyon* (1770) were followed by his first real success, *Le barbier de Séville* in 1775. Its sequel, *Le mariage de Figaro*, which was only performed in 1784 once bans had been lifted and Beaumarchais released from prison, was eagerly anticipated and rapturously received. His subsequent works, the opera *Tarare* (1787) and the final part of the Figaro trilogy, *La mère coupable* (1792) were less successful.

Meanwhile Beaumarchais continued to be active on other fronts. He founded the Société des auteurs dramatiques to protect the rights of authors, and set about publishing the works of Voltaire. He encouraged French support of the Americans in the War of Independence and sought to supply arms from Holland. Such actions qualified him as a patriotic Revolutionary, even though he had a sumptuous house built opposite the Bastille. As the Revolution progressed, however, Beaumarchais was imprisoned, indicted and then exiled to Hamburg. He returned to Paris in July 1796, crippled with debts. He died in 1799.

JOHN WELLS taught modern languages at Eton and has since worked in the theatre as a translator, actor and director. A co-founder of the satirical magazine *Private Eye*, he played the lead in his own farce, *Anyone for Denis?* based on the *Dear Bill Letters*, written with Richard Ingrams.

JOHN LEIGH is a Fellow of Fitzwilliam College, Cambridge and University Assistant Lecturer who specialises in eighteenth-century French literature.

CHRONOLOGY OF BEAUMARCHAIS' LIFE

Year	Age	Life
1732		Born Pierre-Augustin Caron, Paris, 24 January
1745	13	Leaves school in Alfort to start apprenticeship as watchmaker with his father
1753	21	Invents new escapement for watches, an idea copied by Lepaute, a famous watchmaker. Protests to the Académie des sciences
1754	22	The Académie des sciences finds in his favour
1755	23	Becomes Clerk Controller of Royal Household
1756	24	Marries recently widowed Madeleine-Catherine Franquet, 27 November
1757	25	Takes the name Beaumarchais from property belonging to his wife
		Death of his wife, 30 September

CHRONOLOGY OF HIS TIMES

Year	Artistic Events	Historical Events
1733		War of the Polish Succession
1737	Marivaux, *Les Fausses confidences*	
1740	Richardson, *Pamela*	Reign of Maria Theresa (1740–80) Reign of Frederick II (1740–86)
1741	Handel, *Messiah*	War of the Austrian Succession
1742	Voltaire, *Mahomet*	
1746	Diderot, *Pensées philosophiques*	
1748	Montesquieu, *Esprit des lois*	Treaty of Aix-la-Chapelle
1749	Buffon, *Histoire naturelle* (1749–89)	
1750	Rousseau, *Discours sur les sciences et les arts*	
1751	First volumes of the *Encyclopédie* Gray, *Elegy Written in a Country Churchyard*	
1755		Lisbon Earthquake
1756	Mozart born	Seven Years War (1756–63)
1757	Diderot, *Le Fils naturel*	

Year	Age	Life
1758	26	Death of his mother, 17 August
1759	27	Maître de musique and teacher of harp to the daughters of Louis XV
1760	28	Endears himself to Pâris-Duverney, the great financier, by arranging for the king to visit the École militaire, his pet project
1761	29	Buys position of *secrétaire du roi*, thereby acquiring a title of noblility
1762	30	
1763	31	As 'lieutenant-général de la capitainerie de la Varenne du Louvre', judges cases of poaching on the king's land Engaged to Pauline LeBreton, a Creole
1764	32	In Madrid, as emissary of Pâris-Duverney to negotiate commerce with the Spanish. Pursues Joseph Clavijo, who had agreed to marry but subsequently abandoned Lisette, Beaumarchais' sister
1766	34	Breaks engagement with LeBreton With Pâris-Duverney, founds a company to exploit forest of Chinon. His valet absconds with profits
1767	35	*Eugénie* performed at the Comédie–Française, 29 January Writes *Essai sur le genre dramatique sérieux*
1768	36	Marries Geneviève-Madeleine Levêque, a wealthy widow, 11 April Birth of a son, Augustin, 14 December
1770	38	*Les Deux amis ou le négociant de Lyon* performed at the Comédie-Française, 13 January Pâris-Duverney dies, 13 July. Accused by La Blache, his heir, of falsifying documents. A trial follows Death of his wife, 20 November
1772	40	Wins case against La Blache, but faces appeal Death of his son, 17 October
1773	41	Altercation with the Marquis de Chaulnes. Imprisoned in the For-l'Evêque, 26 February Pays a bribe to Mme Goëzman, wife of the judge in his trial who nonetheless judges in favour of La Blache. Attacks Goëzman in *Mémoires à consulter*
1774	42	In London as secret agent. Pursues to Vienna Angelucci-Atkinson, the supposed author of a pamphlet on the sterility of the marriage of Louis XVI and Marie-Antoinette.
1775	43	*Barber of Seville* performed in five acts, 23 February. Not well received. A success when performed in four acts, 26 February
1776	44	Entrusted by the government to send aid to the American insurgents against the English

Year	Artistic Events	Historical Events
1759	Voltaire, *Candide* Johnson, *Rasselas*	
1760	Sterne, *Tristram Shandy* (1760–7)	Reign of George III (1760–1820)
1761	Rousseau, *La Nouvelle Héloïse*	
1762	Rousseau, *Du Contrat social*	Reign of Catherine II (1762–96)
1763	Marivaux dies	
1764	Voltaire, *Dictionnaire philosophique* Walpole, *The Castle of Otranto*	Dissolution of Jesuits in France
1766	Goldsmith, *The Vicar of Wakefield*	
1770		Maupeou reform of Parliament
1773	Goldsmith, *She Stoops to Conquer*	Boston Tea Party
1774	Gluck, *Orphée* Goethe, *Die Leiden des jungen Werthers*; *Clavigo*	Louis XV dies Louis XVI begins reign
1775	Sheridan, *The Rivals*	American War of Independence begins
1776	Gibbon, *Decline and Fall of the Roman Empire* Smith, *The Wealth of Nations*	American Declaration of Independence

Year	Age	Life
1777	45	Birth of a daughter, Eugénie, to Marie-Thérèse Willermaulaz, 5 January
		Equips a fleet transporting provisions and arms to America
		Founds the Société des Auteurs Dramatiques
1779	47	Purchases rights and undertakes to publish the Complete Works of Voltaire in Kehl
		His ship, the *Fier Roderigue*, is destroyed by the British in battle
		Writes the *Observations sur le mémoire justificatif* in reply to an attack by Gibbon
1780	48	Creates the Société littéraire et typographique
1782	50	Adapts Voltaire's *Samson* as an opera
		First performance of Paisiello's opera, *The Barber of Seville*, St Petersburg
1784	52	First performance of *The Marriage of Figaro* at the Comédie–Française, 27 April
		Creates with the proceeds an institution for nursing mothers
1785	53	Incarcerated in Saint-Lazare for allegedly insulting the King in a letter in the *Journal de Paris*
		Marie-Antoinette plays Rosine in a performance of *The Barber of Seville* at Versailles, 19 August
		Founds the Compagnie des Eaux to provide running water for Paris. Attacked by Mirabeau for the project
1786	54	Compromised by the Kornman affair
		Mozart completes *Marriage of Figaro* based on Lorenzo da Ponte's libretto
1787	55	Has a sumptuous house built, opposite the Bastille
		Performance of *Tarare*, opera to music by Salieri
1789	57	Wins case against Kornman and his lawyer, Bergasse
		Elected president of Blancs-Manteaux district, Paris
1790	58	Tarare turned into a constitutional monarch for a new version of the play, 3 August

Year	Artistic Events	Historical Events
1777	Sheridan, *The School for Scandal*	
1778	Voltaire dies Rousseau dies	
1779	Lessing, *Nathan der Weise*	
1781	Schiller, *Die Räuber*	
1782	Rousseau, *Confessions* Laclos, *Les Liaisons dangereuses*	
1783		Peace of Paris ends American War of Independence
1784	Schiller, *Kabale und Liebe*	
1789		Fall of the Bastille
1791	Mozart dies Sade, *Justine* Boswell, *The Life of Samuel Johnson*	Louis' flight to Varennes

Year	Age	Life
1792	50	*A Mother's Guilt* first performed at the Théâtre des Marais Ministry of War entrusts him with purchase and transfer of 60,000 muskets stored in Holland Arms suppliers have him arrested and imprisoned Liberated after intervention of the mistress of the Procurator Flees to London. Jailed there for debts
1793	61	Returns to France but under threat as a proscribed *émigré* Mozart's *Marriage of Figaro* opens in Paris, 20 March Publishes his *Six époques* to defend himself in trying to obtain muskets. Departure for Holland again
1794	62	Seeks refuge in Hamburg. Wife and daughter imprisoned in Paris. Thérèse is forced to divorce him
1796	64	Returns to Paris, crippled by debts
1798	66	Death of Julie, Beaumarchais' sister
1799	67	Death of Beaumarchais, 17/18 May Buried in garden of his home
1822		Remains are transferred to Père Lachaise cemetery

Year	Artistic Events	Historical Events
1792	Rossini born, 29 February	Fall of Monarchy; Battle of Valmy; declaration of republic Revolutionary calendar introduced
1793		Execution of Louis XVI The Terror (1793–4)
1795	Goethe, *Wilhelm Meister* (1795–6)	The Directory (1795–9)
1798	Jane Austen, *Northanger Abbey* Wordsworth, *Lyrical Ballads* Schiller, *Wallenstein* (1798–9)	*Coup d'état* brings Napoleon to power
1816	Rossini, *Il Barbiere di Siviglia*	

INTRODUCTION (1)

I think the only major row we had at the National Theatre in 1970 when we put on Beaumarchais' original stage play of *The Marriage of Figaro* was over the question of Figaro's English accent. The director Jonathan Miller had commissioned me to translate it, and when we came to think about how Figaro would have talked in English I started telling stories about the Cockney photographer Terry Donovan.

Donovan, then a young Jack-the-Lad of great intelligence and charm, had been to the City to raise money for a film he wanted to make called *Yellow Dog*. Afterwards he had described the tiny black leather notebook in which the upper-class banker took notes during his sales pitch. When they came to discuss interest rates the banker had drawled 'Shall we say ten per cent to make it easier with the mathematics?' and Donovan had come back quick as a flash, 'Why don't we say seven an' a 'arf per cent an' *struggle* with the mathematics?'

Both Jonathan Miller and Gawn Grainger, who was playing Figaro, liked the idea, and the character seemed to crackle into life in rehearsal as an enterprising street-trader from the East End of London. Then the theatre authorities arrived to see a run-through, talked about the dignity of a major role in the French classical repertoire, and Figaro became rather more bourgeois.

I still clung to the idea of Figaro as a man of the people.

I heard a story more recently about the board of a small English opera company. They had put on a successful performance of Mozart's *Marriage of Figaro*, were discussing their programme for the coming year, and one less sophisticated member of the board asked why they didn't do a second run of 'the one about the hairdresser'.

All three of these plays are about the same man, but the name Figaro has somehow grown such a thick crust of operatic respectability that we have stopped thinking of him as a hairdresser. We think of him only as a figure in a tie-back wig and a bullfighter's costume, speaking or singing in a foreign language: a charming cultural antique like a pearl-handled cut-throat razor.

But Figaro is still capable of drawing blood.

Even in the Second World War the stage-play of *The Marriage of Figaro* was considered inflammatory enough to be banned by the Nazi authorities throughout the German Occupation of France, and long before Mozart or Rossini took an interest in them all three of these plays had a violent life of their own. This was largely due to the reputation of their author, Pierre-Augustin Caron de Beaumarchais, who had begun life as a watchmaker. It is worth bearing this in mind when examining the construction of his plots, moving, as they do, like clockwork.

Beaumarchais was born in 1732, plain Pierre-Augustin Caron. His father made clocks in Paris, and by the time Caron Junior was twenty-one he had managed, by developing a new balance-wheel, to make a watch so small it would fit inside a ring. He presented it to Marie-Antoinette, sued the court watchmaker who tried to pirate the design, replaced him and became a favourite at Versailles, giving music lessons to the royal princesses.

At court he also married what he thought was a rich widow; in fact she turned out to have no money, but she brought him a title: de Beaumarchais.

Ingenious academics have pointed out that his original title as a watchmaker, Mr Caron Junior, could have given him the name of his main character: *fils* in those days being pronounced *fi*, 'fils Caron' would have sounded very like Figaro. As it was, Figaro became Beaumarchais' spokesman on stage, and the three plays represent a kind of autobiography.

Like Figaro, Beaumarchais as a dramatist began his life in Spain when he was in his early thirties. Until then he was an international business-man, working for a French financier with extensive interests both in Europe and America. Always dabbling in espionage, he was on a secret mission to Madrid when he originally saw the so-called *entremeses* or after-dinner entertainments in private houses that gave him the characters of the comic Spanish barber and the comic *sacristan* who was later to become Don Bazile.

His official reason for being in Madrid was to rescue his sister, who had been seduced and abandoned by a journalist called Clavijo. Determined he should marry her, Beaumarchais arrived in disguise, found Clavijo, struck up an acquaintance with him and began to tell him a long story about an unfortunate French girl betrayed by her Spanish lover. He described to Clavijo how the girl's brother travelled to Madrid to avenge her, and then, throwing back his cloak, proclaimed, 'I, Sir, am that brother!' Goethe thought it was such a good story when he read it in the newspaper in Weimar that he wrote a play called *Clavigo*, but it was only one of a hundred such dramatic episodes in Beaumarchais' own life.

Beaumarchais' first two serious plays, *Eugénie* (1767) and *Les Deux amis* (1770), reflected his character at that time as a successful and slightly smug member of the middle class, dealing as they did in sentimental notions of decent behaviour. They were not a success.

It was in the early 1770s that a series of public scandals stripped Beaumarchais of his complacency and revealed the real Figaro: the tough tradesman's son who had fought his way to the top.

The financier he worked for died, leaving him all his money; Beaumarchais had to spend a lot of time in court beating off rival claimants. The case was settled in his favour, but his major enemy, La Blache, appealed against the judgement. This was followed by a battle over a woman between Beaumarchais and the Marquis de Chaulnes. The Marquis, an absurdly fat man who went about with a monkey on a chain, attacked Beaumarchais in public, tearing his wig off and scratching his face; there was a fight with a knife, and both of them were put in prison.

Meanwhile La Blache's appeal was coming up, and Beaumarchais took the precaution of bribing the wife of the judge who was due to try the case, a man called Goëzman. He sent her a hundred louis and a jewelled watch. In spite of this Goëzman gave judgement in favour of La Blache, and Madame Goëzman very decently returned the watch. She also sent back eighty-five louis, having paid fifteen to the judge's clerk.

Beaumarchais, with the gambler's daring recognisable in such flamboyant chancers even in our own day, publicly demanded the return of the missing fifteen louis, and the court bankrupted him.

Unabashed, he conducted a pamphlet war against Goëzman and his wife for taking the bribe in the first place, and had at least the satisfaction of seeing the judge sacked. Beaumarchais then moved to London until the scandal had died down.

However dented his official reputation may have been in Paris, he was still clearly well thought of in French secret service circles, and trusted by the king. He took a house in Sloane Street, between Knightsbridge and Chelsea – we know the address from a wallpaper sample still in the possession of his descendants – and went to work as a spy for the French government. One of his great friends at the time was the famous Chevalier d'Eon, then gracing the drawing-rooms of Mayfair as a lady of fashion, only occasionally pulling up his skirts to show his battle scars.

The Barber of Seville opened in Paris in 1775, its success enhanced by the author's notoriety, while he divided his time between his espionage job in London and the undercover supply of guns to General Washington, fighting against the British with the help of French military advisers in the American War of Independence. He was never paid for these consignments, and according to one estimate the United States Government still owes him nine million dollars.

In his own preface to the first play, Beaumarchais confesses that the plot of *The Barber of Seville* was a traditional one: his only contribution was to make the characters more intelligent and resourceful.

Figaro, in the stock story of the young lover who rescues a beautiful girl from the hands of an old man, plays the familiar character of the hero's valet. But Figaro is not only more intelligent and more resource-ful, he also has the independence of spirit of the stock Spanish character, the itinerant barber. He has rejoined the Count of his own free will.

That freedom and independence is still more evident in the second play, *The Marriage of Figaro*, even though Figaro and Suzanne are now members of the Count's household.

Written at a time of social unrest that would culminate in the Revolution, *The Marriage of Figaro* was banned by the censor who read the script. Apparently about an indecisive Spanish count who has abolished the *droit de seigneur* and who still wants to have his absolute way with his wife's maid Suzanne, it seemed all too clearly to echo the story of an indecisive king who had allowed a measure of liberal reform and still wanted his absolute way with the French people.

Louis XVI himself rather touchingly told Beaumarchais he would have to demolish the Bastille before the play could be performed without embarrassing the government. As always Beaumarchais fought, organising a semi-public reading at Versailles with a cast that included members of the Royal Family.

Betraying the same fatal indecisiveness, the king gave permission for an amateur performance, allowed Beaumarchais to rehearse for four weeks, and then cancelled it. A few months later he authorised a single performance at a country house. Marie-Antoinette was to have been there, but sent apologies at the last minute.

The publicity campaign was now unstoppable. Beaumarchais challenged the six official royal censors to a public meeting attended by privileged members of Parisian society, going through the play line by line and incorporating any witty suggestions from his fashionable audience as they went along. Madame de Matignon was credited with choosing the colour for Chérubin's ribbon. Beaumarchais continued to abuse the censors, and the king finally ordered his arrest.

Rich friends clubbed together to pay his bail; the king changed his mind again, allowed the play to be performed and the author to be released. Beaumarchais sent a message to say he refused to leave the prison until he had an assurance that the entire Cabinet would attend the first night 'as a gesture of respect to the author'.

Such colossal cheek deserved success, and the opening night at the Comédie-Française in April 1784 was one of the most remarkable in the history of any theatre. Aristocrats paid enormous amounts of money to the actors to be allowed to sleep in their dressing rooms the night before to be sure of getting a seat, and one man who died in the crush in front of the stage during the first act stayed propped upright until the interval, the audience being packed so closely together that it was impossible to get him out any sooner.

Even in his triumph, Beaumarchais was determined to drag up the bribery scandal, paying off a final score to Goëzman by putting him on stage as the foolish stammering judge.

The censor's fears, like those of the Nazi High Command more than 150 years later, were perfectly well-founded: a play that engaged the sympathies of the audience for the servants against the masters was a threat to stable government, and historians mark the first night of *The Marriage of Figaro* as a major milestone on the road to the Revolution.

In the Rothschild Collection at Waddesdon Manor is the desk which Beaumarchais commissioned, following the success of the play, for his new mansion opposite the Bastille. An elaborate and ornate piece of furniture, it is inlaid with the title pages of his works, 'by Citizen Caron de Beaumarchais'.

Citizen Figaro, like Citizen Caron de Beaumarchais, dreamed of a liberal future, of a constitutional monarchy like the household of Aguas Frescas, where they would live in an easier harmony under a benign regime that would respect the dignity of every individual, servant or master alike.

He could hardly have imagined that five years later the old stone fortress he could see through the trees at the end of his garden would be sacked, order entirely overturned, two thousand years of Christian civilisation wiped off the calendar with the declaration of a new Year 1, or that his inlaid desk would be put up as a prize in a state raffle – the ticket is still in the drawer – by the revolutionaries who had cheered his play, or that he himself would be swept into exile in Hamburg where he narrowly escaped with his life.

The final play, *A Mother's Guilt*, was written at the height of the Terror and performed at the Comédie-Française in 1792. By this time all the old liberal illusions have been shattered. Aguas Frescas, the Countess's garden and the grove of chestnuts is sold up and gone; wigs and white stockings have given way to cropped heads and pantaloons; the scented night of romance has given way to a grey dawn of reality, and past infidelities are coming home to roost. An older and more conservative Figaro is left to save his old master and mistress from the Terror, represented by another real-life enemy, a Parisian lawyer called Bégearss, in the role of an Irish villain, an alien force that threatens the utter destruction of the already battered Almaviva family.

It is, apart from being Napoleon's favourite play, one of the first melodramas, with music from the pit sustaining the emotional climaxes and marking dramatic moments, the direct forerunner of a whole race of twentieth-century films and television dramas. During the past 150 years it has rarely been performed. It deserves a sympathetic revival, even if it is not possible to realise Beaumarchais' dying wish that all three plays, 'the whole history of the Almaviva family', should be performed on consecutive evenings. We did admittedly succeed in granting his wish in 1984, when we broadcast the three plays on BBC Radio 3, with Dorothy Tutin as Rosine.

Beaumarchais finally fled the country in 1794, remaining in Hamburg for two years. He returned to a hugely successful revival of *A Mother's Guilt*, and was still devising new money-making schemes – regular commercial air-travel by balloon, a new system to supply Paris with fresh water, and a complete edition of Voltaire using Baskerville's type that he had bought up in England – when he died in his sleep of apoplexy, dreaming perhaps of some new and terrible enemy, in 1799, on the eve of the nineteenth century.

JOHN WELLS

INTRODUCTION (2)

'These days, the general rule is if a line's not worth saying, sing it.'[1] Figaro's observation in *The Barber of Seville* voices an assumption with which Beaumarchais' plays, more familiar to many as operas, appear to have been received. The fame of Mozart's and Rossini's musical adaptations seems not always to have recommended the achievement of the playwright. Yet Beaumarchais owes his reputation largely to these operas which have eclipsed his plays, for the final part of his trilogy, *A Mother's Guilt*, which only became an opera much later, remains largely forgotten.[2]

The three plays excited spectacular reactions, of indignation as much as delight, when they were performed in the eighteenth century, and were soon recognised as influential pieces by contemporary audiences and censors. Their subversive impact is incontestable. Beaumarchais has been identified as one of the many causes of the French Revolution. But his plays should not simply be regarded as a historical curiosity to be conserved in a museum of theatre. So many of Figaro's comments levelled ostensibly at the specific characteristics of 'these days', like that quoted above, have retained or acquired a more general relevance. If some of the satirical pungency has necessarily faded, the virtuosity of the plays continues to render them provoking. These plays engage with problems and personalities which are sometimes parochial or transitory, and they are adapted to the changing tastes of their audiences, but the satire and spirit which perhaps guaranteed their impact then are accompanied by reflections which should endear them to us now. Each play is self-sufficient, but also the component of a trilogy which in its totality exposes more clearly Beaumarchais' earnest attempts to integrate comedy and drama, youth and age, music and morals, and to offer us insights into the complexities of form. All this remains well worth singing *and* saying.

The audacity of Beaumarchais' challenges to authority is still remark-
able. His theatre reflects the tensions of a turbulent century. Born in
1732 when memories of the tyranny of Louis XIV were still stinging,
dead a decade after the storming of the Bastille, Beaumarchais is one of
few important figures who predate, perhaps precipitate, the Revolution
and succeed in surviving it. The vanguard of Enlightenment thought,
Voltaire, Diderot and Rousseau, unhelpfully died before the Revolution,
leaving generations of critics to guess what they would have made of
the events which purported to draw on their ideas. It is nevertheless not
completely clear what Beaumarchais thought of the Revolution or
indeed what it made of him. The brazen revolutionary zeal which
informs his theatre is tempered by a more sober, somewhat disillusioned
awareness of the limitations of human nature and the difficulties in
making good the achievements of innovation.

The very first thing we see in *The Barber of Seville* is a watch. Count
Almaviva, who pulls it out of his pocket as he walks on to the stage,
remarks that time has not moved on as much as could be expected. This
play, like the two which follow, insists on the need to move with the
times. The watchmaker is restlessly aware of time ticking on. Bartholo's
disapproval of inoculation and the *Encyclopédie*, among a litany of
eighteenth-century achievements introduced or applauded by the *phil-
osophes*, signals that the archetypal opposition of good and evil integral
to comedies is to be understood as a battle between an innovative
enlightenment and a retrograde *ancien régime*.[3] The former is validated
unequivocally here. The *philosophes* struggled to reform France which
was toiling under the sway of absolute monarchy and a formidable
Church. Champion of American Independence, publisher of Voltaire,
Beaumarchais shares the impatience of the thinkers of the French
Enlightenment. The play is confident and coherent. Although,
unusually, *The Barber of Seville* was shorn to four acts, it remains
essentially traditional. It is probably indebted to the *parades* and may
have existed in this form prior to its incarnation in five and then four
acts. Comedies end in marriage and Beaumarchais' plays move oblig-
ingly to this conclusion. Their dénouements provide reassuring closure.
Bartholo is vanquished. The Count gets his girl. Figaro will marry. But
the trilogy obeys a sense whereby endings can only be provisional. The
scrutiny of marital fortunes in the succeeding parts of the trilogy induces
a more cautious, complicated view of the artifice of conclusions. With
the exception of Figaro and Suzanne, these comedies of marriage seem
to be succeeded as much by hangovers as honeymoons.

The Marriage of Figaro is as vigorously revolutionary as *The Barber of Seville*, and was an instant *succès de scandale*. *The Marriage of Figaro* was, in the words of Napoleon, the revolution in action already, even if it was written at the behest of a well-placed aristocrat, the Prince de Conti. Whereas the Count was spared the barber's most cutting remarks in the previous play, here he becomes the principal butt of the satire. *The Marriage of Figaro* is altogether more dangerous and disconcerting in the way it forces us to revise our assumptions. Its form is more anarchic, in part because of the way it reshuffles the characters we thought we knew from *The Barber of Seville*. By this second play, the relationships between the protagonists of the previous play are compromised, their achievements complicated. The polarity of good and evil is for a start disturbed by the introduction of many more characters. The introduction of Chérubin, one of those seemingly marginal characters who turn out to be central, adds another dimension to the comedy. Poised on the boundary between childhood and maturity, he embodies the delicacy of moving with the times. It is time to move from the 'château d'Espagne', a fictional fantasy world which is retrograde and unreasonable, although, like the name of the castle, Aguas Frescas, this world connotes a transparency and security which the modern age appears to cloud. Figaro is summoned from 'sleepy, easy-going Spain', the land of romantic fantasies and quixotic illusions, to England, the undisputed seat of modernity in the eighteenth century, the home of reason and cynicism, epitomised by the imprecation 'God Damn!' which the English growl all the time.[4]

The Marriage of Figaro is pulled between Spain and England, *ancien régime* gallantry and cynical enlightenment; Chérubin is in some ways the central character at the frontiers between these states. Chased into this mature, uncertain world, neither boy nor man, he embodies the impossible coalescence of opposites which Beaumarchais strives to achieve in his theatre. One of the supreme achievements of Mozart and Da Ponte is the recognition of the importance of Chérubin whose arias are among the most memorable. Given the fate that awaits him, a fate revealed to us later in *A Mother's Guilt*, Mozart's glorious martial trumpets which call and claim him are endowed with an added poignancy. Beaumarchais dreams of synthesising the gravitas of the adult with the exuberance of youth, or as he says in the preface to *A Mother's Guilt*, of uniting male reason and female ardour to form what he calls a 'moral hermaphroditism'. These plays about marriage try then to achieve a more radical union. Chérubin is both man and woman or neither, innocently cherubic yet also 'a libertine in embryo' who continually anticipates the Count and appears in his place.[5] He embodies an ideal but ultimately elusive harmony of opposites.

But Chérubin is doomed to destruction. *The Marriage of Figaro* is a play already tainted with disillusion. Enlightenment means ridding oneself of delusions and illusions, but this healthy step towards achieving clarity of reason threatens the vitality of the theatre and the comic illusions which are its mainstay. *The Marriage of Figaro* tries to account for the developing thought and changing mores of the century by integrating a more uncomfortable moral dimension alongside the uninhibited *joie de vivre* of *The Barber of Seville*. The dramatic action is thus interrupted by Figaro's lengthy soliloquy in Act V and Marceline's tirade in Act III which burst the traditional bounds of a comedy. The Comédie-Française has regularly omitted this non-theatrical element while Da Ponte had no place for the lengthy expression of such sentiments. The illusion of a coherent fantasy gives way to an exhibition of artifice. The play is contorted into an extraordinary sequence of events, as reunions, scenes of confused identity and moral outbursts multiply. Misshapen and tortuous, *The Marriage of Figaro* is inhabited by different conflicting impulses which are never quite allowed to mesh. Music and morality, satire and sport compete and pull the play in different directions.

In the midst of this confusion, Figaro, a sort of surrogate playwright who plots and pulls the strings, is himself upstaged and he confesses to losing the thread. An inscrutable fate seems to mock his efforts. Events no longer simply take an unpredictable turn. They are now bizarre. Just as Figaro loses his way, so the play seems to follow an erratic course of its own. The length and detail of the prefaces testify to Beaumarchais' desperate attempts to control and explain the messages of his plays but also perhaps betray an implicit recognition that they seem to take on a rather wanton life of their own. As Beaumarchais claims in the preface to *The Marriage of Figaro*, he is not so much the master as the painter of his characters.[6] Like Figaro, the plays are abandoned to a world in which they have to make their own uncertain way and yet there results something positive from the vicissitudes which have to be undergone. Figaro, like Chérubin, is frustrated that he cannot accede to an essential self. Dissimulation and mistaken identity are familiar comic conventions exploited fully here, but they are embroidered with the additional notion that fate hides us from ourselves. Figaro has recesses unfathomable even to himself. While the first play envisages him as 'the Barber', the ingenious valet type familiar from Molière, here in its sequel he is Figaro and only Figaro, endowed with unique properties, solitary in his

confusion. However comical and implausible, the reunion scene trans-
forms Figaro from a stock valet to a human being in search of identity
just as it transforms Marceline into a serious character.

Marceline wrongfoots the audience to which she is the archetypal
hiss-boo character when she suddenly becomes the eloquent and impas-
sioned spokesperson for her sex. The comical attributes of a self are
significantly relativised by its age and gender. Beaumarchais' depiction
of women constitutes what has been called the other revolution in his
theatre.[7] His plays show a world for which one should not be nostalgic,
where women are often at the mercy of men and the comic resolution
of marriage barely disguises ongoing tragedies. Characters who look
good turn out to be bad. By the beginning of the *Marriage* Almaviva
has become a figure more like Bartholo trying to forestall the sort of
marriage he earlier contrived for himself. The dashing hero becomes a
cynical older man. Similarly, while Beaumarchais retains the familiar
satirical butts of the satirist, notably lawyers and doctors, even Bartholo
is endowed with some sense denied usually to the traditional caricature.

Just as Figaro has been decoded as fils Caron, it is difficult to resist
viewing the personality of Figaro as a sort of biographical anagram of
Beaumarchais. The bastard's discovery of his parents has for instance
been said to correspond to the watchmaker's projected integration into
the higher echelons of society. Nevertheless, Figaro is as comprehensible
and no less moving without recourse to biographies of Beaumarchais.
Correlations between play and biography risk simplifying the lively and
unpredictable vision of character which the play depicts. Beaumarchais
eschews the representation of a single central character. His personages
seldom incarnate a single attribute, like avarice or misanthropy *à la*
Molière, but the constituents of character are themselves under ques-
tion. Between and even within the plays character is seldom unitary but
changes in ways which often upset our assumptions and sympathies.

Accordingly, the third play, *A Mother's Guilt*, shifts the emphases
and changes the tone. It opens in a decidedly new age, measured by new
dates. It was written and first performed in Year 1, as 1792 was to be
known in the revolutionary calendar. Allusions to divorce and the
abolition of titles, the enthusiasm for liberty and even a bust of George
Washington, situate the action of the play unmistakably in the post-
revolutionary period. Once again, however, Beaumarchais accommo-
dates innovations but not without misgivings. The Revolution has
occurred, but it has not abolished the past.

In his famous essay *What is Enlightenment?* Kant answered his own
question by arguing that Enlightenment was a process which resulted in

the attainment of maturity. But Beaumarchais regrets that growing up seems to mean growing old. Maturity is not achieved without a little wistful retrospection. Wordsworth enthuses that, at the time of the Revolution, 'to be young was very heaven', but Beaumarchais shows that to be old is more difficult.[8] He is also uneasily aware of that which is lost to the past. Wordsworth's blissful dawn represents more of a twilight for Beaumarchais. Time has again moved on. The joyous strains of music are dulled. The comic and satiric arsenal is used more sparingly, as Beaumarchais attempts to construct a serious model, though he cannot resist transforming an adversary of his into the deceitful Bégearss. Laughter must make way for mature reflection. *A Mother's Guilt* represents a bid to assert order and achieve reconciliation in an age of confusion. An unusual geometric pattern governs the plot. Flaubert remarked that in every revolutionary there is a policeman. The morality which sat somewhat awkwardly alongside the wit in *The Marriage of Figaro* prevails, as Beaumarchais tries to integrate the innovations of eighteenth-century dramatists, particularly those promoted by Diderot. But again he looks back. Figaro, a bastard, owes nothing to authority or patriarchy. He is a secular hero and Anonymous is his only patron saint, he boasts to Brid'oison in the court scene, before discovering that he is actually called Emmanuel.[9] But we are reminded again and again that the action in *A Mother's Guilt*, confined to a single day like *The Marriage of Figaro*, takes place on the feast of Saint Leo. On this day the guilty Rosine secretly thinks of Chérubin who was killed in battle and is lionised as Léon – his real name. At odds with the adoption of the new age and its idioms, she is emotionally and nostalgically governed by the old calendar. The past cannot be expunged entirely. Guilt represents the incursion of the past into the present. Rosine's misdemeanours catch up with her, as Marceline's past error resurfaces.

The scene opens shrouded in mournfully dark colours. *All That Trouble for Nothing*, the play within *The Barber of Seville*, had been described as a picture of spring.[10] Rosine's name evokes flowers and helps to convey an optimistic emergence into the light from the dark and the cold. Now a distinctly autumnal feeling pervades the play. But it turns out to be an Indian summer. Flowers are everywhere, we are informed by a stage direction in this play, first performed, in revised form, in the month of Floréal.[11] As its actual title, *The New Tartuffe*, suggests, the drama aims to rejuvenate Molière and appeal to a time before the Revolution. The play's happy ending also ties up different thematic knots with the past. Just as Léon's name recalls his lost father, so Florestine, whom he marries at the end, guarantees a coherence with Rosine. Florestine allows Rosine to atone and flourish. The resonances of the names, like the persistence of the stock characteristics of Tartuffe, afford a sense of continuity with the past which the revolution seemed to have ruptured. The optimistic blossoming it promises paves the way also for a generation of floral women in the following century, without, for now, the complications with which Violetta and her sisters will be tainted.[12]

The trilogy carries us from Spain to France and through the Revolution, pitching modern thought against grand old fantasies. Youth gives way to age as comedy seeks to integrate morality. Revolutionary, but sensitive to the less glamorous by-products of revolution, Beaumarchais' theatre is spontaneous but increasingly reflective. The trilogy conducts a search for a form suitable to mediate these conceptions. Changes in thought and history had implications for the theatre which sought to embrace and develop these progressions. When we first see Figaro in *The Barber of Seville* he seeks but cannot find the optimal rhyme for the verses he is composing. In the three plays the playwright undertakes a perhaps similarly frustrated quest for a perfect form which can give expression to different imperatives. The plays are distinct and autonomous but the echoes which unite them and the interstices that separate them afford further insights. Read as a trilogy, the plays allow a sense of consecutive development, but they expose also the formal adjustments which Beaumarchais tries to effect in tumultuous years of change. The watchmaker's trilogy urges us to move with the times, but reminds us of the difficulties that accompany age and enlightenment, for ultimately it is perhaps only in the frustrations of uncertainty that maturity can be enjoyed and liberty achieved.

JOHN LEIGH

References

1. See *The Barber of Seville*, p. 4.
2. Darius Milhaud's opera, *La mère coupable*, adapted from Beaumarchais by Madeleine Milhaud, was performed in 1965, while John Corigliano's *The Ghosts of Versailles*, a grand *opéra bouffe* in two acts 'suggested' by *A Mother's Guilt*, was commissioned by the Metropolitan Opera for its centenary in 1991.
3. Voltaire wrote an essay, *Conformez-vous aux temps*, in December 1764, urging France to make reforms and keep pace with other nations.
4. See *A Mother's Guilt* (p. 154) for the reference to Spain and *The Marriage*

of Figaro, Act III (p. 104) for the reference to England. Spain was widely regarded as backward by the rest of Europe. Only the French Revolution seems to have woken it from its slumbers. See Richard Herr, *The Eighteenth-Century Revolution in Spain* (Princeton University Press, 1958), pp. 435–44. Meanwhile these plays are responsible for propagating a French image of Spain, further romanticised in the nineteenth and twentieth centuries by the *Carmen* of Merimée and Bizet and Massenet's *Don Quichotte*.

5. Robert Niklaus, *Beaumarchais: Le Mariage de Figaro* (London: Grant & Cutler, 1983, p. 47).

6. See p. 238.

7. See Michel Delon, 'Beaumarchais et l'autre révolution', *Europe*, 528 (April 1973): 79–88.

8. William Wordsworth, *French Revolution, as it Appeared to Enthusiasts* and *The Prelude*, Book XI, l. 109.

9. *The Marriage of Figaro*, Act III, p. 111.

10. *The Barber of Seville*, p. 38.

11. See *A Mother's Guilt*, Act III, p. 181.

12. See *Violetta and her Sisters: The Lady of the Camellias: Responses to the Myth*, ed. Nicholas John (London: Faber & Faber, 1994).

THE BARBER OF SEVILLE

OR

ALL THAT TROUBLE
FOR NOTHING

A Comedy in Four Acts
BY BEAUMARCHAIS

Which Opened and Closed
At the Comédie-Française in the Tuileries
23 February 1775

I was a father and I could not die. *

DRAMATIS PERSONAE

COUNT ALMAVIVA a Spanish Grandee,
Rosine's unknown admirer

BARTHOLO a doctor, Rosine's guardian

ROSINE a young woman of noble birth, Bartholo's ward

FIGARO a barber of Seville

MASTER BAZILE an organist, Rosine's singing teacher

THE YOUTH (Acts II and IV) Bartholo's elderly servant

WIDEAWAKE (Acts II and IV) Bartholo's other valet,
half-witted and always half-asleep

A NOTARY (Act IV)

AN ALCADE (Act IV) or JUSTICE OF THE PEACE

Several ALGUAZILS, or CONSTABLES, and SERVANTS
with torches.

———————

Act I – A street beneath Rosine's windows: the rest
of the play in the house of Dr Bartholo.

ACT I

A street in Seville, with barred and latticed windows. COUNT
ALMAVIVA *discovered alone, in a long brown cloak and a broad-
brimmed hat. He is pacing up and down. He takes out his watch.*

COUNT: Earlier than I thought – still hours before the time she usually
appears at the window. It can't be helped. Better be here too soon than
miss the first thrill of seeing her. If one of my sophisticated friends at
Court had any idea I was miles away from Madrid, out here every morn-
ing under the windows of a woman I've never even spoken to, he'd think
I was a ghost from the old romantic days of Ferdinand and Isabella!*
But why not? Everybody wants whatever makes them happy: and I'm
only happy when I'm near Rosine. But all the same, following a
woman all the way to Seville when Madrid and the Court have
everything, whatever you want; so easy, so available? That's precisely
what I'm trying to get away from. I am tired of women who want to
be seen with the right people or think it's the right thing to do, or
want to show off. It's so wonderful to be loved for what you are, and
not who you are; if only I could be sure this disguise. . . . Oh damn
him, that's all I needed!

The COUNT *conceals himself.* FIGARO *comes on, with a guitar
slung over his shoulder on a length of ribbon; he is strumming
happily to himself and has a paper and pencil in his hand.*

FIGARO: (*singing*)
>Away with black despair
>It wastes away the days
>When wine is waiting there
>To set us all ablaze.
>Unless we live for pleasure
>Those moments we can treasure
>We'd slave for our bread
>Until we were dead.

Not bad so far, eh? eh?

> Until we were dead
> For idling and drinking
> Which do I love the more?

No, that won't do. There's no competition. I love them both; fifty-fifty, absolutely equal.

> For idling and drinking
> Are what I most adore.

Will that do? 'Most adore'? Oh, why worry? When you're writing lyrics to be sung on stage, nobody bothers about a little thing like that. These days, the general rule is if a line's not worth saying, sing it.

> For idling and drinking
> Are what I most adore.

I'd like a good line to end with, something striking, something brilliant, that would seem vaguely like an original thought.

> *(He goes down on one knee and writes as he sings)*
> Are what I most adore
> At both you'll catch me winking
> I love them more and more.

No good! Boring! That's not right. I need balance, antithesis . . .

> I either lie there thinking
> Or . . .

Oh! Of course! Got it!

> Or dead drunk on the floor.

Well done, Figaro!

> *(He writes as he sings)*
> For idling and drinking
> Are what I most adore
> I either lie there thinking
> Or dead drunk on the floor.
> Or dead drunk on the floor.
> Or dead drunk on the floor.

Hm ... hm ... When it's got the music with it, yet further proof to the critics that I know what I'm doing!

(*He sees* COUNT ALMAVIVA)

I've seen that priest before somewhere.

He stands up.

COUNT: (*aside*) I think I know that man.

FIGARO: No, that's never a priest. Too arrogant, looking down his nose like that ...

COUNT: Dressed in that absurd rig-out ...

FIGARO: No, there's no mistaking him. It's Count Almaviva.

COUNT: I do believe it's that villain Figaro.

FIGARO: In the flesh, your Lordship.

COUNT: You swine! Don't say a word ...

FIGARO: Recognised you at once: that kindly, affectionate way you always used to speak to me: very flattered, Sir, as always.

COUNT: I'd never have recognised you. You have grown so enormously fat.

FIGARO: What do you expect, my Lord? That's starvation for you.

COUNT: You poor thing! But what are you doing in Seville? I thought I recommended you for a job in the Army.

FIGARO: I got it, my Lord; very much obliged.

COUNT: Call me Lindor. Surely you can see from this disguise? I don't wish to be recognised.

FIGARO: I'll be off.

COUNT: On the contrary. I am waiting here on purpose, and two men talking are less conspicuous than one man walking up and down alone. Pretend we're having a conversation. Well, what happened to the job?

FIGARO: The Minister, obviously treating any recommendation from your Excellency with the respect it deserves, had me appointed the same day as a medical orderly.

COUNT: At an Army Hospital?

FIGARO: No. At a stables in Andalusia.

COUNT: (*laughing*) Off to a good start!

FIGARO: As jobs go it wasn't bad: having the key to the drugs and dressings-cupboard I was frequently in a position to sell my fellow human beings medicine of a quality only normally offered to horses ...

COUNT: ... Killing the Spanish like flies I presume ...

FIGARO: Ha! ha! Well, no remedy is infallible: but they did from time to time cure a few hardy yokels from the remoter provinces.

COUNT: Then why did you give it up?

FIGARO: Give it up? It gave me up. I was reported to the authorities. 'When Green-eyed Envy spreads its grasping claws . . .'*

COUNT: Oh, for goodness' sake! You're a poet as well, then? I saw you scribbling on your knee there; singing at this hour of the morning!

FIGARO: That is the very cause of all my troubles, your Excellency. When they told the Minister I was in the habit of composing these artistic offerings, and with considerable skill, though I say it myself; that I was contributing puzzles to the newspapers, that some part-songs I had written were becoming popular: I mean when he discovered I was in print, he took it very badly, and had me relieved of my employment on the grounds that a literary turn of mind is not always compatible with a head for business.

COUNT: Obviously a man of some intelligence! And you didn't argue with him?

FIGARO: I thought I was lucky enough if he'd forgotten all about me; in my opinion people in power are doing us quite enough of a favour when they're not doing us any actual harm.*

COUNT: That is your side of the story. I remember when you worked for me you were a thoroughly bad character.

FIGARO: Oh come along, my Lord, just because you're poor everybody wants you to be honest.

COUNT: Lazy, dissolute . . .

FIGARO: Talking of the morals you look for in a working man, your Lordship, can you think of many employers who would give satisfaction as a valet?

COUNT: (*laughing*) Not bad. And you came back here?

FIGARO: Not straightaway, Sir, no.

COUNT: (*stopping him*) Wait! . . . I thought it was her. . . . Go on talking. I'm still listening.

FIGARO: When I got back to Madrid, I wanted to have another try at exercising my writing talent, and the theatre seemed a likely field in which to shine . . .

COUNT: Oh God!

During the following speech, COUNT ALMAVIVA *continues to watch the window.*

FIGARO: Quite honestly, I don't know why I wasn't more of a success: I filled the stalls with all available help: men with hands the size of carpet-beaters; no gloves or walking sticks allowed, nothing to interfere with the applause; and I swear, before the curtain went up, the critics seemed entirely on my side. Someone else must have bribed them . . . afterwards.

COUNT: Bribed them, eh? That's the failed playwright talking.

FIGARO: I'm not the only one. What other explanation is there? Would you believe it, they actually hissed? But if I ever meet that lot again . . .

COUNT: You'll bore them to death by way of revenge.

FIGARO: I'll never forgive them, never.

COUNT: Oh, won't you? Do you know, in a court of law you're only allowed to go on abusing the judges for twenty-four hours?*

FIGARO: It's twenty-four years in the theatre; a grudge like that will keep me going for a lifetime.

COUNT: I've always found you very entertaining when you're in a rage. But you haven't said what drove you to leave Madrid.

FIGARO: It must have been Providence, your Excellency, seeing that I've had the good luck to run into my old employer again. Having formed the impression that the literary world in Madrid was largely inhabited by wolves, hunting each other in packs, and as you would expect, given all the ridiculous ripping and tearing that goes on, all the swarms of miserable insects, mosquitoes, midges, critics, horse-flies, mean-minded little hacks, journalists, publishers, censors and all the other bloodsuckers that attach themselves to writers, God help them, had done lacerating them and sucked them dry of any last drop of red blood they might ever have possessed; sick of writing, boring even myself, disgusted by everyone else, up to the eyes in debt and not a sniff of any money; in the end, coming to the conclusion that a steady income from pulling a razor is preferable to the unpaid distinction of pushing a pen, I left Madrid, slung my bag over my shoulder and tramped very happily through every province in the country; Castile, La Mancha, Extremadura, Sierra Morena, ending up in Andalusia; in one place they greeted me with open arms, the next they locked me up: wherever I went I rose above it; praised by some, condemned by others, taking risks when I was on a winning streak, cutting my losses when I wasn't. Paying no attention to fools and not afraid of villains; no money, no worries, and shaving anybody; here I am finally, set up in Seville and ready once again to serve you in whatever way Your Excellency requires.

COUNT: How is it you take life so philosophically? You're always so cheerful.

FIGARO: I suppose it's always being miserable. I'm very quick to laugh at anything for fear it might make me weep. Why are you looking up there at the window all the time?

COUNT: Get back!

FIGARO: Why?

COUNT: Back, you fool! It's opening. You'll give me away!

Sc.3

They hide. The lattice on the first floor opens, BARTHOLO *and* ROSINE *appear at the window.*

ROSINE: Fresh air! How lovely! Why is this window always shut?

BARTHOLO: What's that paper you've got?

ROSINE: It's a song from *All That Trouble For Nothing* my singing teacher gave me yesterday.

BARTHOLO: *All That Trouble For Nothing*? What's that?

ROSINE: A new comedy.

BARTHOLO: One of these dramas, is it? More modern rubbish!

ROSINE: I have no idea.

BARTHOLO: Ugh! Ugh! The critics and the Lord Chamberlain's office will know how to deal with that! What a barbaric age we live in!

ROSINE: You're always blaming the poor age we live in!

BARTHOLO: Forgive the liberty! But I cannot see it has produced anything we should be grateful for: every conceivable kind of idiocy: free-thinking, magnetism, electricity, religious tolerance, inoculation, quinine, Diderot's *Encyclopaedia* and dramas . . .*

ROSINE *lets go the paper and it falls into the street.*

ROSINE: Oh, my music! I've dropped my music, listening to you talk! Quick, quick, go down and get it or I'll never see it again!

BARTHOLO: For God's sake, if you want to keep a thing, hold on to it!

He leaves the balcony. ROSINE *looks over her shoulder and then signals down to the street.*

ROSINE: Psst! Psst!

The COUNT *reappears.*

Quick! Pick it up and go!

The COUNT *leaps forward to retrieve the song-sheet and returns to his hiding-place.* BARTHOLO *comes out of the house, looking for it.*

BARTHOLO: Where is it? I can't see it anywhere.

ROSINE: Under the balcony, down there by the wall.

BARTHOLO: A fine wild-goose chase, this is! Did somebody go by?

ROSINE: I didn't see anyone.

BARTHOLO: (*to himself*) And I, kind old soul, come down here to look for it. . . . Bartholo, you are a blithering idiot: let this be a lesson to you: never open a window that overlooks the street.

He goes in again. ROSINE *stays on the balcony.*

ROSINE: I must surely be forgiven in the circumstances: utterly miserable, shut up here all alone treated like a slave, left to the attentions of a man that I detest, it can't be wrong to try and escape!

BARTHOLO *appears on the balcony.*

BARTHOLO: You will go indoors, Madam: if you have lost your music, the fault was entirely mine, but it is an accident that will not occur again, you have my word.

He closes the window and locks it. The COUNT *and* FIGARO   Sc.4
creep back.

COUNT: They have gone in. Now we can see what this music is; it was a trick, I'm sure of that. It's a letter!

FIGARO: And he wanted to know what *All That Trouble For Nothing* was!

COUNT: (*excited, reading*) I should like very much to know why you are so persistent: as soon as my guardian goes out, pretend you're singing: use this tune and make up anything you like as long as you kindly tell me who you are, what your name is, and what you want, since you seem determined to meet a very miserable Rosine.

FIGARO: (*imitating* ROSINE) 'My music! I've dropped my music! Quick, quick, go down and get it!' Ha! ha! ha! ha! Honestly, women! You want to turn a wide-eyed innocent into a calculating little minx, all you have to do is stop her going out.

COUNT: Dear Rosine!

FIGARO: Your Lordship, I am now no longer in the dark as to what the disguise is all about. You are in love, or intend to be.

COUNT: Now you know: but if you tell anybody . . .

FIGARO: Me, tell anybody! I won't waste my breath with swearing on my mother's grave and giving my word of honour: people break that every day of the week: I'll just say this. It is not in my own interest to tell anybody: use that as a guide and you won't go far wrong.

COUNT: Very well then, I'll tell you. By pure chance six months ago, in the Paseo del Prado,* I met a girl; she was so beautiful.... You've seen her! – I had people looking for her all over Madrid. Without success. Only a few days ago I found out that her name was Rosine, that she's the daughter of a Duke, an orphan, and is married to an elderly doctor here called Bartholo.

FIGARO: A sweet little bird, I'll grant you, and it won't be easy stealing her out of the nest! But who told you she was married to the doctor?

COUNT: Everybody did.

FIGARO: It's a story he made up when he got back from Madrid to confuse the competition and keep off other suitors; at the moment he's only her legal guardian, but any minute now ...

COUNT: (*passionately*) Never! Oh, what wonderful news! I'd made up my mind I'd risk everything to commiserate with her on her marriage, and now I find she's free! There's not a moment to lose; I must make her fall in love with me, and rescue her from this terrible life she's been condemned to. You know her guardian then?

FIGARO: As well as I know my own mother.

COUNT: What's he like?

FIGARO: (*quickly*) Oh, he's a plumpish, shortish, youngish, oldish-looking man, greyish hair going to pepper-and-salt, close-shaven, tight-fisted, twisted, ear to the ground, weather-eye open and nose in everything.

COUNT: (*impatiently*) Please! I have seen him! I mean what's he like as a human being?

FIGARO: Oh, an animal. Mean, lecherous, and as far as she's concerned, jealous to the point of insanity. She hates him like poison.

COUNT: So, his personal charm is ...

FIGARO: Non-existent.

COUNT: Even better. Highly moral?

FIGARO: Just barely enough to save him from the gallows.

COUNT: Better still. Teach him a lesson and get what we want into the bargain ...

FIGARO: ... Acting in the public and private interest simultaneously as you might say, my Lord. From a moral point of view quite a *tour de force.*

COUNT: You say he keeps the door locked for fear of other men?

FIGARO: Never lets in anyone: he'd have it bricked up if he could.

COUNT: Ah! Damn, that's not so good. Have you any way of getting in?

FIGARO: Any way of getting in? In the first place, the house I live in is the doctor's property, and he puts me up there gratis and for nothing.

COUNT: Aha!

FIGARO: It's the truth. In return for which I promised to pay him one hundred pieces of gold a year, also gratis and for nothing.

COUNT: (*impatiently*) You are his lodger?

FIGARO: More than that: I am his barber, his medical attendant, his chemist's shop. There's not a shave, a surgical dressing or an enema inside that house that is not administered by this hand, always at your service, sir.

COUNT: (*hugs him*) Oh, Figaro, you're my friend, my lucky star, the answer to all my problems and I worship you!

FIGARO: Amazing! I have something you want and social barriers just disappear! Talk about mad passion . . .

COUNT: Oh, Figaro, you're so fortunate! You'll see my Rosine! You'll see her! Do you realise how lucky you are?

FIGARO: Now only someone in love could say a thing like that! I'm not in love with her! Now, if you could go instead of me.

COUNT: If we could distract the attention of whoever's looking after her . . .

FIGARO: That's what I was thinking of.

COUNT: For just twelve hours!

FIGARO: Give people enough to bother about on their own account and they won't come bothering you.

COUNT: How very true! And . . .?

FIGARO: (*thoughtfully*) A thought was running through my head whether the chemist's shop might not provide us with some innocent little device.

COUNT: That would be criminal!

FIGARO: I'm not trying to do them any harm! They all need medicine now and then. It just means me giving it to them all at the same time.

COUNT: But he's a doctor; he might suspect something!

FIGARO: We must act so fast he hasn't time to suspect anything. I have an idea! The Horse Guards are due in town . . .

COUNT: I know their Colonel.

FIGARO: Good. Turn up at the Doctor's front door in cavalry uniform; bring a billeting order; he'll have to take you in, he won't have any alternative; and I'll see to everything else.

COUNT: Excellent.

FIGARO: It might not even be a bad idea if you'd had a bit to drink.

COUNT: Why?

FIGARO: ... So you can lead him rather more of a dance while giving the illusion you're entirely out of your mind.

COUNT: Why?

FIGARO: So he won't think there's anything afoot and believe you've come to his house to sleep rather than get up to anything.

COUNT: What an extraordinarily brilliant thought! But you won't be coming in yourself?

FIGARO: Oh, yes, I'll be there all right. We'll be very lucky if he doesn't see through the disguise, even though he doesn't know you from Adam. And otherwise how would I let you in again?

COUNT: You're right.

FIGARO: Perhaps you can't manage a character as difficult as that. A cavalryman. ... In his cups.

COUNT: You're joking. (*He puts on a drunken voice*) Doctor Bartholo's residence, if I am not mistaken, my good man?

FIGARO: Not bad; no really. Perhaps the legs might be a little more inebriated ... (*more drunkenly*) Doctor Bartholo's residence ...

COUNT: Oh come on! That's how a working-man gets drunk.

FIGARO: That's the right way: just for the fun of it.

COUNT: The door's opening!

FIGARO: It's our man: out of the way till he's gone.

Sc.5   *The* COUNT *and* FIGARO *hide*, BARTHOLO *comes out of the house shouting back over his shoulder.*

BARTHOLO: I shall be back in just a moment: don't let anyone in. (*To himself*) So stupid to have come downstairs. Her asking should have made me think twice. ... And Bazile still hasn't come! He was supposed to make all the arrangements for my marriage to be celebrated discreetly first thing tomorrow morning ... and no sign of him! I must go and see what can be keeping him.

Sc.6   *He goes. The* COUNT *and* FIGARO *emerge from hiding.*

COUNT: What did he say? Secretly marrying Rosine tomorrow morning?

FIGARO: My Lord, if it's going to be difficult, all the more incentive to get started.

COUNT: Who's this Bazile? What's he got to do with the marriage?

FIGARO: A miserable little runt who gives her singing lessons, music-mad, shifty, always short of money, faints clean away at the sight of silver, and very easy to come to an understanding with, your Lordship. (*Looking up at the window*) She's there! She's there!

COUNT: Who is?

FIGARO: At the window. Up there! Up there! Don't look, don't look!

COUNT: Why not?

FIGARO: She said in the letter 'Pretend you're singing'. So, sing! Just sing! Doesn't matter what. . . . Go on! She's there! She's there!

COUNT: She seems keen even though she doesn't know who I am. I've told people here my name is Lindor, so I'll stick to it. All the more wonderful if she'll have me.

(*He opens* ROSINE's *music*)

But how can I sing anything to this tune? I can never think of a rhyme . . .

FIGARO: (*deliberately*) Anything that crosses your mind, your Lordship, will be perfect. Being in love is no time for literary criticism. Here, have my guitar.

COUNT: But what do I do with it? I'm absolutely hopeless.

FIGARO: Oh, surely. Your sort can do everything. Use the back of your hand; thrum, thrum, thrum. . . . You get caught singing in Seville without a guitar! You'd be recognised in a flash, and bang goes your disguise!

FIGARO *flattens himself against the wall beneath the balcony.*
The COUNT *sings, strolling to and fro and accompanying himself*
on the guitar.

COUNT:

Though in disguise I could dare to adore you
You do but ask, I tell you my name,
I name my name, though it fills me with shame
I am your slave, I'll do anything for you.

FIGARO: (*whispering*) Well done, I must say. Keep it up, your Lordship!

COUNT:

A man in love, a man in the street,
My name is Lindor, no one you would know,
Not a name you can drop, not a man who could throw
Fame or fortune at your feet . . .

FIGARO: Amazing! Couldn't have done it better myself, and I'm a serious poet.

COUNT:

> Each day at dawn, if I know you'll appear
> I'll sing of love you may never return
> Enough for me if I see you and yearn
> Enough for me if you're happy to hear.

FIGARO: Oh! Sheer genius! Allow me . . .

He comes forward, kneels and kisses the hem of the COUNT's
cloak.

COUNT: Figaro?
FIGARO: Your Excellency?
COUNT: Do you think she heard it?

ROSINE: (*singing behind the window*)

> His voice is charming, dear Lindor
> And I shall love him more and more.

The sound of a window being slammed shut.

FIGARO: Now do you think she heard?
COUNT: She's shut the window; someone must have come into the room.
FIGARO: Oh! The poor little thing, you could hear the emotion from the way her voice shook. It worked, my Lord!
COUNT: You see, that was the scheme she suggested! 'His voice is charming, dear Lindor.' How clever! How brilliant!
FIGARO: How crafty! How madly in love!
COUNT: Do you think she's serious, Figaro?
FIGARO: Serious, Sir? She'll break through those iron bars.
COUNT: That's fixed, then: I shall love Rosine for ever and ever, always!
FIGARO: You forget, Your Lordship, she's not listening.
COUNT: Mr Figaro, I will say only this: that woman is going to be my wife: and if you are of assistance to me and see to it she doesn't find out who I am . . . you know what I mean, you know me . . .
FIGARO: All right, I surrender. Come along Figaro, my lad, this could make your fortune.
COUNT: We must go. We don't want to draw attention to ourselves.
FIGARO: (*quickly*) Right. I go in, and making use of my professional training, I wave my magic wand and ping, guards asleep, love awakens, jealousy led up the garden path, any counter-attack nipped

in the bud, all resistance swept away. Now, Your Lordship, you come to me, army uniform, the billeting order, and money.

COUNT: Money? What for?

FIGARO: (*quickly*) Money, for God's sake, plots do not work without money.

COUNT: Have no fear, Figaro, I'll bring ample supplies.

FIGARO: (*going off*) I'll be back in a moment.

COUNT: Figaro?

FIGARO: What is it?

COUNT: What about your guitar?

FIGARO: (*coming back*) Forget my guitar? I must be going mad!

Going off again.

COUNT: And where do you live, you idiot?

FIGARO: (*coming back*) Ah! It must be the excitement. The shop's just round the corner: blue paint, leaded windows, sign outside with three bleeding cups, a Hand with an Eye in the middle, and the motto Consilio Manuque, The Nimble Brain, the Swiftness of the Hand, FIGARO.

[*He runs off*]

ACT II

Sc.1 ROSINE's *apartment. The window upstage is shuttered with an*
iron grill. ROSINE, *alone, with a candlestick in her hand. She takes*
a piece of paper from the table and begins to write.

ROSINE: Marceline's ill: the servants are all busy: no one will see me
writing. I don't know whether these walls really have eyes and ears,
or whether it is my lynx-eyed guardian has some evil genie that tells
him everything the moment it happens, but I can't say a word or
make a move without him knowing about it! Oh, Lindor!
(She seals the letter)
I must seal this letter anyway, even though I have no idea when or
how I shall ever get it to him. I saw him through the grill there having
a long talk to Figaro, the barber. He's a good man: I think he feels
sorry for me sometimes; if I could just talk to him for a moment!

Sc.2   *Enter* FIGARO.

ROSINE: *(taken aback)* Ah, at last, Mr Figaro! Oh, I'm so happy to see
you!
FIGARO: I trust you're well, Madam?
ROSINE: Not very well, no, Mr Figaro. I think I may be dying of
boredom.
FIGARO: I believe you: you'd have to be a fool to flourish on it.
ROSINE: Who was that you were having such an interesting conver-
sation with down there? Not that I could hear, but . . .
FIGARO: Oh, a young student, a cousin of mine: a very promising lad;
highly intelligent, imaginative, talented and very good-looking, I'd
have said.
ROSINE: Oh very, I agree. And his name?
FIGARO: Lindor. Not a penny in the world; but if he hadn't left Madrid
in such a hurry he could be very successful there.
ROSINE: He will be, Mr Figaro, I'm sure he will. A young man of the
kind you are describing could never fail to be recognised sooner or
later.

FIGARO: (*aside*) Very good. (*Aloud*) But he has one serious handicap that will stop him ever getting very far.

ROSINE: A handicap, Mr Figaro! Are you sure?

FIGARO: He's in love.

ROSINE: In love! And you call that a handicap?

FIGARO: Well, to be frank, only on account of his being born poor.

ROSINE: Oh! Life is so unfair! And did he tell you the name of the girl he is in love with? I shouldn't be so inquisitive . . .

FIGARO: You are the last person on earth, Madam, to whom I would reveal a confidence of that nature.

ROSINE: (*quickly*) Why, Mr Figaro? I can keep a secret: this young man, a member of your family: it's only natural I should be interested in him: do tell me.

FIGARO: (*with a knowing look*) Try and picture the prettiest little girl in the world, kind, affectionate, quiet, neat as a pin, amazingly attractive; glimpse of an ankle, tiny little waist, long back, beautifully shaped arms, little pink lips, and her hands! Cheeks! Teeth! Eyes!

ROSINE: She lives here in Seville?

FIGARO: In this very parish.

ROSINE: In this street perhaps?

FIGARO: Very near me.

ROSINE: Oh, how wonderful . . . for your cousin I mean. And the girl . . .

FIGARO: I didn't say her name?

ROSINE: (*quickly*) That is the only thing you forgot, Mr Figaro. Tell me, tell me quick, if someone were to come in, I'd never know.

FIGARO: You absolutely insist, Madam? Very well ! Officially she's your guardian's legal ward.

ROSINE: My guardian?

FIGARO: Doctor Bartholo, yes, Madam.

ROSINE: (*with emotion*) Oh, Mr Figaro . . . I don't believe you, I really don't . . .

FIGARO: What is more he's desperate to come and tell you so himself.

ROSINE: You're making me so frightened, Mr Figaro.

FIGARO: Why? Frightened! That's quite the wrong reaction, Madam! You start fearing the worst, the worst will happen. And another thing: I have just disposed of all your watchdogs for you till the morning.

ROSINE: If he loves me, he must prove it to me by remaining absolutely calm.

FIGARO: Oh Madam, how can anybody be in love and stay calm? I pity young people nowadays, having the awful choice: in love and never a moment's peace, or a quiet life and not being in love.

ROSINE: (*averting her eyes*) A quiet life and not being in love would be ... .

FIGARO: Oh, not worth living. In fact I am told that being in love and never having a moment's peace is preferable in polite society; and, personally, if I was a woman ...

ROSINE: (*embarrassed*) Why certainly, a young lady can't prevent a young gentleman from admiring her.

FIGARO: Indeed. And my cousin admires you very very much indeed.

ROSINE: But if he did anything silly, Mr Figaro, he'd ruin everything for us.

FIGARO: (*aside*) He'd ruin everything for us! (*Aloud*) But if you wrote him a little letter, telling him he mustn't; people take a letter seriously.

She gives him the letter she has just written.

ROSINE: I haven't time to write this one again, but when you give it to him, tell him ... do be sure to tell him ... (*she listens*)

FIGARO: No one there, Madam.

ROSINE: ... That I am doing this purely as a friend, and nothing else.

FIGARO: Oh, obviously. I mean, love is something else entirely.

ROSINE: Purely as a friend, I hope that's clear. I am only afraid that when he finds how impossibly difficult it is he'll ...

FIGARO: ... Just float away and vanish like a will o' the wisp? Madam, always remember: a draught may blow out a candle but it makes a bonfire burn like blazes, and we are that bonfire. You don't know how passionate he is! Just talking he gives off such a heat I nearly burst into flames myself and I'm only a mere bystander.

ROSINE: Oh heavens! That's my guardian. If he were to find you here. ... Go through the little room with the harpsichord, and down the stairs as quietly as you can.

FIGARO: Have no fear. (*Aside*) This letter is worth more than anything I can tell him.

Sc.3   *He goes off through the little room.*

ROSINE: Oh, I can't bear it! Once he's safe outside. ... Oh, I'm so fond of him. Dear Figaro! Such a good, honest man and so kind to his poor cousin! Here comes the prison governor. Where's my needle-work? (*She blows out the candle.*)

Sc.4   ROSINE *sits down, and takes up an embroidery frame.*

BARTHOLO: (*enters in a rage*) Oh! Hell and damnation! The lunatic! The criminal hooligan! Figaro! For pity's sake, can't a man leave his own house for a moment without knowing for certain the moment he comes back . . .

ROSINE: What can have made you so angry, Sir?

BARTHOLO: That damned barber! He's just crippled the entire household at a stroke. He gives Wideawake a sleeping draught, the Youth a sneezing powder; he bleeds Marceline's foot: every man jack of them, including the mule. . . he's blindfolded it! The poor creature can't see anyway, and he slaps a hot poultice over its face! He owes me a hundred crowns, so he's trying to run me up bigger bills. Just let him bring them to me, that's all! And no one out there in the hall. Anyone could walk into this room: it's like a public thoroughfare.

ROSINE: And who would ever burst in here but you, Sir?

BARTHOLO: I prefer to be suspicious without reason than to expose myself to unnecessary risk through not taking sufficient trouble: there are people everywhere, scheming men, who will stop at nothing. . . . This very morning, if I am not mistaken, someone very craftily picked up that sheet of music of yours while I was on the way down to retrieve it. Oh! I . . .

ROSINE: You just love reading significance into everything that happens! The piece of paper could have blown away, a passer-by could have picked it up: how do I know?

BARTHOLO: Blown away, a passer-by! There is no wind, Madam, and there is no such thing as a passer-by! It is always someone stationed there on purpose to pick up pieces of paper women pretend to drop by mistake.

ROSINE: Pretend, Sir?

BARTHOLO: Yes, Madam, pretend!

ROSINE: (*aside*) The cunning old devil!

BARTHOLO: But there'll be no more of that: because I am going to have this lattice welded shut.

ROSINE: Why stop there? Why not have all the windows in the house bricked up? Turn a prison into a dungeon; there'd be very little difference!

BARTHOLO: Those that open on the street you mean? Not a bad idea. . . . At least the barber didn't come in here. Or did he?

ROSINE: You have your suspicions about him too, I expect?

BARTHOLO: As I have about everybody else.

ROSINE: Well, at least you're frank.

BARTHOLO: Oh! Trust everybody, and you soon have a good kind wife to be unfaithful to you, good kind friends to run away with her, and good kind servants to help them do it.

ROSINE: So! You wouldn't even credit me with the moral strength to resist Mr Figaro?

BARTHOLO: How the hell can any man ever begin to understand anything as peculiar as a woman? I've seen more than one case of where moral strength can get you.

ROSINE: (*in a rage*) Well, Sir, if it is enough merely to be a man to sweep us all off our feet why do I find you so singularly unattractive?

BARTHOLO: (*stunned*) Why? Why? You haven't answered my question about the barber.

ROSINE: (*beside herself*) Very well then, yes. He came into my room; I saw him: I spoke to him. I will even confess that I thought he was very kind: and I hope you're so cross you choke to death of apoplexy!

[*She goes*]

Sc.5

BARTHOLO: Oh, the Jews! The dogs! Call themselves servants! The Youth! Wideawake! Wideawake, damn you!

Sc.6   *Enter* WIDEAWAKE *yawning, half asleep.*

WIDEAWAKE: Sir? Aah! Ah! Ah!

BARTHOLO: Where have you been, you diseased cretin? What were you doing when that barber came in here?

WIDEAWAKE: Sir, I was . . . ah, aah, ah . . .

BARTHOLO: Devising some prank, no doubt? And you didn't see him.

WIDEAWAKE: Certainly I saw him, because he thought I was very poorly: well, that was what he said: and I must be, and all, 'cos I started aching and paining all over: from no more than hearing him asking me how I was . . . Ah! Ah! Ah!

BARTHOLO: (*imitating him*) 'From no more than hear . . .' Where's that idle youth? Giving this young innocent drugs without me writing a prescription! There's more to this than meets the eye.

Sc.7   THE YOUTH *comes in, in the guise of an old man with a crutch.*
                  He sneezes several times.

WIDEAWAKE: (*still yawning*) The youth?

BARTHOLO: Do you think you might have stopped sneezing by the end of the week?

THE YOUTH: That's more than fifty . . . fifty times . . . just like that! (*He sneezes*) I'm a wreck!

BARTHOLO: What! I asked both of you whether somebody had been into Rosine's apartment and neither of you told me that that Barber . . .

WIDEAWAKE: (*continuing to yawn*) Oh, I didn't know Mr Figaro counted as a somebody. . . . Aah! Aah!

BARTHOLO: I'll bet the cunning little skunk has come to some understanding with him.

WIDEAWAKE: (*bursting into tears*) Me? Understanding?

THE YOUTH: (*sneezing*) Oh but, Sir, you're so . . . unjust!

BARTHOLO: Unjust! Unjust to your sort, you miserable wretch? I am your employer; that means I am automatically always right.

THE YOUTH: (*sneezing*) But, mercy on us, Sir, if it's true . . .

BARTHOLO: If it's true! If I don't want it to be true, I say it isn't true! Start admitting you ragamuffins to be in the right and you'd soon see what would become of established authority.

THE YOUTH: (*sneezing*) You can sack me for all I care. It's terrible working here, driven like slaves we are.

WIDEAWAKE: (*weeping*) If you're one of nature's gentlemen they treat you like filth.

BARTHOLO: All right, get out, nature's gentleman! (*He imitates them*) 'Atishoo, waah!!' One sneezes in my face, the other yawns in it.

THE YOUTH: Oh, Sir, on my honour, if it weren't for the young lady life in . . . life in this house would be intolerable!

[*He goes out sneezing.*]

BARTHOLO: A fine state Figaro's left them all in! I was right: the swine's trying to pay me back my hundred crowns without breaking into his capital.

(*Enter* BAZILE. FIGARO, *hiding in the harpsichord room, appears Sc.8 from time to time, eavesdropping*)

Aha! Master Bazile, come to give Rosine her music lesson.

BAZILE: That's the least of our troubles.

BARTHOLO: I came to your house: you weren't there.

BAZILE: I was out on business on your behalf. You may as well hear it. There's some very disturbing news!

BARTHOLO: For you?

BAZILE: No, for you. Count Almaviva's in town.

BARTHOLO: Not so loud! The one that had people looking for Rosine all over Madrid?

BAZILE: He's taken lodgings in the Plaza Major and goes out every morning in disguise.

BARTHOLO: There can't be any doubt about it: this requires my attention. What are we to do?

BAZILE: If he was an ordinary member of the public there'd be no difficulty in disposing of him.

BARTHOLO: Yes, ambush him, late at night, heavily armed ... protective clothing ...

BAZILE: *Deo omnipotente!* And compromise yourself! Stir up a scandal, that's the way, and once it's on the boil, have him slandered by experts. *Cosi va bene!*

BARTHOLO: A strange way of disposing of a man!

BAZILE: Slander, Sir? You don't know the half of it: never despise slander. I've seen some very distinguished men come very near to being destroyed by it. Believe me, there is no piece of gossip, however unimaginative, no tale of horror, however outrageous, no story, however absurd that you can't get accepted as the gospel truth by the idle classes in a city of any size, if you go about it the right way: and we have people here who do it brilliantly! It'll start as a whisper, a rumour, skimming along like a swallow before the storm, a dull buzz *pianissimo*, never stopping, scattering the poison as it goes. Someone else laps it up and *piano, piano,* slides it in your ear, so cleverly. The damage is done: it grows, it gets about, it gains momentum, and *rinforzando* passes from mouth to mouth doing its wicked work; then suddenly no one knows how, you see the slander there threatening, hissing, gathering strength, growing before your very eyes, it takes off, spreads its wings, twisting like a whirlwind, all-enveloping, carrying all before it, overturning all opposition, exploding and thundering till it has become, thanks be to heaven, a general outcry, a public crescendo, a universal chorus of hate and condemnation. There's not a man alive can stand against that!!!

BARTHOLO: You really do talk the most awful drivel. What possible bearing, Bazile, has a *piano* or a *crescendo* on my present situation?

BAZILE: What do you mean, what bearing? The normal practice for disposing of an enemy: in this case to prevent yours from ever getting here.

BARTHOLO: Getting here? I hope I shall be married to Rosine before she even knows the Count exists.

BAZILE: In that case you haven't a moment to lose.

BARTHOLO: And who will do all this, Bazile? I asked you to take charge of all the details in this matter.

BAZILE: Yes. But you have rather soft-pedalled on the expenses, and in preserving the harmony of law and order, a marriage between a commoner and a member of the nobility, misleading the Court, and an obvious circumvention of the law all create discord: they can only be resolved, as we say in music, by something unexpected in the left hand.

BARTHOLO: (*giving him money*) You must do as you like: but I want this over and done with.

BAZILE: That is what I call talking. Tomorrow everything will be completed; all you have to do today is to prevent anyone informing your ward.

BARTHOLO: Trust me. Will you come back tonight, Bazile?

BAZILE: Don't count on it. I shall devote myself entirely to the arrangements for your marriage for the rest of the day: don't count on it.

BARTHOLO: (*going with him*) Allow me.

BAZILE: No, Doctor, please, there's no need to come down.

BARTHOLO: Yes, there is. I want to lock the front door after you've gone.

FIGARO *comes out of the harpsichord room.*   Sc.9

FIGARO: Oh! How good of him to take the trouble! Lock it, lock the front door: and I shall open it again for the Count when I go out. He's a big villain, that Bazile. Fortunately he's an even bigger fool. You need some standing in society, to be well-connected, have a famous name, a title – in a word be someone of real importance – if you're going to have any success slandering anybody in polite society. Bazile!! Even if it was malicious gossip no one would believe him!

ROSINE *runs in.*   Sc.10

ROSINE: What! You're still here, Mr Figaro?

FIGARO: Very lucky for you I am, Miss. Your guardian and your music teacher thought they were alone in here; they were talking very frankly and openly.

ROSINE: And you were listening, Mr Figaro? Surely you know that's wrong?

FIGARO: Listening? All the same it's the best way I know of hearing things. I'd better tell you: your guardian is making arrangements to marry you tomorrow.

ROSINE: Oh God!

FIGARO: Have no fear, we'll keep him so busy he won't even have time to think about it.

ROSINE: He's coming back: go down by the back stairs! You frighten me to death!

FIGARO *runs off.* BARTHOLO *returns.*

ROSINE: It seems you have had company, Sir?

BARTHOLO: Master Bazile: I was seeing him out, very necessary under the circumstances. I expect you would rather it had been Mr Figaro?

ROSINE: I assure you I have no feelings on the matter.

BARTHOLO: I'd like to know what it can have been the barber was so desperate to tell you.

ROSINE: If you seriously want to know he gave me a report on Marceline's health, which is none too good from what he tells me.

BARTHOLO: Gave you a report! I am prepared to bet he had been paid to bring you some kind of letter.

ROSINE: Who from? Perhaps you could tell me that?

BARTHOLO: Oh! Who from? From someone women never mention by name. How should I know? Perhaps an answer to the piece of paper you threw out of the window.

ROSINE: (*aside*) He hasn't missed a single thing. (*Aloud*) If it were true it would be no more than you deserve.

BARTHOLO *looks at* ROSINE's *hands.*

BARTHOLO: And it is true. You've been writing.

ROSINE: (*embarrassed*) Don't tell me you intend to force me to confess to that. That would be entertaining, wouldn't it?

BARTHOLO: (*taking her right hand*) Why should I do that? Not at all; but the ink is still on your finger! Eh? Naughty Señora!

ROSINE: (*aside*) Damn the man!

BARTHOLO: (*still holding her hand*) A woman always thinks she is safe, when she is alone.

ROSINE: Oh! Of course! And that proves it, I suppose? Stop it, Sir, you are twisting my arm. I burned myself doing some embroidery too near the candle, and I've always been told the best remedy is dipping it in ink as soon as possible: so I did.

BARTHOLO: So you did. Then let's just see if a second witness will corroborate the evidence of the first. This writing-case contained, I know for a fact, six sheets of writing paper: I count them every morning and did so today.

ROSINE: (*aside*) Oh, I'm such a fool! (*Aloud*) The sixth.

BARTHOLO: (*counting*) Three, four, five.... I see it isn't there; the sixth.

ROSINE: (*averting her eyes*) The sixth, I used to make into a bag for some sweets I sent to the little Figaro girl.

BARTHOLO: The little Figaro girl? And this quill which was quite new, I wonder what can have turned it black? Was it writing the little Figaro girl's address?

ROSINE: (*aside*) The man has a real talent for jealousy! (*Aloud*) I used it to re-trace the outline of a flower that wasn't very clear on the waistcoat I am embroidering for you on the frame.

BARTHOLO: Ah! How touching! In order to be believed, my child, you would do better not to blush every time you tell another lie; but you haven't learned that yet.

ROSINE: Oh! And who would not blush, Sir, when you draw such prurient conclusions from perfectly innocent behaviour?

BARTHOLO: I'm sure I'm wrong: burning your finger, dipping it in the ink, making a sheet of paper into a bag for sweets for the little Figaro girl, designing embroidery for my waistcoat on the frame! What could be more innocent than that? But why heap lie upon lie to conceal one single fact? 'I am alone, no one can see me; I can lie, he'll never know': but the tip of your finger is still covered in ink! The quill is still black, the paper is still missing: nobody can think of everything. But there is one thing you may be certain of Señora: when I go into town I shall see to it the front door is double-locked.

Enter the COUNT *in cavalry uniform, apparently slightly drunk and singing.*   Sc.12

COUNT: 'Come, let us awake her . . .'

BARTHOLO: But what's that man doing here? A soldier? Go to your room, Señora.

COUNT: 'Come let us awake her.'
(*moving towards* ROSINE)
Which of you two ladies, I wonder, goes by the name of Doctor Balordo? (*Whispering to* ROSINE) I'm Lindor.

BARTHOLO: Bartholo!!

ROSINE: (*aside*) He said Lindor!

COUNT: Bath-hello: Bark-hello, I don't care about that. All I want to know is which of you two ladies. . . . (*To* ROSINE, *showing her a piece of paper*) Take this letter.

BARTHOLO: Ladies! Well obviously I am! Ladies! Go to your room, Rosine, this man would appear to have taken drink.

ROSINE: That is why I think I ought to stay, Sir. You are alone. Sometimes a woman's influence . . .

BARTHOLO: Go inside, go inside: I am not afraid.

[*She goes*]   Sc.13

COUNT: Oh! Now I recognise you. You're just like your official description.

BARTHOLO: (*to the* COUNT *who is putting the letter in his pocket*) What is that you are trying to conceal in your pocket?

COUNT: I am trying to conceal it in my pocket so you won't find out what it is.

BARTHOLO: My official description? These people always talk as if they were still in the barrack room!

COUNT: You can't think there's any problem compiling your official description?

> Bald as a badger, teeth all wobbly
> Eyes akimbo, nose all nobbly
> Madder than a Hottentot . . .
> Old bow-legged Jeremiah
> One side down and one side higher
> On his chin a hideous spot
> Ugly, yes, but nice he's not
> Paunch hangs down and always dribbling
> So contrary, cross and quibbling
> Sleeps alone, all slime and slobbery
> Dreams of rape and highway robbery
> Nasty smell and spell-concocter
> Quite the darling little Doctor!

BARTHOLO: What is that supposed to mean? Have you come here to insult me? Now you just get out of this house this minute!

COUNT: Get out of this house! I say! That's no way to talk! Can you read, Doctor Halfaloaf?

BARTHOLO: So, another impertinent question!

COUNT: Ah! You need feel no shame! I'm a doctor too; if anything more so . . .

BARTHOLO: What?

COUNT: General Practitioner to every horse in the regiment. That is why they made a point of billeting me on a colleague.

BARTHOLO: Are you daring to compare me to a mere vet?

COUNT: We veterinary men can do
> So little when compared to you
> Your greater knowledge, greater skill

> (*He sings*)
> Will bring you victory, come what will

> For each new day the doctor tries
> To fight disease and claim the prize
> At least the patient always dies.

Now, is that entirely polite?

BARTHOLO: It is no worse than I would expect of an ignorant sawbones like yourself! Maligning the most esteemed, the greatest of all professions, bringing the greatest benefit to all humanity.

COUNT: And considerable benefit to those who practise it.

BARTHOLO: What a profession! It has achieved some of the most brilliant triumphs on this earth!

COUNT: And its failures can be buried very quickly underneath it!

BARTHOLO: It is very obvious to me, you uncouth person, that you are only accustomed to talking to horses.

COUNT: Talking to horses? Oh Doctor! How you, as a witty doctor. . . . Surely you know the old saying? Veterinary surgeons always cure their patients and never say a word to them: doctors are always talking to theirs . . .

BARTHOLO: And never cure them, I suppose?

COUNT: You said it. I didn't.

BARTHOLO: Who the hell can have sent me this confounded drunk?

COUNT: Did you say something terribly affectionate?

BARTHOLO: For the last time, what do you want? What are you here for?

COUNT: (*pretending to be suddenly very angry*) Right, that does it! Now he's in a filthy temper! What do I want? Can't you see what I want?

ROSINE *comes running in.*   Sc.14

ROSINE: Oh please, Trooper, don't be angry. Please don't. (To BARTHOLO) Be gentle with him, Sir: he's not quite right in the head!

COUNT: You're quite right: he's not quite right, but we're all right and what's more we're in the right. I'm polite, you're a delight, but that's enough of that! The truth is you are the only person in this house I have any desire to have anything to do with!

ROSINE: What can I do to help you, Trooper?

COUNT: Really nothing of any consequence, child. And if my speech should seem somewhat slurred . . .

ROSINE: I'll get the gist of it.

COUNT: (*showing her the letter*) No. You must understand what I'm saying to the letter, to the letter. All I want . . . I tell you this as a

gentleman, and an officer, that I would like to go to bed with you
immediately.

BARTHOLO: Is that all?

COUNT: That's all. Here, read this love letter our billeting officer has
written you.

BARTHOLO: Let me see.

The COUNT *hides the letter and gives him another piece of paper.*
BARTHOLO *reads.*

'Doctor Bartholo will billet, provision and provide a bed . . .'

COUNT: (*emphatically*) A bed.

BARTHOLO: '. . . for one night only to the above-named Lindor, also
known as Brains, a cavalryman in the Royal . . .'

ROSINE: It's him, it's really him!

BARTHOLO: (*quickly, to* ROSINE) What was that?

COUNT: Well? Who's in the wrong now, Doctor Baccherole?

BARTHOLO: You'd think this man actually enjoyed mangling my name
in any way that takes his evil fancy. Damn you! Halfaloaf, Baccherole.
And tell your impertinent billeting officer that since my last visit to
Madrid I am exempt from lodging the military.

COUNT: (*aside*) Oh damn! How very annoying!

BARTHOLO: Aha! My friend! That makes you cross doesn't it? Sobered
you up a bit? But don't let it delay you. Go on, make yourself scarce!

COUNT: (*aside*) I nearly gave myself away! (*Aloud*) Make myself scarce?
Being excused the military doesn't mean you're excused good man-
ners, I trust! Make myself scarce, indeed! If you are exempt I shall
need to see the warrant; I may not be able to read, but I shall soon
see what's what.

BARTHOLO: It won't make any difference. It's in my writing-desk.

He goes to fetch it. The COUNT *speaks from the same position.*

COUNT: Oh, my beautiful Rosine.

ROSINE: Lindor, is it really you?

COUNT: Take this letter at least.

ROSINE: Careful, he's still watching us.

COUNT: Get your handkerchief ready. I'll drop it.

He moves towards her.

BARTHOLO: Easy, Trooper! Easy, Sir! I don't like people examining my
wife quite as closely as that, thank you.

COUNT: Your wife?

BARTHOLO: Who else do you think she is?

COUNT: I thought you must be her great-grandfather on her father's mother's side; certainly on the very elderly side. There must be at least three generations between her and you.

BARTHOLO: (*reading from a parchment*) 'Upon the testimony of good and faithful witnesses . . .'

The COUNT *strikes the parchment, knocking it out of*
BARTHOLO's *hands.*

COUNT: What do I need with all the gobbledy-gook?

BARTHOLO: You realise, Trooper, if I call the servants, I can have you disciplined here and now and it will be nothing less than you deserve?

COUNT: A fight eh? Oh, I'm all for a fight. That's my job, that is: I am a fighting man, you know. (*Showing the pistol in his belt*) See this pistol. . . . This'll blow 'em off course a bit. Perhaps you've never seen a battle, Madam?

ROSINE: No, and I do not wish to see one.

COUNT: Oh, for sheer fun there's nothing like a fight. Picture the scene. (*Pushing* BARTHOLO) There! Enemy on one side of the ditch, all the lads on the other! (*Whispering to* ROSINE, *showing her the letter*) Ready with your handkerchief. (*He spits on the floor. Then aloud*) That's the ditch there: all clear? Right!

ROSINE *takes out her handkerchief, and the* COUNT *drops the letter between them.*

BARTHOLO: (*stooping*) Aha!

The COUNT *retrieves the handkerchief.*

COUNT: Hold it! Just as I was about to initiate you in the finer points of my profession. . . . A very virtuous wife, I must say! Is this or is it not a love letter from another man that just fell out of her pocket?

BARTHOLO: Give it me, give it me!

COUNT: Gently does it, Grandpa! Everyone's entitled to their privacy. How would you feel if a prescription for syrup of figs had fallen out of your pocket?

ROSINE: (*putting out her hand*) Oh, I know what it is, Trooper. Thank you.

She takes the letter and puts it in the pocket of her apron.

BARTHOLO: Will you get out???

COUNT: Very well, I will get out: farewell, Doctor; no hard feelings.

Your servant, dear one: pray that death will spare me for a few more battles yet: I've never felt a more passionate desire to live!

BARTHOLO: I said get out. If I had any credit of that kind with the Grim Reaper . . .

COUNT: Credit with the Reaper? Honestly, Doctor, after all you've done for him, I can't believe he'd refuse you anything.

Sc.15

[*He goes off*]

BARTHOLO: (*watching him go*) I thought he'd never go. (*Aside*) I must disguise my true feelings.

ROSINE: You must admit, Sir, he was very amusing, the young Captain. Even though he was drunk you could see he wasn't stupid by any means; even quite an educated man.

BARTHOLO: I am only happy, my dear love, that thanks to my firmness we are now both shot of him. But aren't you dying for us to read the paper he gave you?

ROSINE: What paper?

BARTHOLO: The one he pretended to pick up so he could give it to you.

ROSINE: Oh that! That was a letter from my cousin who's an officer in the army. It fell out of my pocket.

BARTHOLO: I could have sworn he took it out of his.

ROSINE: But I recognised it straightaway.

BARTHOLO: Surely there's no harm in my looking at it?

ROSINE: Except I don't know what I've done with it.

BARTHOLO: (*pointing to the pocket*) You put it there.

ROSINE: Oh! I can't have been thinking.

BARTHOLO: No, I'm sure you weren't. You'll see, it will be some silly bit of nonsense.

ROSINE: (*aside*) If I don't get him into a rage, there'll be no way of refusing.

BARTHOLO: Give it me, dearest heart.

ROSINE: But how dare you insist on such a thing, Sir? I suppose you don't believe me again?

BARTHOLO: What about you! What possible reason could you have for not showing it to me?

ROSINE: I have already told you, Sir, that piece of paper is the letter from my cousin that you gave me yesterday already opened, nothing else: and while we're on the subject, I may as well tell you quite frankly I find your taking that particular liberty extremely irritating.

BARTHOLO: I don't understand!

ROSINE: Do I go prying into papers that come for you? Why should you presume to touch those that are addressed to me? If you do it out of jealousy I find it insulting: if you are merely taking advantage of a position of authority you have no right to in the first place I find it even more disgusting!

BARTHOLO: Disgusting? You've never talked to me like this before.

ROSINE: If I have kept my temper till now that is no reason to go on persecuting me!

BARTHOLO: What do you mean, persecuting you?

ROSINE: It's unheard of, daring to open someone else's letters.

BARTHOLO: If they're addressed to my wife?

ROSINE: I am not your wife yet! But why should your wife have the privilege of suffering an indignity you wouldn't inflict on any other living soul?

BARTHOLO: You are trying to change the subject and distract my attention from that note, which is no doubt a missive from some lover! But don't worry, I shall see it!

ROSINE: You will not see it. If you come any closer I shall run out of this house and throw myself on the mercy of the first person I meet. I shall ask them for a room.

BARTHOLO: And they won't let you have one.

ROSINE: That remains to be seen.

BARTHOLO: This is not France. There they always presume a woman is in the right; but to spare you the trouble of indulging that particular fantasy, I shall go and lock the front door.

[He goes off]

ROSINE: Oh God! What can I do? Put my cousin's letter there instead. I'll make him sit up and beg for that.

She exchanges the letters, putting the cousin's letter in her pocket so that it is sticking out a little. BARTHOLO *comes back.*

BARTHOLO: Ah! I hope now you will allow me to see it.

ROSINE: By what right, if you please?

BARTHOLO: That which is most generally recognised: the right of whoever happens to be stronger.*

ROSINE: You can kill me if you like. I'm not going to give it to you.

BARTHOLO: (*stamping his foot*) Madam! Madam!

ROSINE *falls in an armchair and pretends to faint.*

ROSINE: Oh, it's so humiliating!

BARTHOLO: Give me that letter! If you make me angry I may not be answerable for my actions!

ROSINE: (*turning away*) I'm so miserable!

BARTHOLO: What's the matter with you?

ROSINE: What have I to look forward to?

BARTHOLO: Rosine!

ROSINE: Oh, I am so angry!

BARTHOLO: She is not well.

ROSINE: I feel so faint! I think I may be dying.

BARTHOLO: (*aside*) Hurrah! The letter! I can read it now without her realising!

He feels her pulse and takes out the letter, turning away as he tries to read it.

ROSINE: (*still turning away*) What have I done to deserve this?

BARTHOLO *drops her arm.*

BARTHOLO: (*aside*) Why am I so desperate to read it when I'm terrified what I may find?

ROSINE: Oh, poor Rosine!

BARTHOLO: It may be some perfume you've been using. . . . It has been known to cause convulsions of this kind.

He holds the letter behind the chair, as he feels her pulse. ROSINE *raises her head slightly, gives him a knowing look, nods, and lies back without speaking.*

BARTHOLO: (*aside*) Oh God! It's the letter from her cousin. . . . Damn it! Why do I have to be so jealous? I'll never hear the end of this! At least she mustn't know I've read it!

He helps her up and slips the letter back in her pocket.

ROSINE: (*sighing*) Oh . . .

BARTHOLO: Well! Nothing too serious, my dear. Touch of the vapours, that's all: pulse didn't flicker for a moment.

He goes to get a bottle from the table against the wall.

ROSINE: (*aside*) He's put the letter back. It worked!

BARTHOLO: My dear Rosine, a little restorative liqueur.

ROSINE: I don't ever want anything from you ever again! Leave me alone!

BARTHOLO: I must confess I may have been over-hasty about the letter.

ROSINE: The letter's nothing to do with it. It's the way you ask that's so repulsive.

BARTHOLO: (*on his knees*) Forgive me; I did acknowledge immediately that I was in the wrong. Look, I'm on my knees. I'm ready to make amends.

ROSINE: Oh yes, I have to forgive you! And you still think that letter isn't from my cousin.

BARTHOLO: Whether it's from someone else or from him, I have no desire to question you further.

ROSINE: (*offering him the letter*) There, you see: if you ask me properly, you can have whatever you want. Read it.

BARTHOLO: Your frank and open manner would allay all my suspicions, were I still unfortunate enough to harbour any.

ROSINE: Then read it, Sir!

BARTHOLO: (*drawing back*) God forbid I should ever insult you by doing such a thing.

ROSINE: If you are going to refuse, Sir, I shall be very cross indeed.

BARTHOLO: Take it as an act of atonement, an indication I trust you absolutely. I am going upstairs to see poor Marceline; Figaro, for some reason I can't understand, has let some blood from her foot; won't you come with me?

ROSINE: I'll come up in a moment.

BARTHOLO: There, we have made peace, my darling; give me your hand. If only you could love me! Oh, how happy you would be!

ROSINE: (*averting her eyes*) If you could make me happy I should love you very much.

BARTHOLO: Oh, I'll make you happy, I'll make you happy, you've no idea how happy I'll make you!

[*He goes off*]   *Sc.16*

ROSINE: (*watching him go*) Oh Lindor! And he says he'll make me happy! I must read the letter. It's already nearly got me into terrible trouble. (*She reads and cries out*) Oh! Too late! I should have read it sooner: he says I ought to start a serious quarrel with my guardian; that was such a good one and now I've let it die down. When I picked up the letter I'm sure I must have gone as red as a beetroot. Oh, my guardian is right. I have an awful lot to learn about the ways of the world: my guardian's always telling me, there are women who can seem absolutely serene whatever happens; but in the end a bad husband could make a wicked woman out of anyone – even the most innocent girl in the world!

ACT III

Sc.1   BARTHOLO, *alone and in despair.*

BARTHOLO: She's so angry again! She's so angry again! Just when I thought I'd calmed her down! Now, who the hell can have put it into her head she doesn't want any more music lessons from Master Bazile? She knows he's making the arrangements for the marriage. . . .
(There is a knock at the door)
You do everything on earth to make women happy: they're not satisfied about one little tiny point, one little thing. . . .
(The knocking is repeated)
Who can that be?

Sc.2   The COUNT *comes in, in academic dress.*

COUNT: May peace and happiness be upon this house and all who dwell herein.

BARTHOLO: *(belligerently)* A prayer very appropriate at this present time! What do you want?

COUNT: Sir, my name is Alonzo, bachelor of arts, licenciate . . .

BARTHOLO: If you're a music teacher I've already got one.

COUNT: Pupil of Master Bazile, the organist at the Convent, who has I believe the privilege of expounding musical technique to the lady of the house.

BARTHOLO: Bazile! Organist! Privilege. . . . Yes, I am already aware of that!

COUNT: *(aside)* Here we go again! *(Aloud)* A sudden indisposition: he is obliged to stay in bed.

BARTHOLO: Stay in bed! Bazile! Thank God he let me know: I'll come at once.

COUNT: *(aside)* Oh damn the man! *(Aloud)* When I say in bed, Sir, I mean in his room.

BARTHOLO: Whatever it is, if it's keeping him at home: lead the way, I'll be right behind you!

COUNT: (*embarrassed*) Sir, I was instructed. . . . No one can hear us?

BARTHOLO: (*aside*) This is some trick. (*Aloud*) Oh no, mysterious doings afoot, no doubt. Speak out quite fearlessly . . . if that is possible.

COUNT: (*aside*) Horrible old man! (*Aloud*) Master Bazile told me I should inform you . . .

BARTHOLO: Speak up, I am deaf in one ear.

COUNT: Oh, certainly! (*Raising his voice*) That Count Almaviva, who had taken lodgings in the Plaza Major!!!

BARTHOLO: (*terrified*) Not so loud, not so loud!

COUNT: (*even louder*) . . . moved out this morning!!! As it was I who first informed him that Count Almaviva . . .

BARTHOLO: Not so loud. Not quite so loud, please!

COUNT: (*just as loudly*) . . . was in the city, and it was I who found out that Señora Rosine had written to him!!!

BARTHOLO: Written to him? Look, let's sit down and have a chat about all this in a more friendly atmosphere. You found out, you say, that Rosine . . .

COUNT: (*proudly*) I most certainly did. Bazile, alarmed on your behalf that a correspondence had been entered into, did ask me to show you her letter; but given the way you take things . . .

BARTHOLO: For heaven's sake, I'd say I was taking this extremely well! But would it not be possible for you to speak a little less loudly?

COUNT: You said you were deaf in one ear.

BARTHOLO: Forgive me, forgive me, Señor Alonzo, if you find me suspicious or impolite; but I am surrounded by people trying to trick me, trying to trip me up. . . . And your appearance, your age, your manner. . . . Forgive me, forgive me. Well, where's the letter?

COUNT: If you talk like that, Sir, of course: but I'm sure there's someone eavesdropping on us.

BARTHOLO: What? But who? The servants have all been knocked out cold. Rosine had a tantrum and locked herself in her room! There's been all hell let loose. All the same I'll go and make quite certain.

He goes and cautiously opens ROSINE'*s door.*

COUNT: (*aside*) Why am I such a fool? I can't let him see the letter. I'll try and get out without him seeing me! I should never have come in the first place! I suppose I could show it to him. If I could warn Rosine, letting him see it would be a stroke of genius.

BARTHOLO: (*returning on tiptoe*) She is sitting at the window with her

back to the door, re-reading a letter from her cousin in the army I
took the precaution of opening. . . . Now, let me see hers.

The COUNT *gives him* ROSINE'*s letter.*

COUNT: Here. (*Aside*) That's my letter she is reading.

BARTHOLO: (*reading*) 'Now I know your name and who you are . . .'.
Oh, how devious! That's her handwriting, no doubt about it!

COUNT: (*terrified*) Not so loud!!

BARTHOLO: Oh, I'm so obliged to you, dear kind friend!!

COUNT: Oh, when it's all over, if you feel you're in my debt, that is of
course up to you as my employer. . . . On the question of the work
Master Bazile is engaged in with the lawyer . . .

BARTHOLO: The lawyer? On my marriage?

COUNT: I presume so. He instructed me to inform you that everything
can be ready by tomorrow. So, if she resists . . .

BARTHOLO: She'll resist all right.

The COUNT *tries to take back the letter.* BARTHOLO *keeps it.*

COUNT: That will be the moment I can be of some assistance; we'll
show her this letter, and if needs be . . . (*more conspiratorially*) I will
take it a step further and tell her I had it from another woman the
Count had given it to as a proof of his love; you watch, she'll be so
upset, so ashamed, she'll give in immediately, just to spite him.

BARTHOLO: (*laughing*) A little slander! My dear man, now I'm con-
vinced you are sent by Bazile! But so it won't seem like a conspiracy
between the two of us, might it not be as well if she'd already met
you?

COUNT: (*suppressing his excitement*) That was rather what Master
Bazile had in mind. But how? It's late: there's so little time . . .

BARTHOLO: I will say that you come instead. You can give her a lesson,
can't you?

COUNT: For you, Sir, anything! But be careful: you know all the old
stories about people pretending to be music teachers: it's a very old
trick, you often see it used as a comic device on stage: what if she
suspects something?

BARTHOLO: When I'm the one that introduces you? Not a chance. You
look more like the lover in disguise than someone secretly in cahoots
with me.

COUNT: Really? So you think my appearance might actually help in the
deception?

BARTHOLO: I guarantee nobody, however shrewd, would ever see through this. She is in a terrible temper tonight. But I'm sure the moment she sees you. . . . Her harpsichord is in this little room in here. Make yourself at home; I'll go and pit myself against the elements and bring her in.

COUNT: Not a word about the letter.

BARTHOLO: Not until the crucial moment! That would ruin everything. No, no, nod's as good as a wink! I'm no fool, I can tell you that.

[He goes]   Sc.3

COUNT: Done it! Phew! He's hard work and no mistake, the miserable old devil! Figaro's absolutely right about him. Even I could tell I was lying; that made me seem even slower and clumsier: and those eyes! God, if I hadn't suddenly thought of the letter there's no doubt about it, I'd have been outside that door again, looking like a blithering idiot. Oh heavens, now they're arguing in there. What if she won't see me?

(He listens at the door)

What's she saying? She won't leave her room, so it hasn't worked!

(He goes back to listen)

No, she's coming: I mustn't let her see me straightaway.

He goes into the harpsichord room.   Sc.4

ROSINE: (pretending to be angry) Nothing you have to say can make any difference whatsoever, Sir! My mind is made up; I don't want to hear any more talk about music.

BARTHOLO: Do listen, my dear: Señor Alonzo is a pupil and a friend of Master Bazile, chosen by him to be one of our witnesses. You'll find the music soothing, I promise you.

ROSINE: Nonsense! You can just get rid of him! Sing this evening, indeed! And where is this music teacher you're so terrified of offending? I'll give him his marching orders soon enough, and Master Bazile for that matter!

(She sees the COUNT)

Oh!

BARTHOLO: What's the matter?

ROSINE: (with both hands pressed against her heart, in great confusion) Ah! Oh God, Sir! . . . Ah! Oh God, Sir!

BARTHOLO: She is having another of her turns! Señor Alonzo!

ROSINE: I am not having another of my turns! . . . I just turned round and. . . . Oh!

COUNT: You turned your ankle, Madam?

ROSINE: What? Yes, I turned my ankle. It was terribly painful!

COUNT: So I saw!

ROSINE: (*looking at the* COUNT) It caught me here! My heart!

BARTHOLO: Sit down, you must sit down! Why are there no comfort-
able chairs in here?

He goes to get one.

COUNT: Oh, Rosine!

ROSINE: This is very reckless of you!

COUNT: I have so many things I absolutely have to tell you.

ROSINE: He'll never leave us alone together for a moment.

COUNT: Figaro is on the way. He'll think of something.

BARTHOLO: (*bringing an armchair*) Here, my darling, do sit down – I
am afraid, Dominie, there is no chance of her taking her lesson this
evening: another day. Goodbye.

ROSINE: (*to the* COUNT) No, wait, it's already beginning to hurt a great
deal less. (*to* BARTHOLO) I realise I was in the wrong, Sir. I'd like to
do as you did, do something to show you I'm sorry.

BARTHOLO: Ah! Such a dear sweet little girl you are underneath it all!
But after anything as upsetting as that, my dear, I can't allow you to
exert yourself in any way. Goodbye, Goodbye, Sir.

ROSINE: (*to the* COUNT) Do wait Señor Alonzo, please! (*To* BAR-
THOLO) I shall think, Sir, you are not in the least concerned about
my happiness if you prevent me from showing how sorry I am by
having my lesson.

COUNT: (*aside, to* BARTHOLO) Don't antagonise her, Sir, if you have
any faith in me at all.

BARTHOLO: Then that is settled, my little love-bird. I am so far from
any desire to displease you I shall stay here all the time and listen to
you practising.

ROSINE: Oh no, Sir: I know you're not the slightest bit interested in
music.

BARTHOLO: I promise you, this evening I shall find it quite enchanting!

ROSINE: (*to the* COUNT, *aside*) This will kill me!

COUNT: (*taking up a piece of music from the desk*) Is this the one you
want to sing, Madam?

ROSINE: Yes, it is a very charming piece from *All That Trouble For
Nothing*.

BARTHOLO: It's always *All That Trouble For Nothing*!

COUNT: It is the very latest thing. This is a description of spring; quite
vividly portrayed. If you'd care to try it, Madam . . .

ROSINE: (*looking at the* COUNT) I'd love to: how thrilling, a picture of spring! Everything in nature is young. The end of the winter, when you suddenly feel more intensely: as if you'd been shut up in prison, and offered the chance of freedom for the first time!

BARTHOLO: (*whispering to the* COUNT) She always has very romantic ideas.

COUNT: (*whispering to* BARTHOLO) You know what she's talking about though, don't you?

BARTHOLO: Good Lord!

> *He goes and sits down in the armchair previously occupied by*
> ROSINE.

ROSINE: (*singing*)

> When o'er the plain
> Love once again
> Summons the spring
> Then lovers sing;
> All is new made,
> See her invade
> New life impart
> To each bud and young heart;
> Now o'er the hill
> Flocks roam at will,
> Sweet echoes repeat
> The lambs' timid bleat,
> Gambolling free
> And leap o'er the lea;
> Sap is flowing
> All is growing,
> Flowers unheeding
> Sheep are feeding
> At peace, without fear
> The watchdog is near;
> But Lindor, the swain
> Trembles and sighs
> To gaze once again
> In his shepherdess's eyes.

> *The same music is repeated. Listening to the song,* BARTHOLO *has fallen asleep. The* COUNT, *during the coming reprise, risks taking* ROSINE's *hand and covers it with kisses.*

> Far from her home

See the shepherdess roam
Singing so sweet
Her lover to greet
Thus by her play
Love has its way
Say can he hear?
The danger is clear;
Sweet piping is heard
The song of each bird
Her budding young charms
Her childish alarms
Scarce seventeen
Though far from serene;
All excites her
All delights her
Lindor is by
Sees her draw nigh
Then she is there
He bounds from his lair
Holding her fast
Happy at last
She feigns alarm

(ROSINE *is singing more slowly, and seems about to swoon: now she breaks off in mid-phrase*)

To feel his strong arm.

There is a short reprise. The orchestra follows the singer, playing more and more softly and coming to an end as she does.

Heart to heart
Softly sighing
Swear love undying
Never to part
Pliant and pleasing
Playfully teasing
Soon her swain
Is forgiven again
If jealous eye
Dare there to pry
Our lovers combine,
Take infinite care

> Betraying no sign
> Cupid above
> A presence malign
> Adds spice to their love.

The absence of the noise that has lulled BARTHOLO *to sleep now awakens him. The* COUNT *rises to his feet,* ROSINE *and the orchestra suddenly begin again with the remainder of the tune.*

COUNT: Indeed, it's a very charming piece: the young lady phrases it very intelligently . . .

ROSINE: You flatter me, Sir; I'm sure that any glory should go to you, as my teacher.

BARTHOLO: (*yawning*) Do you know, I think I may possibly have nodded off for a moment during that charming piece. My patients, you know, the sick. Always on the go, on my rounds, round and round and round like a top; the moment I sit down, my poor legs . . .

He gets up and pushes the chair back.

ROSINE: (*whispering to the* COUNT) Where's Figaro?

COUNT: (*whispering*) We must play for time.

BARTHOLO: But Señor Alonzo, as I've often said to old Bazile: couldn't she learn something more amusing than all these grand arias? They're always going up and down all the time, all those trills – hee, ho, ah, ah, ah, ah? They always sound to me as though they ought to be performed at funerals! Now the little songs we used to sing when I was younger: they were very easy to learn. I knew a lot of them in the old days . . . for instance . . .

During the introductory accompaniment he scratches his head, trying to remember the tune, and as he sings he snaps his fingers, only dancing with his knees like an old man.

(*he sings*)

> Rosine, do but try me
> A glass of wine will buy me –
> The husband of your dreams . . .

(*To the* COUNT, *laughing*) In the song it's Belinda, you see – 'Belinda, do but try me' – but I sang Rosine instead, to make it more entertaining, more applicable to the present situation. Ha, ha, ha, ha! Very good, what?

COUNT: (*laughing*) Ha, ha, ha! Oh yes. Wonderful. Wonderful!

Sc.5   FIGARO *appears upstage.*

BARTHOLO: (*singing*)
                Rosine do but try me
                A glass of wine will buy me
                The husband of your dreams!
                No Adonis as it seems
                But when it's dark at night
                I think I'd dare to claim
                Just shut your eyes, blow out the light, –
                We all look much the same.

He repeats the refrain, still dancing. FIGARO, *behind him, imitates*
his movements.

                No Adonis as it seems. . . .

(*He sees* FIGARO) Ah! Come in, Barber; come in, do. Oh, you're a charmer, you are!

FIGARO: (*bowing*) So my mother used to tell me, Sir; but I have grown in some very peculiar directions since those days. (*Aside, to the* COUNT) Well done, Your Lordship!

During this entire scene the COUNT *does his best to talk to*
ROSINE, *but he is prevented every time by quick looks from*
BARTHOLO, *always on his guard. This creates a dumb show*
among all the actors, which is independent of the dialogue
between BARTHOLO *and* FIGARO.

BARTHOLO: I expect you have come to adminster more laxative all round? Bleed and drug and demolish my entire household?

FIGARO: No, Sir, we can't have fun all the time; but my regular duties apart, Sir, I hope you're satisfied that when there's a call for my services I am a man of initiative who goes to work with a will.

BARTHOLO: A man of initiative who goes to work with a will! What would you say, as a man of initiative, to that wretched man yawning, stumbling round half asleep? Or to the other one who has spent the last three hours sneezing fit to blow the top of his head off and spatter his brains about? What would you say to them?

FIGARO: What would I say to them?

BARTHOLO: Yes.

FIGARO: Well, I'd say. . . . Well, damn it! I'd say 'Bless you' to the one that's sneezing, and 'Go to bed!' to the one that's yawning. That advice entirely gratis and will not appear on the bill.

BARTHOLO: It had better not! But you'd charge me for the bleeding and the drugs no doubt, if you thought you'd get away with it! And that was your initiative too, was it, slapping the mule round the face with a mustard plaster? I suppose you thought a hot poultice would restore its eyesight?

FIGARO: Well, if it doesn't restore its eyesight it won't mind being blindfolded, will it?

BARTHOLO: Just you let me find a bill for that! If there's one thing I can't stand, it's the senseless squandering of money!

FIGARO: Well, Sir, the way I see it, the only choice a man has got is either to be a fool or a lunatic, and in a case where I can't see any prospect of making a profit, I think at least I can have a bit of fun. Enjoy life, that's my motto. Who knows if the world'll still be there in three weeks' time?

BARTHOLO: You'd do better, my philosophical friend, to pay me the hundred crowns you owe me, with the interest, and stop this tomfoolery. I'm warning you!

FIGARO: Are you casting aspersions on my honesty, Sir? Your hundred crowns! I wouldn't deny they're yours for a moment! I'd rather have that debt hanging over me till my dying day!

BARTHOLO: And do tell me, how did little Miss Figaro like the sweeties that you brought her?

FIGARO: Sweeties? What are you talking about?

BARTHOLO: You know, the sweets in the bag made out of a piece of writing paper, this morning.

FIGARO: Well I'll be damned if I . . .

ROSINE: (interrupting him) I hope you remembered to tell her they were from me, Mr Figaro: I did ask you specially.

FIGARO: Oh! Oh! The sweets this morning you mean? Oh, how can I be so stupid! They'd completely slipped my mind! Oh, they were excellent, Madam. First class.

BARTHOLO: Excellent! First class! That's right, barber, cover your tracks! A highly moral line of business you're in, Sir!

FIGARO: What are you talking about, Sir?

BARTHOLO: And one that will enhance your reputation, no end.

FIGARO: I'll do my best to live up to it, Sir.

BARTHOLO: Live down to it, you mean!

FIGARO: Whichever you prefer, Sir.

BARTHOLO: You have a damn cheek, Sir! Now you listen to me! When I'm arguing with a conceited dolt I am not in the habit of giving in.

FIGARO: (*turning his back on him*) Ah, that is where we differ, Sir. I always do.

BARTHOLO: Eh? What was that he said, Señor Alonzo?

FIGARO: Your trouble is you think you're dealing with some village barber who's never touched anything in his life but a razor. Now you may not know it, Sir, but in Madrid I earned a living as a man of letters, and if it hadn't been for the other writers getting jealous . . .

BARTHOLO: Well, why didn't you stay there, instead of coming back here and taking someone else's job?

FIGARO: We all do the best we can: put yourself in my position . . .

BARTHOLO: Put myself in your position? God, I'd say some stupid things!

FIGARO: You're not doing so badly, Sir. What would your colleague say, day-dreaming over there?

COUNT: (*suddenly coming to his senses*) What, me? But I'm not a doctor!

FIGARO: Aren't you? Oh. Seeing you here, diagnosing about, I thought you must be, as it were, engaged in the same pursuit!

BARTHOLO: (*angrily*) Well, what brings you here this time? Another letter to deliver to this lady by the second post? Do say if you'd prefer to be left alone!

FIGARO: Why must you always shout at all of us poor souls? Heavens above, Sir, I've come to shave you, that's all. It is your day today, isn't it?

BARTHOLO: Come back later!

FIGARO: Oh, that's right, come back later! The whole garrison on parade for enemas first thing in the morning. I only got the contract knowing the right strings to pull. So you can imagine how much time I've got to hang about! Now, if you would kindly step into your consulting room, Sir . . .

BARTHOLO: No, I will not kindly step into my consulting room. Just a minute! What's wrong with shaving me in here?

ROSINE: (*contemptuously*) What exquisite manners!! Why not? After all, I only have to live in here!

BARTHOLO: You're getting angry again! Forgive me, my dear, you shall finish your lesson. This is only so I shouldn't miss a moment of the pleasure of listening to you.

FIGARO: (*whispering to the* COUNT) We'll never get him out of here! (*Aloud*) Come on, Wideawake, where's the Youth? The basin, the hot water, all the gentleman's things . . .

BARTHOLO: Oh call them, by all means. You realise they were so done for, utterly shattered and wrung out, after what you've done to them, I had to send them to bed?

FIGARO: All right, I'll go and fetch it all myself. Everything up in your bedroom, isn't it? (*Whispering to the* COUNT) This'll get him outside!

BARTHOLO *takes out his bunch of keys.*

BARTHOLO: (*after a moment's thought*) No, no, I'll come myself. (*Whispering to the* COUNT *as he goes out*) Keep an eye on them, eh?

FIGARO: I nearly had him then! He was just going to give me the whole   *Sc.6* bunch. There must be the key to the lattice in among them somewhere.

ROSINE: It's the brand-new one.

BARTHOLO: (*coming back: aside*) So! I can't think what I can have   *Sc.7* been doing, leaving that confounded barber alone in here. (*To* FIGARO) Take these! (*He gives him the bunch of keys*) In my study, underneath the desk: but don't touch anything.

FIGARO: For heaven's sake! Fat lot of good that'd be, knowing how suspicious you are! (*Aside, as he goes off*) There: I've always said honesty was the best policy!

BARTHOLO: (*whispering to the* COUNT) That's the clown that brought   *Sc.8* the letter from the Count.

COUNT: (*whispering*) Looked very untrustworthy to me.

BARTHOLO: (*whispering*) Last time he'll catch me napping!

COUNT: (*whispering*) I think as far as all that's concerned the worst is over.

BARTHOLO: (*whispering*) All things considered, I thought it was wiser to send him up to my room than leave him alone with her.

COUNT: (*whispering*) They couldn't have said a word without me overhearing it.

ROSINE: What perfect manners you both have, gentlemen, whispering all the time! And what about my music lesson?

A sound of breaking china is heard off-stage.

BARTHOLO: (*crying out*) What's that? That bloody barber's dropped everything down the stairs. That china was priceless! My intimate utensils!

                                        [*He rushes out*]   *Sc.9*

COUNT: Well done, Figaro! Very clever! We mustn't waste a second. Let me see you tonight, Madam. You must! It's vital I talk to you, so I can rescue you before that man makes you a slave for life.

ROSINE: Oh, Lindor!

COUNT: I can climb up to this window here. Oh, and the letter you wrote me this morning, I had to . . .

Sc.10   BARTHOLO *returns, followed by* FIGARO.

BARTHOLO: I was right; everything broken, smashed to smithereens!

FIGARO: All this fuss he's making about a little accident like that. You can't see a blind thing on those stairs.
(*He shows the key to the* COUNT)
This key caught my eye on the way up.

BARTHOLO: You should concentrate! Caught your eye on a key! What a brilliant man!

FIGARO: Oh yes, Sir, they don't come much cleverer than me!

Sc.11   BAZILE *comes in.*

ROSINE: (*aside: alarmed*) Don Bazile!

COUNT: (*aside*) Oh heavens!

FIGARO: (*aside*) It's the devil himself.

BARTHOLO: (*stepping forward to greet him*) Ah! Bazile, my friend, so glad to see you've recovered. No unpleasant complications? I must confess Señor Alonzo very much alarmed me when he told me you weren't well: ask him, I was about to come and see you; in fact if he hadn't stopped me . . .

BAZILE: (*in amazement*) Señor Alonzo?

FIGARO: (*stamping his foot*) What? Another interruption! I spend two hours trying to shave one miserable chin! What a way to earn a living!

BAZILE: (*looking from one to the other*) I wonder, gentlemen, whether you'd be very kind, and tell me . . .

FIGARO: You have a nice long talk to him after I've gone.

BAZILE: But all the same, I should . . .

COUNT: What you should do, Bazile, is shut your mouth. Do you think that you could possibly tell this gentleman anything he doesn't already know! I have explained that you asked me to give the music lesson because you couldn't come.

BAZILE: (*more astonished*) Music lesson! Alonzo! . . .

ROSINE: (*aside, to* BAZILE) Oh, do be quiet!

BAZILE: Now she's at it!

COUNT: (*whispering, to* BARTHOLO) Whisper to him! Tell him we're in this together.

BARTHOLO: (*aside, to* BAZILE) Don't give us away, Bazile! For heaven's sake don't say he's not a music teacher! You'll ruin everything!

BAZILE: Ah! Ah!

BARTHOLO: (*aloud*) No doubt about it, Bazile, you've taught him very well! An extremely talented man!

BAZILE: (*taken aback*) Taught him? (*Whispering*) I came to tell you the Count has moved out of his lodgings.

BARTHOLO: (*whispering*) I know that, you fool! Be quiet!

BAZILE: (*whispering*) But who told you?

BARTHOLO: (*whispering*) He did, obviously!

COUNT: (*whispering*) I did of course! Just listen!

ROSINE: (*whispering, to* BAZILE) What's so difficult? Just be quiet!

FIGARO: (*whispering*) Eh?? You clumsy great lout!! Are you deaf?

BAZILE: (*aside*) For pity's sake! Please! Who are we trying to deceive? Everybody's in the secret except me.

BARTHOLO: (*aloud*) Well, Bazile, what news of the lawyer?

FIGARO: Look! You have got all night to talk about the lawyer!!

BARTHOLO: (*to* BAZILE) Only one question: are you happy about the lawyer?

BAZILE: (*startled*) About the lawyer?

COUNT: (*smiling*) You mean you haven't seen the lawyer?

BAZILE: (*growing impatient*) What? No, I haven't seen the lawyer!

COUNT: (*aside to* BARTHOLO) You don't want him to start talking about all this in front of her! Tell him to get out!

BARTHOLO: (*whispering to the* COUNT) You're quite right. (*To* BAZILE) But what can have made you so ill so suddenly?

BAZILE: (*angrily*) I don't understand!

COUNT: (*slipping a purse into his hand*) Yes you do! Doctor Bartholo is asking what you are doing here, when you are obviously ill?

FIGARO: He's as white as a sheet.

BAZILE: Oh, I see . . .

COUNT: Go to bed, Bazile dear: you are not well and you are causing us grave anxiety: you ought to go to bed!

FIGARO: You should see your face! You look terrible! Go to bed!

BARTHOLO: There's no question, the man reeks of fever, you can smell it a mile off. Go to bed!

ROSINE: Whatever made you get up in the first place? It's probably contagious. Go to bed!

BAZILE: (*utterly astonished*) Go to bed?

ALL: Yes!

BAZILE: (*looking at them all*) Well, gentlemen, I think it might be no bad thing if I were to go home: I haven't really been feeling quite myself ever since I got here.

BARTHOLO: I'll see you tomorrow then: if you're better.

COUNT: Bazile! I'll come and see you first thing in the morning.

FIGARO: Believe me, wrap up warm and stay in bed.

ROSINE: Goodnight, Master Bazile!

BAZILE: (*aside*) I'm dammed if I understand what's going on! If it wasn't for the money . . .

ALL: Goodnight, Bazile, goodnight!

BAZILE: (*going*) Oh, very well. Goodnight, then, goodnight.

Sc.12   *They all go with him, laughing.*

BARTHOLO: (*with an air of authority*) That man is by no means well.

ROSINE: Did you see his eyes? The way they were wandering?

COUNT: I expect it was coming out in the fresh air.

FIGARO: Did you notice how he was muttering to himself? What a feeble piece of work is man, eh? (*To* BARTHOLO) Ah! You've made your mind up at last, have you?

He pushes an armchair as far as possible from the COUNT, *and holds up a cloth.*

COUNT: Before we finish, Madam, there's something most important I must tell you if we are to make any progress at all; it has been such a privilege to teach you . . .

He goes closer and whispers to her.

BARTHOLO: (*to* FIGARO) Just a moment! It seems to me you're doing that on purpose: coming up and standing in front of me so I can't see . . .

COUNT: (*whispering to* ROSINE) We have the key to the lattice; we'll be here at midnight.

FIGARO: (*knotting the cloth round* BARTHOLO's *neck*) Can't see what? Now, if it was a dancing lesson, I'd have you down there so you could watch; but a singing lesson. . . . Ow! Ah!

BARTHOLO: What is it?

FIGARO: Something's gone in my eye!

He puts his face close to BARTHOLO's.

BARTHOLO: Don't rub it, then!

FIGARO: The left one! Would you be so kind as to blow in it, fairly hard, I wonder?

BARTHOLO *takes hold of* FIGARO's *head, looks over the top of it, pushes it violently away and goes over behind the lovers to listen to what they are saying.*

COUNT: (*whispering to* ROSINE) About the letter you wrote: I'd got myself so tied up just now, trying to think of some excuse to stay.

FIGARO: (*warning them from a distance*) Ahem! Ahem!

COUNT: (*whispering*) I was desperate: I thought I'd got into this disguise for nothing.

BARTHOLO: (*appearing between them*) This disguise for nothing . . .

ROSINE: (*terrified*) Oh!

BARTHOLO: Very good, Madam, please feel no qualms on my account. What! Before my very eyes, in my presence, you dare to behave in this abominable manner?

COUNT: Are you all right, Doctor?

BARTHOLO: Alonzo! You snake in the grass!

COUNT: Doctor Bartholo, if you are subject to fits of the kind I happen, quite by chance, to be witnessing at this moment, I am not surprised at the aversion this young lady feels at the prospect of becoming your wife.

ROSINE: His wife! How could I ever spend my life with a jealous old man like this? He thinks he's making me happy, condemning me to spend the best years of my life locked up like a slave!

BARTHOLO: What? What did I hear you say?

ROSINE: Yes, and I don't mind who else hears it either! I will give myself gladly, body and soul, to any man who can rescue me, by force if necessary, from this hideous prison where I and everything that I possess are held in defiance of every law that was ever written!!!

[ROSINE *goes off*]   Sc.13

BARTHOLO: I am so angry I shall choke!!

COUNT: You must admit, Doctor, it isn't easy for a young wife . . .

FIGARO: Oh yes, young wife, him being so elderly . . . preys on an old man's mind.

BARTHOLO: What! When I caught them in the act! You infernal barber!! Do you know what I'd like to do??

FIGARO: I'm going: he's gone mad.

COUNT: So am I. He's definitely gone mad!

FIGARO: He's gone mad! He's gone mad!

They go off. BARTHOLO *chases after them.*   Sc.14

BARTHOLO: I've gone mad!! The filthy swine, trying to corrupt the morals of that innocent young girl! Fiends out of hell, sent to torment me, the devil take 'em all back where they came from! I've gone mad! I saw them! As plain as I can see this music stand ... shamelessly brazening it out in front of me! Bazile's the only person who can explain all this! I must send for him. Hullo! Somebody! ... Oh, I'd forgotten. No one there. Send a neighbour: a passer-by, what does it matter? All this is driving me out of my mind! It's driving me out of my mind!

The sound of a storm is heard.

ACT IV

BARTHOLO: What do you mean, Bazile, you've never clapped eyes on him in your life? You seriously expect me to believe that?

BAZILE: However often you asked me I'd still give you the same answer. If he gave you the letter from Rosine, then it can only have been someone sent by the Count. But from the size of his gift to me, it could have been the Count himself.

BARTHOLO: Is that likely? But on the question of the present. What did you think you were doing accepting it? Eh?

BAZILE: Well, you looked as though you knew all about it: I had no idea what was going on; and in a case that's hard to judge I always think a large payment in cash is an unanswerable argument. And then, you know the old proverb, a fool and his money . . .

BARTHOLO: I know, are soon . . .

BAZILE: . . . don't grow on trees!

BARTHOLO: (*surprised*) Oh!

BAZILE: Yes, I have arranged quite a lot of little proverbs like that: variations on the original theme as it were. But, down to brass tacks: what do you plan to do?

BARTHOLO: If you were in my place, Bazile, surely you'd do everything in your power to possess her?

BAZILE: Oh goodness me, no Doctor! It's the same with any bit of property: it doesn't matter if it's yours; the real pleasure's in having the use of it: in my opinion marrying a woman who doesn't love you is laying yourself open . . .

BARTHOLO: You would be afraid some mishap might occur?

BAZILE: Ha, ha! Well, Sir. . . . There are always enough of those. I wouldn't force her, not against her inclinations.

BARTHOLO: Very obliged, Bazile. But I'd rather have her crying at having to have me, than me dying to have her and not having her.

BAZILE: You mean it's a matter of life and death? Then you must marry her, Doctor, marry her!

BARTHOLO: I intend to. Tonight!

BAZILE: Goodbye then. And remember, when you're talking to her, make them seem as evil as you can!

BARTHOLO: You are quite right.

BAZILE: Slander, Doctor, slander! Always the best way in the end.

BARTHOLO: This is the letter from Rosine that Alonzo gave me; he also let slip, against his will, the best method of using it to work on her.

BAZILE: Goodbye: we'll all be here at four o'clock.

BARTHOLO: Why can't you come earlier?

BAZILE: It can't be done. The Notary has a previous engagement.

BARTHOLO: A wedding?

BAZILE: Yes, at the barber's. At Figaro's; he's marrying his niece.

BARTHOLO: His niece? He hasn't got a niece!!

BAZILE: That's what they told the Notary.

BARTHOLO: That clown must be part of the conspiracy, damn it!

BAZILE: You weren't thinking . . . ?

BARTHOLO: Good God, those people are on their toes! Wait, man, I am uneasy. Go back to the Notary's. Bring him here immediately.

BAZILE: It's pouring with rain! I wouldn't send a cat out on a night like this. However, you can rely on me, Sir, at your service at all times. What are you doing?

BARTHOLO: Coming with you, as far as the front door: you know they employed Figaro to maim all the servants, don't you? I'm all alone!

BAZILE: I have my lantern.

BARTHOLO: Bazile, this is my own master-key. You take it. I'll be expecting you. I shall wait up. And whoever comes, other than the Notary and yourself, they will not get in here tonight.

BAZILE: You're taking a great deal of trouble. But better safe than sorry, what?

Sc.2   *They both go off.* ROSINE *comes out of her room.*

ROSINE: I thought I heard someone talking. It's gone midnight. Lindor can't be coming now! Such dreadful weather should have made it easier for him. He'd have been sure of not being seen. Oh Lindor! Perhaps he wasn't telling me the truth! What's that noise? Oh God, it's my guardian. I must go back to my room!

Sc.3   BARTHOLO *comes in with a light.*

BARTHOLO: Ah, Rosine! Since you're still up . . .

ROSINE: I am on the way to bed, Sir.

BARTHOLO: Terrible weather like this, you won't sleep, and I have something very urgent I must discuss with you!

ROSINE: What do you want me for, Sir? You have all day to torment me; isn't that enough?

BARTHOLO: Rosine, listen to me!

ROSINE: I'll listen to you in the morning.

BARTHOLO: One moment, please!

ROSINE: (*aside*) What if he comes?

BARTHOLO: (*showing her the letter*) Do you recognise this letter?

ROSINE: (*recognising it*) Oh God!

BARTHOLO: Rosine, I don't propose to reproach you: at your age everyone makes mistakes; but I am fond of you: now listen . . .

ROSINE: Please! No more! I can't bear it!

BARTHOLO: This letter you wrote to Count Almaviva . . .

ROSINE: (*amazed*) Count Almaviva!

BARTHOLO: You must realise what an atrocious man he is, this Count: as soon as he received it, he went round showing it off like a hunting trophy: I was sent it by some woman he gave it to, merely as proof of his devotion to her.

ROSINE: Count Almaviva!

BARTHOLO: You find it hard to believe that anyone would do anything so horrible. It's lack of experience of the world, Rosine, makes you young women so trusting and gullible; but you must see you were being lured into a trap! The woman had me informed of the true facts, presumably to be rid of a rival as dangerous as you. I tremble to think of it! A fiendish conspiracy between Almaviva, Figaro and the other man, Alonzo, who claimed he was a pupil of Bazile's.

That's not his name, of course: he's just some pimp employed by the Count. They were going to drag you away to a hell where there would have been no escape, ever!

ROSINE: (*overwhelmed*) How horrible! What, Lindor? What . . . the young man?

BARTHOLO: (*aside*) Aha! Lindor, is it?

ROSINE: All for Count Almaviva. . . . For another man . . . ?

BARTHOLO: That was what I was told when I was given your letter.

ROSINE: (*indignantly*) Oh how humiliating! I'll show him, though! Sir, I believe you wished to marry me?

BARTHOLO: You know my very violent feelings for you!

ROSINE: If I haven't entirely alienated them by my behaviour, I am yours.

BARTHOLO: Good. The lawyer's on his way. We'll have it signed and sealed tonight.

ROSINE: That is not all; Oh God, as if I hadn't been humiliated enough already! You may as well know: any moment now the filthy liar is going to try and climb in through that window. They managed to steal your key to the lattice.

BARTHOLO: (*looking at his bunch of keys*) The thieves! Oh, my darling child, I'm never going to leave you alone, ever again!

ROSINE: (*terrified*) Oh Sir! What if they're armed?

BARTHOLO: You're right; that would prevent me having my revenge. Go up to Marceline's room: shut yourself in there and double-lock the door. I'll go and turn out the watch, and lie in wait for them outside the front door. Have him arrested as a common burglar: we shall be revenged and rid of him at the same time! And, I swear, my love will more than make up for all this and much, much more!

ROSINE: (*in despair*) Only forgive me for being so foolish! (*Aside*) God knows, I'm punishing myself enough.

BARTHOLO: (*going out*) Off to prepare the ambush! At last! She's mine!

Sc.4   [*He goes*]

ROSINE: How could his love make up for anything? Oh, I'm so miserable!

(*She takes out her handkerchief and gives way to tears*)

What can I do? He'll come. I'll stay, and pretend I don't know, just so I can see him for a moment as he really is: in his true colours. The foul way he has behaved will be enough to protect me against him! Oh! I shall need it. He has such a fine face, and such a kind way with him, such a gentle voice ... and he's only procuring for some vile, lascivious man I've never seen! Oh I'm so miserable, so miserable! Oh heavens! They're unlocking the lattice!   [*She runs off*]

Sc.5   FIGARO *appears at the window, wrapped in a cloak.*

FIGARO: (*off-stage*) Somebody's just run out of the room! Shall I go in?

COUNT: (*off-stage*) A man?

FIGARO: No.

COUNT: (*off-stage*) Then it must have been Rosine. The sight of your ugly face probably gave her a fright.

FIGARO: (*jumping down into the room*) My God, I think it did. Well here we are at last! Through thunder, lightning and the heavens opening!

The COUNT *appears, also wrapped in a long cloak.*

COUNT: Give me your hand.
 (He jumps down)
We've done it!

FIGARO: *(throwing off his cloak)* Both soaked to the skin, like a pair of drowned rats! Charming weather to go courting, I must say. How do you like the evening air, Your Lordship?

COUNT: Glorious night for lovers.

FIGARO: Not so nice for the comic servant. What happens if someone catches us?

COUNT: You're with me, aren't you? There's something worries me a great deal more than that: how are we going to persuade her to leave here tonight?

FIGARO: You have the advantage of three passions dominant in the fairer sex: love, hate and terror.

COUNT: *(peering into the darkness)* I can't come straight out with it and tell her the lawyer's at your house waiting to marry us! She'll think I'm mad! She'll think I'm forward.

FIGARO: If she calls you forward you can call her cruel. Women love it when you call them cruel. And another thing: if she loves you as much as you hope she does, you can tell her who you really are; she won't have any doubts about your intentions after that!

FIGARO *lights all the candles on the table.* ROSINE *appears.* Sc.6

COUNT: Here she is, Rosine! My beautiful one!

ROSINE: *(very controlled)* I was beginning to think you weren't coming, Sir.

COUNT: Oh, how sweet of you to be so anxious! Madam, I have no right to take advantage of the circumstances to ask you, poor as I am, to share my life: but wherever you may choose to take refuge, I swear on my honour . . .

ROSINE: Sir, if I had not intended to give you my hand as well as my heart, you would not be here. If there is anything irregular about our meeting in this way it was justified by necessity.

COUNT: You mean it, Rosine? You'll be the wife of a poor man – no family, no fortune!

ROSINE: Family and fortune are of no importance: it's a matter of pure chance who has them and who hasn't; but if you promise me your intentions are honourable . . .

COUNT: *(kneeling at her feet)* Oh, Rosine! I adore you!

ROSINE: (*indignantly*) Stop it! You despicable hypocrite! How dare you desecrate. . . . You adore me. Go on! You're no threat to me any more; I was only waiting for you to say that so I could hate you. But before I leave you to the mercy of your own conscience . . . (*she weeps*) you may as well know I was in love with you: that I was completely happy hoping I could share your poverty. Lindor, you're so vile! I was going to leave everything to come away with you. But the cowardly way you've taken advantage of my kindness, and the humiliating truth about this hideous Count Almaviva you meant to sell me to, are sufficient evidence of just how weak I was. Do you recognise this letter?

COUNT: (*eagerly*) Your guardian gave it you?

ROSINE: (*proudly*) Yes, and I am very grateful that he did.

COUNT: Oh God, I'm so happy! I gave it to him. I was in such trouble, earlier, I gave it him to make him trust me; I could never find an opportunity to tell you that I'd done it. Oh Rosine, so it's true! You honestly do love me!

FIGARO: Well, Your Lordship, you were looking for a woman who would love you for yourself . . .

ROSINE: 'Your Lordship'? What does he mean?

The COUNT *throws back his long cloak, revealing a magnificent costume underneath.*

COUNT: Oh my dearest, I love you more than any other woman in the world! I can't lie to you any longer: the man you've made so happy, kneeling at your feet, is not Lindor: I am Count Almaviva, I am desperately in love with you, I have spent six months searching for you, and never found you until now.

ROSINE: (*falling into the* COUNT's *arms*) Oh!

COUNT: (*alarmed*) Figaro?

FIGARO: Don't be alarmed, Your Lordship. Happiness is a very agreeable emotion and it's never fatal. There, there, she's coming to already. My God, she's beautiful!

ROSINE: Oh Lindor! Oh Sir! What have I done! I said I'd marry my guardian tonight!

COUNT: You, Rosine?

ROSINE: Think of the punishment! I would have spent my whole life despising you. Oh Lindor! Isn't it the most terrible torture on earth to have to hate when we know we were made to love?

FIGARO: (*looking out of the window*) Your Lordship! Our retreat has been cut off! Somebody's taken the ladder away!

COUNT: Done what?

ROSINE: (*confused*) Yes, it was me! I mean the Doctor. This is what comes of being so gullible! He tricked me. I told him everything, I gave everything away! He knows you're here, he's gone to get the watch!

FIGARO: (*still at the window*) Your Lordship! Someone's coming in the front door!

ROSINE: (*running into the* COUNT's *arms, terrified*) Oh, Lindor!

COUNT: (*firmly*) Rosine, you love me. I'm not afraid of anyone; and you are going to be my wife. Let me have the luxury of punishing this horrible old man . . . in my own way.

ROSINE: No, no; have pity on him, dear Lindor! I'm far too happy to want any revenge!

Enter BAZILE *and the* NOTARY   *Sc.7*

FIGARO: Your Lordship, it's the lawyer!

COUNT: And he's got Bazile with him!

BAZILE: I don't believe it!

FIGARO: What a fortunate coincidence!

BAZILE: This is a disaster!

NOTARY: Are these the parties to be joined in matrimony?

COUNT: Yes, Sir. You were to have married Señora Rosine and myself tonight, at Figaro the barber's house; but we preferred to hold the ceremony here for reasons I'll explain. Have you the contract?

NOTARY: So, I have the honour of addressing His Excellency the Count Almaviva?

FIGARO: Precisely.

BAZILE: (*aside*) He can't have given me the master-key for this!

NOTARY: Only I have here two marriage contracts, Your Lordship: just to be sure there's no confusion: this is yours: and this is the other, between a Señor Bartholo and Señora . . . also Rosine. The young ladies are no doubt two sisters of the same name . . .

COUNT: I think we should sign it nevertheless. I'm sure Master Bazile will be kind enough to serve as second witness.

They sign.

BAZILE: But, Your Excellency. . . . I don't understand.

COUNT: My dear Bazile, whatever we do, you're either confused or amazed.

BAZILE: Your Lordship! What happens if the Doctor . . . ?

COUNT: (*throwing him a purse*) Don't be childish! Sign it!

BAZILE: (*astonished*) Oh! Ah!

FIGARO: What is so difficult about signing your name?

BAZILE: (*weighing the purse*) Nothing! Not now! Only when I have given my solemn word of honour, it takes a very convincing argument . . .

Sc.8   *He signs:* BARTHOLO *enters with a* JUSTICE OF THE PEACE, *constables and servants carrying torches. He sees the* COUNT *kissing* ROSINE's *hand, and* FIGARO *enfolding* BAZILE *in a grotesque embrace.*

BARTHOLO: (*crying out and seizing the* NOTARY *by the throat*) Rosine, here with these burglars! Arrest the lot of them! This one won't escape . . . I've got him by the scruff!

NOTARY: I am your lawyer.

BAZILE: He's your lawyer. Is this some joke?

BARTHOLO: Oh! Bazile! Why are you here?

BAZILE: More to the point, why weren't you?

JP: (*pointing to* FIGARO) One moment; I know this man. What are you doing in this house in the middle of the night?

FIGARO: Middle of the night? Oh, come on, Sir, it's more like morning than night. Besides I am a member of the retinue of His Excellency Count Almaviva.

BARTHOLO: Almaviva?

JP: So they are not burglars!

BARTHOLO: Never mind that! Anywhere else, my Lord, I am Your Excellency's very humble servant; but you will appreciate that social distinctions are in this instance of no consequence. Please be so kind as to leave my house.

COUNT: Yes, social distinctions are of no consequence here: but what is of consequence is the fact this lady has just given proof she prefers me to you, in freely promising to become my wife.

BARTHOLO: What did he say, Rosine?

ROSINE: What he says is true. Why are you so surprised? Tonight I was going to take my revenge on a man who lied to me. Well, I've taken it!

BAZILE: I did tell you it was the Count himself, Doctor, didn't I?

BARTHOLO: What do I care? Call this a marriage? Where are the witnesses?

NOTARY: Everything is entirely in order. The document was signed in the presence of these two gentlemen here.

BARTHOLO: What, Bazile? You were a witness?

BAZILE: What else could I do? This man is a fiend. He seems to have an inexhaustible supply of convincing arguments.

BARTHOLO: I don't give a damn about his arguments! I shall exercise my legal authority.

COUNT: You have abused it for so long, Sir; it's no longer yours to exercise.

BARTHOLO: This young lady has not yet reached the age of consent.

FIGARO: She has just declared her independence.

BARTHOLO: Nobody asked for your opinion, slyboots!

COUNT: This lady is beautiful and nobly born; I am a gentleman, young and more than able to support her; she is my wife; we are now equal members in an honourable estate: do you presume to dispute it?

BARTHOLO: She is mine, and no one is ever going to take her away from me!

COUNT: She is no longer under your jurisdiction. She is now under the protection of the law; and this gentleman you brought here yourself will safeguard her from any violence you wish to do to her freedom. A true magistrate is always ready to defend the rights of the oppressed.

JP: Certainly. And this continuing futile resistance to an eminently respectable marriage would suggest to me some anxiety about his administration of his ward's financial affairs, of which the Court will require a full account.

COUNT: Oh, his consent is enough. I shan't ask for anything else.

FIGARO: ... except a note discharging me of the hundred crowns I owe him: let's not lose our heads.

BARTHOLO: (provoked) They were all in this together, all against me; I've stirred up a hornet's nest.

BAZILE: What hornet's nest? You can't have the lady, Doctor, but do take into account you still have her money and ...

BARTHOLO: Oh, stop it, Bazile! Leave me alone! Money is all you think about. What do I care about the money? Very well, I'll keep it: but don't think for one moment that is why I changed my mind. . . .

He signs.

FIGARO: (laughing) Ha, ha, ha, Your Lordship: they're like two peas in a pod!

NOTARY: But gentlemen, I must confess I'm lost! Are these not two ladies of the same name?

FIGARO: No, Sir, they are only one lady!

BARTHOLO: (miserably) And I took the ladder away so no one would interrupt the marriage ceremony! Beaten! I should have had more servants.

FIGARO: More sense, Doctor, more sense. But let's face it, when a couple have the luck to be young, and in love, and set out to fool an old man, whatever he does to prevent it, he'll still be asking himself at the end why he took All That Trouble For Nothing!

ONE MAD DAY

OR

THE MARRIAGE OF FIGARO

A Comedy in Five Acts
BY BEAUMARCHAIS

Performed for the first time
By The Comédiens Français ordinaires du roi
27 April 1784

'Neath the teases of our courting
'Tis let reason be our guide.
(Vaudeville in the play)

DRAMATIS PERSONAE

COUNT ALMAVIVA Lord High Sheriff of Andalusia

THE COUNTESS his wife

FIGARO his manservant and steward of the castle

SUZANNE maid of honour to the Countess and betrothed to Figaro

MARCELINE the housekeeper

ANTONIO gardener at the castle, uncle of Suzanne
and father of Fanchette

FANCHETTE daughter of Antonio

CHERUBIN the Count's Page

BARTHOLO a doctor from Seville

BAZILE music master at the castle

GUTSMAN BRID'OISON a local magistrate

DOUBLE-MAIN Clerk of the Court, Brid'oison's Secretary

USHER

LACKEY

GRIPE-SOLEIL a young goatherd

YOUNG SHEPHERDESS

PEDRILLO the Count's huntsman

SERVANTS, PEASANTS, PEASANT WOMEN

The action of the play is set in the Castle of Aguas Frescas, twenty
miles from Seville.

AUTHOR'S NOTES ON THE CHARACTERS

COUNT ALMAVIVA Needs to be played with great nobility, but also with charm and informality. His lack of any moral fibre should not make him any less the 'perfect gentleman' as far as his manners are concerned. In the bad old days it was by no means unusual for our betters to be very irresponsible when it came to adventures with the fair sex. The part is all the harder to do justice to for being one with which the audience can never identify.

THE COUNTESS A prey to conflicting emotions, should be very restrained in showing her feelings, and keep her anger well in check: above all there must be nothing that detracts from her charm and innocence in the eyes of the audience. It is one of the most difficult parts in the play.

FIGARO It is impossible to over-emphasise how important it is for anyone playing this part to immerse himself absolutely in the character. If he were to see in it anything other than common sense, leavened with a sense of humour and a quick wit, or, worse be tempted to overplay it in any way, he would coarsen a role that has been described as a challenge to the talents of any actor capable of grasping its many subtleties and rising to its overall demands.

SUZANNE A clever, entertaining girl, always laughing, but without the pertness of the traditional cheeky maid in French comedy.

MARCELINE Is an intelligent woman, emotional by nature, but chastened by experience and her earlier mistakes. If the actress playing the part can find the necessary dignity to rise to the moment of high moral seriousness after the recognition scene in Act IV, she will add a great deal to the value of the work.

ANTONIO Should be only mildly drunk, and this should gradually wear off, so that by Act V we are barely aware of it.

FANCHETTE Is a child of twelve, and very innocent.

ACT I

A half-furnished room: stage centre a large high-backed armchair:
FIGARO *is measuring the floor with a yardstick:* SUZANNE *in front*
of a looking-glass, pinning up a chaplet of orange blossom.

FIGARO: Nineteen feet by twenty-six . . .

SUZANNE: Look, Figaro, that's my little hat: do you think it's better now?

FIGARO: Nothing could be lovelier, my sweet one. . . .
      (*He takes her by the hands*)
Oh, that's a sight for a loving husband's eyes: a beautiful girl on her wedding day, with flowers in her hair, declaring before all the world that she's a virgin . . .

SUZANNE *slips away from him.*

SUZANNE: What are you measuring, my son?

FIGARO: I am looking to see, Suzanne my love, how the beautiful bed His Lordship's giving us will go in here . . .

SUZANNE: In this room?

FIGARO: He says that we can have it.

SUZANNE: Well, I don't want it.

FIGARO: Why not?

SUZANNE: I don't want it.

FIGARO: But why not?

SUZANNE: I don't like it.

FIGARO: It is usual to give a reason.

SUZANNE: What if I don't want to?

FIGARO: Oh, the moment that they're sure of us . . .

SUZANNE: Having to prove I'm right would be admitting that I could be wrong. Are you my devoted slave or are you not?

FIGARO: You take against the most comfortable room in the castle, in between the two apartments. In the night, if Her Ladyship's not well, she can ring from her side and whizz – two steps and you'll be with her. If His Lordship should want some thing, all he has to do is tinkle from his side, and bang – hop, skip and a jump, I'm there!

SUZANNE: Very good! But when he's been and tinkled in the morning and sent you off on some good long errand for him, whizz – two steps and he'll be at my door, and hop, skip and a jump and bang!

FIGARO: What precisely do you mean by that?

SUZANNE: You'll have to listen quietly . . .

FIGARO: Oh God! What is it?

SUZANNE: What it is, my dear, is that now he's tired of making love to all the local beauties, Count Almaviva is thinking of something rather nearer home, here in the castle: not his wife though: it's yours, you see, he has designs on. And that is what Bazile tells me every morning when he is giving me my singing lesson.

FIGARO: Bazile! Oh, my sweet girl, if anyone deserved a good birching to thrash some backbone into him . . .

SUZANNE: And you thought, you little innocent, this dowry that he's giving me was your reward for being his blue-eyed boy?

FIGARO: I'd surely done enough to deserve it . . .

SUZANNE: Then you may as well know that he thinks it will persuade me, some time when he and I are all alone, to let him have his *droit de seigneur** like in the old days: and you know how miserable that was . . .

FIGARO: I do! And if he hadn't done away with his disgusting Rights when he was wed, I never would have married you on his estate . . .

SUZANNE: Well, if he did give them up he is now regretting it: and your wife's the one he wants to buy them back from, today.

FIGARO: Oh, if only there were some way that I could catch him, the treacherous brute: set a trap he'd fall into and then keep the dowry . . .

SUZANNE: Plots and money! Now you're in your element!

(*A bell rings off-stage*)

That'll be Her Ladyship awake: she told me specially I was to be the first to speak to her on my wedding day . . .

FIGARO: Is there something behind that too?

SUZANNE: The shepherd says it's lucky for neglected wives! Goodbye, my fine Figaro of a man. Think about our little plot!

FIGARO: You have no idea how much I love you!

SUZANNE: Nag! Nag! Nag! When will you leave off saying that all day?

FIGARO: When I have a chance of proving it all night!

Sc.2   *The bell rings again:* SUZANNE *runs off, then turns and blows*
                              FIGARO *a kiss.*

FIGARO: Beautiful girl! Always laughing and blooming, happy and funny and loving and delicious. But very virtuous!

(*He walks up and down, rubbing his hands*)

Well, master! My dear master! So that is what you're giving the bridegroom is it? I was wondering, after he'd said I was to be steward of this castle, why he should take me with him when he goes to be ambassador, as his official runner. I see, Your Lordship. While I was galloping one way, he'd be leading her off in the other. Spattered with muck and breaking my back for the honour of your family, and you deigning to exert yourself in the increase of mine! Touching act of gratitude, I must say! But you are doing too much, my Lord. Performing the official functions for your master and your valet both at once! Deputising for the King and me in foreign parts . . . it's too much, by a long chalk, it's too much. And as for you, Bazile, you piddling little villain, I'll teach you to mock the afflicted! I'll. . . . No, I'll fool them into thinking I know nothing and let them trip each other up. Careful now, this is the great day, Mister Figaro! First, you have to have your little ceremony earlier, so as to be more sure of being married: beat off that Marceline that's drooling for you like a mad thing, frustrate His Lordship's lustful little schemes, thrash Master Bazile's ar . . .

Enter BARTHOLO *and* MARCELINE.   *Sc.3*

. . . ah! The enormous Doctor! The party is complete. Good morning, my very dear Doctor! Can it be my marriage brings you to the castle, I wonder?

BARTHOLO: Ah, my dear sir! No.

FIGARO: It would be very generous of you . . .

BARTHOLO: True, and extremely foolish.

FIGARO: When I had the misfortune to cause so much trouble at your own!

BARTHOLO: You mad chatter-box.

FIGARO: Farewell, Marceline. Are you still intending to sue me? 'Where there's no love, must hatred take its place?'* I leave it in the Doctor's hands.

BARTHOLO: What?

FIGARO: She'll tell you soon enough.

[*Exit* FIGARO]

BARTHOLO *watches* FIGARO *go.*   *Sc.4*

BARTHOLO: Buffoon! And unless he is flayed alive, I would opine he'll die of overweening arrogance with the thickest, most insolent skin in the . . .

MARCELINE: So, there you are at last, eternal Doctor. Still so grave and ponderous a creature might die waiting for your succour, just as another creature on one occasion eloped, in despite of your precautions . . .

BARTHOLO: Still malicious and provocative, I see. Well, who is it that makes my presence in the house so necessary then? Has His Lordship had some accident?

MARCELINE: No, Doctor. I don't know how I should define His Lordship's condition: he is jealous, and a libertine.

BARTHOLO: Oh, a libertine from boredom, jealous out of vanity: that goes without saying.

MARCELINE: This very day, for instance, he is marrying our Suzanne to his man Figaro, on whom he is squandering, for their marriage . . .

BARTHOLO: Which His Excellency has made necessary . . .

MARCELINE: Not entirely: but whose consummation His Excellency desires to celebrate discreetly with the bride . . .

BARTHOLO: . . . Figaro's? Surely that's a proposition he'll agree to?

MARCELINE: Bazile assures me not.

BARTHOLO: That other lousy villain living here as well? It's a den of thieves! And what's he doing here?

MARCELINE: All the mischief he is capable of. But the worst thing in him that I find is this tedious passion for me he has had for such an age.

BARTHOLO: I would have rid myself of his attentions twenty times by now.

MARCELINE: How?

BARTHOLO: By marrying him.

MARCELINE: You cruel, insipid sniggerer! Why don't you rid yourself of mine for the same price? Don't you owe it to me? Where is the memory of the troth that you once plighted? Where is the remembrance of our little Emmanuel, the fruit of an abandoned love that was to lead to matrimony?

BARTHOLO *takes off his hat.*

BARTHOLO: Was I called out from Seville to listen to these drivellings? This renewed attack of matrimonial fever has seized you in a very violent form . . .

MARCELINE: Very well, we will not speak of it again. But if nothing has been efficacious in persuading you of the justice of marrying me, help me at least to marry someone else.

BARTHOLO: By all means! Let us speak of it immediately! But what mortal abandoned by heaven and the female race . . . ?

MARCELINE: Oh, who else could it be, Doctor, but handsome, gay, kind, Figaro.

BARTHOLO: That scab?

MARCELINE: Never cross, always good-humoured, abandoning the fleeting moment to delight, caring for the future as little as for the past: simply delectable. But he is a monster.

BARTHOLO: And his Suzanne?

MARCELINE: She would never have him, the scheming hussy, if you were to assist me, Doctor dear, to make him honour an obligation that he has to me . . .

BARTHOLO: On his wedding day?

MARCELINE: They stop some that have gone very far indeed: and if I didn't fear to air a woman's little secret . . .

BARTHOLO: Have they any, from a doctor?

MARCELINE: Oh, you know that I have none from you: we women are so passionate, but timid: a certain charm may vainly beckon us toward pleasure, and yet the most adventurous of our sex will hear within herself a voice that says 'Be beautiful if you can, virtuous if you wish; but be discreet, you must!' So, since discretion at least is so essential and every woman senses the importance of it, let's terrify that Suzanne first of all, by threatening to divulge the advances that are being made to her.

BARTHOLO: And where will that lead?

MARCELINE: To her continuing, as shame takes her by the throat, to refuse the Count, who, in order to be revenged, will support the objections I have made to her marriage: thus mine becomes assured.

BARTHOLO: She's right! Zounds, it's a good trick, having my old housekeeper marry the ruffian that abducted my young ward.

MARCELINE: And who thinks he can amuse himself still further by withering my hopes!

BARTHOLO: And who on one occasion robbed me of a hundred crowns that still hang very heavy on my heart.

MARCELINE: Oh the voluptuous rapture!

BARTHOLO: Of punishing a criminal!

MARCELINE: Of marrying him, Doctor, marrying him!!

Sc.5   Enter SUZANNE, *carrying a nightcap with a broad ribbon in it, and a dress.*

SUZANNE: Marrying him! Marrying him! Who? My Figaro?

MARCELINE: Why not? You are!

BARTHOLO: The wondrous logic of a woman in a rage! We were saying, Suzanne, how fortunate he is to possess you . . .

MARCELINE: Not counting His Lordship but we don't talk of that . . .

SUZANNE: It is fortunate, Madam, that your jealousy is as well-known as your claims upon Figaro are ill-founded!

MARCELINE: One might have rendered them more binding had they been staked in the manner yours have, Madam.

SUZANNE: The manner, Madam, that any woman of intelligence would use . . .

MARCELINE: One attribute the child entirely lacks: but innocent, as a fumbling old judge.

BARTHOLO: Farewell, our Figaro's pretty bride!

MARCELINE: (*curtseying*) And His Lordship's secret concubine!

SUZANNE: (*curtseying*) And one that esteems you vastly, Madam.

MARCELINE: (*curtseying*) You are such a pretty woman, Madam.

SUZANNE: (*curtseying*) Hardly, Madam: but pretty enough to make you miserable.

MARCELINE: (*curtseying*) And above all with such a blameless reputation . . .

SUZANNE: (*curtseying*) No, Madam, it is old governesses should have blameless reputations!

MARCELINE: Old governesses! Old governesses!

BARTHOLO: Marceline!

MARCELINE: Come, Doctor, I will positively not endure it any longer. (*She curtseys*) Good-day, Madam.

Sc.6   [*Exit* MARCELINE *and* BARTHOLO]

SUZANNE: Be off with you, Madam! Be off with you, you pompous old baggage!

(*She throws the dress over a chair*)

Now I don't know what I came to fetch.

Sc.7   Enter CHERUBIN, *running in.*

CHERUBIN: Oh Suzette, I've been peeping through the keyhole for hours; I was waiting for a moment when I could have you on my own. . . . Oh, it's so sad you are going to be married and I have to go away!

SUZANNE: What has my marrying got to do with it?

CHERUBIN: He's giving me the sack.

SUZANNE: Chérubin what have you been up to?

CHERUBIN: He caught me last night with Fanchette, your cousin. I was going through her little part with her; she has to be a virgin in the masque tonight. He wasn't half angry when he saw me! He said 'Get out! You little. . . .' I couldn't say the vulgar word he used in front of a woman. 'Get out, and this is the last night you ever spend beneath this roof.' If Her Ladyship, my beautiful godmother, doesn't manage to put in a good word for me it's all up, Suzanne. I shall never know again the bliss of seeing you!

SUZANNE: Seeing me! Me? It's me now, is it? It's not my mistress you're secretly in love with any more then?

CHERUBIN: Oh, Suzette, she's so noble and so beautiful, but she terrifies me.

SUZANNE: And I don't, you mean? So I'm the sort that you can take a liberty with?

CHERUBIN: You know very well, you naughty girl, I'd never take the liberty of taking a liberty. But you're so fortunate! Seeing her every minute of the day, talking to her, putting her clothes on in the morning and taking them off at night, pin by pin. . . . Oh Suzette, I'd give. . . . What's that you've got there?

SUZANNE: (affectedly) Oh God! A nightcap that is fortunate enough to have known the bliss of tying up your beautiful godmother's hair . . .

CHERUBIN: Her ribbon! Give it me, sweetheart!

SUZANNE snatches it away from him.

SUZANNE: Oh, no you don't! Sweetheart! You're very familiar, aren't you? If you weren't such a scruffy little twopenny-ha'penny . . .
(CHERUBIN *takes the ribbon from her*)
Oh, in three or four years I swear you'll be the biggest little rip. . . . Will you give me back that ribbon?

She tries to take it: CHERUBIN *pulls a sheet of music out of his pocket.*

CHERUBIN: Let me! Oh, let me keep it, Suzette! I'll give you my ballad in exchange. . . . And when the memory of your lovely mistress makes my every waking moment misery, the thought of you will shed the only gleam of happiness still able to warm the cockles of my heart!

SUZANNE: I'll warm your cockles for you, you little perisher! Think you're talking to your Fanchette, do you? You get caught with her, you're in love with Her Ladyship, and you come giving me your fibs on top of that!!

CHERUBIN: I know: it's true. I don't know what's happening to me any more: for some time now I've been feeling a strange pain in my chest here: my heart starts palpitating every time I see a woman: words like 'love' and 'desire' make it stop altogether and then go on very fast indeed. In fact I feel such a desperate need to say 'I love you' to somebody, I say it when I'm on my own, out running in the park, to your mistress, to you, to trees, to clouds, to the wind that carries them away, along with everything I say: lost on the wind. . . . I met Marceline yesterday . . .

SUZANNE: Ha ha ha!!

CHERUBIN: Why not, she's a woman. She isn't married. Isn't married . . . a woman . . . words like that are so beautiful: so interesting . . .

SUZANNE: He's going mad.

CHERUBIN: Fanchette's sweet. She listens to me at least. You don't.

SUZANNE: Oh dear, what a pity. . . . Now you listen to me, young man!

She tries to take the ribbon again. CHERUBIN *runs away, adopting his mock-heroic tone again.*

CHERUBIN: Very well! You see, I'll lay down my life before I let you have it! If you're not happy with the price I'll add a thousand kisses . . .

He begins to chase her.

SUZANNE: You'll get your face slapping a thousand times, if you come any closer! I'll tell my mistress of you, I will! I'll tell His Lordship, I'll say 'You did right, Your Lordship, we wanted you to sack him: he's a little thief!' You send him packing back to his parents, for a rotten little egg that's always giving himself airs he's in love with Her Ladyship, and trying to kiss me on the rebound!

Sc.8   CHERUBIN *sees the* COUNT *coming and dives behind the armchair in terror.*

CHERUBIN: Shh . . .

SUZANNE: What are you so frightened of all of a sudden?

CHERUBIN: I'm done for!

SUZANNE *turns and sees the* COUNT, *and tries to stand in front of the armchair.*

SUZANNE: Oh!

COUNT: You seem disturbed, Suzette! You were talking to yourself, and your poor darling heart's beating.... It's easy enough to understand, on a day like this ...

SUZANNE: My Lord, what do you want me for? If they found you alone with me ...

COUNT: I've only got a moment to explain my plans. Now listen....

He sits down in the armchair.

SUZANNE: I'm not listening.

COUNT: Just one word. You know the King has made me his ambassador in London. I am taking Figaro with me: I shall put him in an excellent position, and as it's a wife's duty to follow her husband ...

SUZANNE: If only I dared to speak!

COUNT: Speak, say what you like, my love. It's a privilege that I intend to grant to you for ever, so you may as well take advantage of it straightaway.

SUZANNE: I don't want it my Lord. I don't want it. Please leave me alone.

COUNT: Very well, but tell me.

SUZANNE: Well, when Your Lordship eloped with your own wife from the Doctor's house and married her for love; when Your Lordship did away for her sake with that awful *droit de seigneur* ...

COUNT: ... that made the little girls so miserable! Oh, those wonderful rights of a seigneur! If only we could have a talk about it all this evening in the garden when it's getting dark ... such a small favour that I'm asking, and I'd show you how grateful I was ...

BAZILE: (*off-stage*) His Lordship isn't in his rooms!

COUNT: Who's that calling?

SUZANNE: Oh, I am so unhappy!

COUNT: Go and tell them that they can't come in!

SUZANNE: And leave you here?

BAZILE: (*off-stage*) His Lordship was with Her Ladyship: he came from there. I'll go and see ...

COUNT: And nowhere I can hide. Ah, behind this chair. It's barely big enough: but make them go as quickly as you can ...

SUZANNE stands in his way: he pushes her gently, and she gives way, putting herself between him and CHERUBIN: as the COUNT crouches down where he is hiding, CHERUBIN runs round and

jumps into the chair, pulling up his knees and cowering. SUZANNE
throws the dress over him and stands in front of the chair.

Sc.9   *Enter* BAZILE.

BAZILE: You wouldn't have seen His Lordship, Miss?

SUZANNE: Why should I have seen him? Leave me alone!

BAZILE: If you were more reasonable, there'd be nothing odd about
my asking. Figaro is looking for him.

SUZANNE: In that case he is looking for a man that wants to do him
more harm than anyone on earth, apart from you!

COUNT: *(aside)* I'll just see how he serves me.

BAZILE: Does wishing to do a woman good mean that you want to do
her husband harm?

SUZANNE: Not by your disgusting standards, you are so corrupt!

BAZILE: What is being asked of you? Something you're going to
squander in vast amounts on someone else. Thanks to the sacred
ceremony, what the world denied you yesterday, they will insist you
have tomorrow.

SUZANNE: You are beneath contempt.

BAZILE: Of all the deadly serious things in life, marriage being the most
ridiculous, I was thinking . . .

SUZANNE: Filthy thoughts! Who gave you permission to come in here?

BAZILE: There, there. Don't be so cantankerous! May Heaven grant
you patience! Nothing will come of it unless you . . . want it. But
don't think either I consider Mister Figaro is what is hindering His
Lordship. And when that little page has gone . . .

SUZANNE: Chérubin?

BAZILE: *Cherubino di amore*, constantly fluttering about you, prowling
about outside again this morning, waiting to come in the moment I
went out: now tell me if that isn't true?

SUZANNE: That is a barefaced lie! Go away, you evil man!

BAZILE: One is an evil man because one is aware of what is going on. I
suppose that ballad is addressed to you, as well, the one he is so
secretive about . . . ?

SUZANNE: Oh yes, I'm sure it is!

BAZILE: Unless he made it up for Madam. To tell the truth, when he
serves at table, they do say he looks at her with a strange expression
in his eyes. But, by heaven, he'd best not overplay his hand in that
direction. His Lordship's *vicious* when it comes to anything like that.

SUZANNE: And it's very wicked of you to go spreading such rumours and ruining a poor unfortunate child that's already in his master's bad books as it is!

BAZILE: Would I have invented it? I only mention it because everybody's talking about it.

The COUNT *stands up.*

COUNT: What do you mean, everybody's talking about it?

SUZANNE: Oh heavens!

BAZILE: Ha ha!

COUNT: Bazile, go and have him thrown out of the house this minute!

BAZILE: Oh, I'm sorry I came in . . .

SUZANNE: Oh God, Oh God!

COUNT: She's fainted. Sit down my dear.

SUZANNE *pushes them away.*

SUZANNE: I do not want to sit down. Taking liberties, coming in here, it's unforgivable!

COUNT: There are two of us, my dear. You are in no danger whatsoever . . .

BAZILE: I must say I am desperately sorry for having made that joke about the page when you were listening. I only did it to find out what she felt about him: because seriously . . .

COUNT: Fifty florins, a horse, and have him sent back to his parents.

BAZILE: Your Lordship! For a little joke?

COUNT: He's a little libertine. I caught him last night with the gardener's daughter.

BAZILE: With Fanchette?

COUNT: And in her bedroom.

SUZANNE: Where Your Lordship no doubt had some business to be seeing to as well.

COUNT: I rather like that!

BAZILE: Straw in the wind!

COUNT: No, I was looking for her uncle, Antonio, my drunken gardener, to give him his instructions. I knock on the door, it is a long time being opened, your cousin seems flustered, I become suspicious, and as I talk I look about me. . . . There was a kind of curtain behind the door for hanging coats, I don't know, covering clothes: without appearing to be doing anything, I so very gently, very gently, and lift the curtain . . .

(*He demonstrates, lifting the dress from the armchair*)
And who do I see but. . . .

(He sees CHERUBIN)

Aha!!

BAZILE: Ha ha!

COUNT: This trick's as good as the other one.

BAZILE: Even better.

COUNT: Most accomplished, young lady! Barely a bride and you
indulge in this variety of subterfuge! So that was why you wished to
be alone? In order to entertain my page! As for you, Sir, with your
predictable manner of carrying on, all that we needed was for you,
with no consideration for the feelings of your godmother, to make
advances to her lady's maid! But I will not allow Figaro, a man that I
esteem and love, to be the victim of this kind of underhand deception.
Was he with you, Bazile?

SUZANNE: There was no deception and no victim: he was here all the
time that you were talking to me.

COUNT: I hope you're lying when you say that: his cruellest enemy
would not dare to wish him that misfortune!

SUZANNE: He was begging me to ask Her Ladyship to prevail on you
to have him pardoned. Your coming in frightened him so much he
used that chair to hide himself.

COUNT: That is a damned lie! I sat down in that chair when I came in.

CHERUBIN: Oh dear, Your Lordship . . . I was cowering down behind it.

COUNT: Yet another untruth! That is the position I myself was occu-
pying! About a moment ago!

CHERUBIN: Pardon me, Sir, but that was when I hid inside the chair.

COUNT: So you wriggled round like a serpent, did you? You little
snake! You were listening!

CHERUBIN: On the contrary, my Lord, I was trying not to!

COUNT: Oh, the disloyalty of it! *(To* SUZANNE) You will not marry
Figaro!

Singing off-stage.

BAZILE: Control yourself, there's someone coming.

The COUNT *drags* CHERUBIN *out of the armchair and on to his
feet.*

COUNT: He'd like to stay there and blaze it out in front of everyone!

Sc.10   *Enter the* COUNTESS, FANNY, PEASANTS *and* PEASANT WOMEN:
FIGARO *carrying a diadem decorated with white plumes and a
veil, talking to the* COUNTESS.

FIGARO: Madam, you're the only one that can persuade him . . .

COUNTESS: You see, my Lord, they credit me with powers I don't possess but as what they are asking for is not unreasonable . . .

COUNT: What is it you want?

FIGARO: My Lord, your serfs are so touched by your having done away with certain distressing Rights, out of love for Her Ladyship . . .

COUNT: Well? The Rights you refer to no longer exist. What are you trying to say?

FIGARO: That it's time your being so virtuous and so good a master received more general acclaim: It's such a blessing to me in my present circumstances that I'd like to be the first to celebrate it at my wedding.

COUNT: You're not serious, my old friend: doing away with a humiliating privilege like that is merely coming to terms with honesty. We Spaniards may want to conquer beauty with our charm, but to demand the first and sweetest enjoyment of it as a servile due, that is the tyranny of a Visigoth, not the kind of privilege a Lord of Castile could countenance . . .

FIGARO: Then let this innocent creature that owes the preservation of her virtue to your wisdom, receive from you in public this insignia of virginity, decorated with plumes and white ribbons, to symbolise the purity of your intentions: and let it be a part of every wedding ceremony, with a hymn sung by the choir, to keep the memory fresh for evermore . . .

Girls sing first two lines of 'Young Bride'.

COUNT: If I didn't know that being a lover, or a poet, or a musician entitles anyone to any kind of lunancy . . .

FIGARO: All together friends.

ALL: Your Lordship! Your Lordship!

Girls sing second two lines of 'Young Bride'.

SUZANNE: Why be shy of praise when it's so well deserved?

COUNT: (*aside*) Treacherous slut!

FIGARO: Look at her, Your Lordship! There'll never be a prettier bride to show how great a sacrifice you've made!

SUZANNE: You leave my looks out of it and get on with praising his Lordship's virtue!

COUNT: (*aside*) It's a game, all this.

COUNTESS: I agree with them, my Lord: and the ceremony will be always dear to me, because it owes its inspiration to the wondrous love that you once had for me . . .

COUNT: And, Madam, have for you still: it is to that authority I yield.

ALL: Three cheers for His Lordship! Hip-hip! Hooray!

Girls sing 'Conveying You Safe'.

COUNT: (*aside*) Trapped!! (*Aloud*) In order for the ceremony to be more imposing, I would only ask that it be delayed till later in the day. (*Aside*) I must have Marceline found at once!

FIGARO *goes to* CHERUBIN.

FIGARO: Well, you little monkey, you're not clapping?

SUZANNE: He's very unhappy: His Lordship is dismissing him.

COUNTESS: Oh Sir, I beg you, spare him!

COUNT: He does not deserve it.

COUNTESS: Oh but he's so young . . .

COUNT: Not so young as you imagine!

CHERUBIN: I've been thoughtless, Sir, in what I've done, I know, but never in the least bit indiscreet in what I've said . . .

COUNT: Very well, that will suffice!

FIGARO: What can he mean?

COUNT: That will suffice! That will suffice! Everyone demands that he be pardoned: very well, I grant it, and I will go still further. I will give him a company in my regiment.

Company applaud.

ALL: Three cheers for His Lordship!! Hip! Hip! . . .

COUNT: But only on condition that he leaves this instant and goes to enlist in Catalonia!

FIGARO: Oh Your Lordship, tomorrow!

COUNT: Immediately. I insist!

CHERUBIN: I obey.

COUNT: My boy. Say goodbye to your godmother and ask her for her protection.

CHERUBIN *kneels before the* COUNTESS, *unable to speak.*

COUNTESS: Since we are not allowed to keep you even for today, you must go. There's a new life waiting for you: go and do well. Be a credit to your master. Remember this house, where your being young has been so much indulged. Be obedient, honest and brave, and we'll believe we have some part in your successes . . .

CHERUBIN *gets up and goes back to his place.*

COUNT: You are very moved, Madam.

COUNTESS: I don't deny it. What will become of a child thrown into a career as dangerous as that? He is related to my family, and besides he is my godson.

COUNT: (*aside*) I see that Bazile was right. (*Aloud*) My boy, kiss Suzanne . . . for the last time.

FIGARO: Why, my Lord? He'll be coming to spend his winters here. Kiss me too then, Captain.

(*He kisses him*)

Goodbye, Young Chérubin. You'll be leading a different life from now on, lad: by God, no more creeping round the ladies' quarters: no more sugar buns and cream for tea: no more games of he and blind man's buff! Old soldiers, Lord love us, all weatherbeaten, half in rags: a great big heavy musket: left turn! right turn! Quick march! And off you go to glory: and don't go breaking step, unless you see a bullet coming for you!

SUZANNE: Oh shame on you! How horrible.

COUNTESS: What a thing to tell the child!

COUNT: (*aside*) Where's Marceline? It's very strange that she's not here.

FANCHETTE: Your Lordship.

COUNT: Fanchette.

FANCHETTE: She went to the village down the little path by the farm.

COUNT: And when is she coming back?

BAZILE: When it shall please God in his infinite wisdom . . .

FIGARO: Then please God it never please Him ever.

FANCHETTE: The doctor was giving her his arm.

COUNT: You mean the doctor's here?

BAZILE: She had to take it first.

COUNT: He couldn't have come more opportunely.

FANCHETTE: She seemed ever so cross; she was talking at the top of her voice as she was going along, then stopping and going like this with her arms, and the doctor was going like that to her to soothe her. She looked so angry. And I heard her talking about my cousin Figaro . . .

COUNT: Cousin-to-be.

FANCHETTE: Your Lordship, have you forgiven us for last night?

COUNT: Good morning, my child, good morning. Come Madam, let us go in. Bazile, you will call at my rooms.

FIGARO: (*aside to* SUZANNE) Have we beaten him?

SUZANNE: (*aside to* FIGARO) You sweet boy . . .

They all go off, except FIGARO, *who brings back* BAZILE *and*
                        CHERUBIN.

FIGARO: The ceremony has been accepted: my wedding tonight will
follow as a matter of course. But we must rehearse it well: we mustn't
be like actors that give their worst performance when the critics are
in. We have no second night to make up for it: we have to know our
parts today.

BAZILE: Mine is more difficult than you'd think . . .

        FIGARO, *behind* BAZILE's *back, makes thrashing movements.*

FIGARO: And you have no idea of the rewards in store . . .

CHERUBIN: My friend, you forget that I am going away . . .

FIGARO: And you would like to stay?

CHERUBIN: Of course I would!

FIGARO: Then we must resort to subterfuge: no complaining when you
leave: your travelling cloak across your shoulder, let them see you
pack your bags, let them see your horse is at the gate: gallop as far as
the farm: return on foot by the back way. His Lordship will believe
you've gone: stay out of his sight, that's all, and I promise you I'll
placate him when the wedding's over.

CHERUBIN: But little Fanchette doesn't know her part!

BAZILE: What the devil have you been teaching her then? You haven't
left her alone for a week!

FIGARO: You have nothing else to do today: go and give her a lesson,
for pity's sake!

BAZILE: Have a care, young man, have a care: her father isn't happy
about it: she's had a spanking already: she won't be studying under
you, Chérubin. Chérubin, you will make that little girl unhappy. The
pitcher that goeth often to the well . . .

FIGARO: Oh you fool! You and your ancient proverbs! All right, you
old book-worm, what saith the wisdom of the nations? 'The pitcher
that goeth often to the well . . .'

BAZILE: 'May get a belly-full!'

FIGARO: He's not so stupid after all, he's not so stupid. . . .

ACT II

A luxurious bedroom, with a bed in an alcove on a dais. The main door to the room is upstage right, and there is a closet door downstage left. Upstage a door leading to the women's quarters and a window. SUZANNE *comes in upstage right with the* COUNTESS, *who throws herself into an armchair.*

COUNTESS: Shut the door, Suzanne, tell me everything exactly as it happened.

SUZANNE: There's nothing that I haven't told you, Madam.

COUNTESS: What, Suzanne, you mean he wanted to seduce you?

SUZANNE: Oh no! His Lordship wouldn't put himself to all that trouble for a servant. He tried to buy me.

COUNTESS: And the little page was in the room?

SUZANNE: Hiding behind the big armchair, he was. He came to ask me if I could prevail on you to have him pardoned . . .

COUNTESS: Oh? Why didn't he come to me? Was I likely to have refused him, Suzette.

SUZANNE: That's what I said . . . but what with being so sad at leaving, and most of all about leaving you, Your Ladyship . . . 'Oh Suzette she's so noble and beautiful, but she terrifies me!'

COUNTESS: When I've always been the one that has protected him . . .

SUZANNE: Then he saw the ribbon of your nightcap I was holding: he just pounced on it!

COUNTESS: My ribbon? Oh, he's such a child! So, my poor Suzanne, in the end my husband told you . . .

SUZANNE: That if I wouldn't listen to him he'd take Marceline's side against me.

The COUNTESS *gets up, and walks up and down, using her fan very violently.*

COUNTESS: He does not love me any more, at all.

SUZANNE: Then why is he so jealous?

COUNTESS: Like every other husband, my dear: it's simply pride. Oh, I have loved him too much: I've wearied him with my attentiveness and tired him with my loving. That's the only fault that he can find in me. But I don't want your confessing this to get you into trouble. You shall marry Figaro. Whatever happens, he's the only one can help us: is he coming?

SUZANNE: The moment that he sees the hunt go off.

COUNTESS: Open the window on the garden a little. It is so hot here.

SUZANNE: There's His Lordship now, riding through the garden and Pedrillo behind him, with two, three, four greyhounds . . .

COUNTESS: Then there's still time. There's someone at the door, Suzette . . .

SUZANNE: It's my Figaro, oh it's my Figaro!

Sc.2   (*She opens the door and* FIGARO *comes in.*)

My dear love, come, Her Ladyship is desperate to see you . . .

FIGARO: And you're not, I suppose, my little Suzikins? Her Ladyship has no reason to be desperate, no reason at all: after all, what's all the trouble about? A mere nothing: His Lordship finds my wife delightful and would like to have her as his mistress. And it's very natural that he should . . .

COUNTESS: Figaro, how can you be so flippant about something that could cost every one of us our happiness?

FIGARO: Who says so, Madam?

SUZANNE: Instead of feeling sorry for us when we're in trouble . . .

FIGARO: Isn't it enough if I take charge? Now, to act methodically, as he does . . . we have first of all to moderate his lust for what belongs to us by making him less certain of what belongs to him . . .

COUNTESS: That's true: but how . . . ?

FIGARO: It's already done, my Lady: an idle tale put out about Your Ladyship . . .

COUNTESS: About me? Are you out of your mind?

FIGARO: No, but he will be!

COUNTESS: A man as jealous as that?

FIGARO: So much the better: if you're going to win a game against a man like that, all you need to do is get his blood up: that's what women understand so well. Then bait him till he's glowing red with rage, let him have a sniff of a plot and you can lead him anywhere you want to by the nose: into the Guadalquivir. I had an anonymous letter given to Bazile, warning His Lordship that there's an amorous young gentleman going to try and get in to see you tonight during the ball.

COUNTESS: And you're prepared to gamble with the truth like that at my expense . . . ?

FIGARO: There are very few, My Lady, I would have dared to risk it with for fear of hitting on the truth.

COUNTESS: So I shall be obliged to thank you for it . . .

FIGARO: But you must confess there's something rather charming in having his day divided up for him, so that he'll spend time roaming round and cursing after his own wife that he'd set aside for dallying with mine. . . . He'll be so confused he won't know which way to turn: will he gallop back along this road, watch that one? Think of the turmoil in his mind! Think of it! There he is, racing after some poor exhausted hare! Our wedding will be over before we know it, he'll have had no time to object, and he'll never dare oppose it with Your Ladyship here . . .

SUZANNE: No, but that crafty Marceline will.

FIGARO: Oh pooh, that should worry me: send word to His Lordship you'll be in the garden at dusk.

COUNTESS: You mean that you have no objection to her going?

FIGARO: Of course I have. I make someone else dress up in Suzanne's clothes: if we catch His Lordship *in flagrante*, how can he deny it?

SUZANNE: Who will wear my clothes?

FIGARO: Chérubin.

COUNTESS: He's gone.

FIGARO: I don't think he has. Have I your permission to proceed?

SUZANNE: Trust him to handle a plot.

FIGARO: Oh, two or three or four at once: all very involved and complicated. I should have been in politics.

SUZANNE: Politics? I've always heard it's very demanding work . . .

FIGARO: Three little words: steal, borrow and beg. That's the secret . . .

COUNTESS: He has so much confidence he is beginning to inspire me with it . . .

FIGARO: That is my intention.

SUZANNE: So?

FIGARO: While His Lordship's out I'll send Chérubin down to you. Put his hair up, dress him: I'll shut him in again and give him his instructions, and then, your Lordship, Tarah! Take your partners!!

[*Exit* FIGARO]   *Sc.3*

The COUNTESS *opens a patch box.*

COUNTESS: God, Suzanne, what do I look like? That young man coming. . . . You'll see, I shall be most severe with him . . .

SUZANNE: Let's make him sing his song.

She gives the COUNTESS *the sheet of music.*

COUNTESS: . . . My hair is so untidy . . .

SUZANNE: All I have to do is pin up that curl and then you'll be ever so much more severe with him, Madam . . .

COUNTESS: What did you say, Suzanne?

Sc.4   *Enter* CHERUBIN, *pretending to be bashful.*

SUZANNE: Come in, Officer.

CHERUBIN: Oh, it hurts me so much to be called that, my Lady. It reminds me that I have to leave this house . . . and a godmother, who is so kind . . .

SUZANNE: And so beautiful.

CHERUBIN: Oh yes!

SUZANNE: 'Oh yes!' Look at the innocent young man with his long hypocritical eyelashes! Come, pretty little bluebird, sing your ballad to Her Ladyship.

COUNTESS: Take my guitar.

The COUNTESS, *who is sitting down, follows the music.* SUZANNE, *standing behind her chair, plays the introduction, looking at the music over her mistress's shoulder.* CHERUBIN *is in front of her, looking down. This tableau corresponds exactly to the beautiful engraving by Vanloo,* * The Spanish Conversation.

CHERUBIN: (*singing*)
    'Twas where a rill was breaking
    My heart, oh my heart it is aching
    For her I was forsaking
    I felt the salt tears flow.

    I felt the salt tears flow
    I let my head hang low
    My trusty dagger taking
    My heart, oh my heart, it is aching
    I carved with hand a-quaking
    Her name upon a tree.

> Her name upon a tree
> What though the King could see
> The Queen then, pity taking
> My heart, oh my heart, it is aching
> Quoth 'Page, what ails thee, making
> Thee sadly so to sigh?
>
> Thee sadly so to sigh?'
> I shyly made reply
> 'Queen, though the camp is waking
> My heart, oh my heart, it is aching
> The lady I'm forsaking
> I'll love until I die.'*

COUNTESS: It has a certain naïve feeling: it's rather sentimental.

SUZANNE: Oh he's a very sentimental young man. By the way, Officer, did we tell you? To enliven this evening's entertainment we wanted to know beforehand if one of my dresses would fit you . . .

COUNTESS: I'm afraid it won't.

SUZANNE: He's nearly the same size as I am. Let's take his coat off first . . .

She takes it off.

COUNTESS: And what if somebody came in?

SUZANNE: Are we doing anything wrong? I'll lock the door.
            (*She runs and locks the door*)
   I want to see him with his hair done up . . .

COUNTESS: On the dressing table. Bring one of my bonnets.

[*Exit* SUZANNE]   Sc.5

   Until the moment that the ball begins the Count won't know you're in the house. We'll tell him afterwards we thought of it to fill the time until your Commission arrived . . .

CHERUBIN: Oh dear, My Lady, I've already got it: he gave it to Bazile to give to me.

COUNTESS: Already? He does not believe in wasting time.
            (*She reads the Commission that* CHERUBIN *gives her*)
   They were in such a hurry they've forgotten to put the seal on it.

Re-enter SUZANNE.   Sc.6

SUZANNE: The seal? On what?

COUNTESS: On his Commission.

SUZANNE: Already?

COUNTESS: That's what I said. Is that my bonnet?

SUZANNE: It's the prettiest one there is.

> CHERUBIN *kneels down as* SUZANNE *puts the bonnet on his head,*
> *singing with pins in her mouth.*

> Won't you turn and look at me,
> Johnny, tra la, my love, my liege.

Oh Madam, he's sweet!

COUNTESS: Can you arrange the collar in a rather more feminine way?

SUZANNE: There. But look how pretty he is as a girl, the little urchin.
Oh, I'm jealous. You're not to be as pretty as that, do you hear?

COUNTESS: Don't be so silly! The sleeve needs turning back to make
the cuffs sit better.

> (*She pushes up* CHERUBIN'*s sleeve*)

What's this he has on his arm? A ribbon?

SUZANNE: And a ribbon of yours! I'm very glad you've seen it, Madam!
I've already told him that I'd tell. If His Lordship hadn't come in I'd
have got it back off him. I'm nearly as strong as he is.

COUNTESS: There's blood on it!

> *She unties the ribbon.*

CHERUBIN: This morning when I thought that I was leaving I was
putting the curb-chain on my horse, and he lifted his head and the
snaffle scratched my arm.

COUNTESS: No one ever put a ribbon on a . . .

SUZANNE: Certainly not one they stole. Look what it's done. Oh, his
arm's so white! Like a woman's. Whiter than mine is, look, my Lady!

COUNTESS: You'd be more useful fetching me a plaster.

Sc.7   SUZANNE *pushes* CHERUBIN'*s head away, laughing, and makes*
him fall over on his hands and knees: she goes through the door
downstage left into the closet. The COUNTESS *doesn't say anything*
for a moment and looks at the ribbon: CHERUBIN *devours her*
with his eyes.

As for the ribbon, Sir . . . As it is the one whose colour suits me best I
was extremely cross at losing it . . .

Sc.8   *Re-enter* SUZANNE.

SUZANNE: Where's the ribbon he had tied round his arm?

She gives the COUNTESS *sticking plaster and scissors.*

COUNTESS: When you get your clothes for him, take the ribbon from another night-cap.

SUZANNE *goes off through the door upstage to the women's*   Sc.9
quarters, taking CHERUBIN's *coat.*

CHERUBIN: The one that you took off would have cured me in less than no time.

COUNTESS: Has it some special property? This is much better.

CHERUBIN: When a ribbon has . . . tied up someone's hair, or touched the skin of . . . someone . . .

COUNTESS: Oh do be quiet, child! Do stop talking nonsense for a moment!

(As she is wiping his eyes with a handkerchief there is a knock at the door)

Who could be knocking at my door like that?   Sc.10

COUNT: *(off-stage)* Why are you locked in?

COUNTESS: It's my husband! God Almighty! You with your coat off and your shirt undone! Alone with me! You look as though you're half undressed. . . . He must have read the letter. . . . He's so jealous!

COUNT: *(off-stage)* Why won't you open this door??

COUNTESS: Because I'm . . . alone!

COUNT: Alone? Who's that you are talking to, then?

COUNTESS: You, I imagine!

CHERUBIN: After what happened last night and this morning, he'd murder me!!

CHERUBIN *runs to the closet, goes in and shuts the door behind*   Sc.11
him: the COUNTESS *locks it, removes the key and runs to open the*
door upstage right. Enter the COUNT.

COUNTESS: What a terrible mistake! What a terrible mistake!

COUNT: You are not in the habit of locking yourself in . . .   Sc.12

COUNTESS: I was going through some old clothes . . . some old clothes with Suzanne. She has just gone to her room for a moment.

COUNT: You seem and sound extremely agitated.

COUNTESS: That's hardly surprising! Not in the least surprising, I can assure you. . . . We were talking about you. She's . . . gone, as I say.

COUNT: You were talking about me? I was anxious; that is what made me come back. . . . As I was getting on to my horse I was given a letter.... I'm sure that there's no question of its being true ... but all the same it unsettled me ...

COUNTESS: What? What letter, Sir?

COUNT: It must be confessed, Madam, that you and I are surrounded by ... some very mischievous people. I am informed that during the day someone I believed was not here will try to seek an assignation with you....

(*A chair falls over in the closet*)

What is that noise I hear?

COUNTESS: Noise?

COUNT: Someone overturned a piece of furniture ...

COUNTESS: I ... heard nothing, myself.

COUNT: Then you must be most excessively preoccupied!

COUNTESS: Preoccupied? With what?

COUNT: Madam, there is someone in this closet!

COUNTESS: Oh? And who are you suggesting that it is, Sir?

COUNT: That is what I am asking you! I have only just arrived ...

COUNTESS: Well, it's.... It's Suzanne, obviously, putting clothes away ...

COUNT: You said she went into her room.

COUNTESS: I said that she had gone ... or gone in there: I don't know which ...

COUNT: If it is Suzanne, why should you be so visibly disturbed?

COUNTESS: Disturbed? By my lady's maid?

COUNT: Whether it is by your lady's maid I couldn't say: but disturbed, unquestionably ...

COUNTESS: You find her most disturbing, certainly.... I would say, Sir, you were more preoccupied with her than I was.

COUNT: I am so preoccupied with her that I wish to see her this very instant!!

COUNTESS: I am sure you wish to see her very often, but your suspicions are without the least foundation.

Sc.13   *Enter* SUZANNE, *carrying clothes, pushing open the door upstage.*

COUNT: Then they should be all the easier to dispel!
                (*He goes to the closet and shouts*)
Suzanne! I order you to come out!

COUNTESS: She is practically naked, Sir.

COUNT: If she is so afraid of being seen, she can at least say something. Answer me, Suzanne, are you in this closet?

SUZANNE, *who has stood listening by the door, hides in the alcove.*

COUNTESS: Suzanne, I forbid you to answer that. (*To the* COUNT) Is there no limit to your tyranny?

COUNT: Very well. Since she will not speak, whether she is dressed or not, I am going to see her!

The COUNTESS *goes to stand with her back to the door.*

COUNTESS: Anywhere else, I am powerless to prevent it, but I hope that in my own apartments . . .

COUNT: And I hope in a moment I shall know who this mysterious Suzanne is! Asking for the key, I see, would be a waste of time: but there's a very simple way of breaking down a flimsy door like this! Hello! Somebody!!

COUNTESS: Call your servants in! Make a public exhibition of yourself for the sake of one suspicion. We shall be the laughing stock of the entire household!

COUNT: Very well, Madam. . . . It is true, I can do it alone. I am going instantly to fetch the necessary implements from my rooms. But so that everything remains the same, you will be so good as to accompany me quietly and without making an exhibition of yourself, since such behaviour is so alien to your nature. . . . I imagine that you won't refuse me anything as simple as that?

COUNTESS: Oh Sir, who could ever dream of disobeying you?

COUNT: Aha! I was forgetting the door to your maids' room: I shall lock it as well, in order that you be fully vindicated.

He goes and locks the upstage door, taking the key with him.

COUNTESS: (*aside*) Oh gracious heaven! How could I have been so disastrously foolish?

COUNT: Now that this room is sealed, would you please accept my arm . . . And as for the Suzanne in the closet she will have to be so good as to wait for me . . .

COUNTESS: Truly, Sir, this is the most odious adventure!

The COUNT *takes her out and locks the bedroom door behind*   Sc.14
him. SUZANNE *immediately comes out from the alcove, runs to the closet, and whispers through the keyhole.*

SUZANNE: Come out, Chérubin, come out. It's Suzanne! You can open the door and come out now! Unlock the door from the inside and come out.

CHERUBIN *unlocks the door.*

CHERUBIN: Oh Suzette, what a dreadful scene!

SUZANNE: You must escape, there isn't a moment to lose!

CHERUBIN: But which way shall I go?

SUZANNE: I don't know, but you must escape!

CHERUBIN: What if there's no way out?

SUZANNE: After what happened last time when you met him, he'd slaughter you, and that'll be the end of us as well. Go and tell Figaro . . .

CHERUBIN: Perhaps the garden window isn't too high . . .

SUZANNE: It's up one pair of stairs! It isn't possible! Oh my poor mistress! And my wedding! Oh heavens above!

CHERUBIN: It's over where the melons are: I might spoil a bed or two . . .

SUZANNE: He's going to kill himself!

CHERUBIN: Yes, I would throw myself down headlong rather than have her come to any harm! Give me a kiss for luck!

He kisses SUZANNE *and jumps out of the window.*

Sc.15   SUZANNE: Oh!!

(*She falls into a chair, then gets up, goes cautiously to the window
and looks out*)

He's miles away already. Now I must take his place as quickly as I can. . . . Your Lordship, you can break the lock now if it gives you any satisfaction . . . and I'll be damned if I am going to say a single word.

Sc.16   *She goes into the closet and locks the door behind her. The* COUNT
and the COUNTESS *come back into the room. The* COUNT *has a
crowbar in his hand; he throws it on the chair.*

COUNT: Everything exactly as I left it.

COUNTESS: Is it possible that vanity alone can drive an honourable man to these excesses?

COUNT: Love or vanity, you will open that door, or I shall . . .

COUNTESS: Stop, Sir, stop, I beg you! Do you think I have no self-respect?

COUNT: Anything you please, Madam, but I insist on seeing who is in this closet!

COUNTESS: Very well, Sir. You shall see. But listen . . . quietly . . .

COUNT: So it is not Suzanne?

COUNTESS: At least it's no one ... you have any cause to fear ... we were planning a diversion for this evening ... a very innocent one, it's true, I swear to you ...

COUNT: You, swear?

COUNTESS: ... That we had not, either of us, any thought of giving you offence ...

COUNT: Either of us? It is a man.

COUNTESS: It is a child, Sir.

COUNT: Who is it??

COUNTESS: I hardly dare to tell you.

COUNT: I'll kill him!!

COUNTESS: Oh God!

COUNT: Tell me!!!

COUNTESS: Young ... Chérubin.

COUNT: Chérubin! That insolent little.... So, my suspicions and the letter are confirmed!

COUNTESS: Oh Sir, don't think ...

COUNT: (*aside*) Whichever way I turn it's always that confounded page! (*Aloud*) Come, Madam, open the door. I see it all now: you would not have been so moved at taking leave of him this morning, he would have gone the moment that I told him to, you would not have added so much fabrication to your tale about Suzanne, and he wouldn't have been so painstakingly concealed if there wasn't something criminal afoot!

COUNTESS: He thought that you'd be angry if you saw him.

COUNT: Come out, you little wretch!!!

COUNTESS: Oh Sir, your anger makes me tremble for him. Do not believe unworthy thoughts, I beg of you.... And just because you find him half undressed ...

COUNT: Undressed?

COUNTESS: Unfortunately yes. He was going to put on women's clothes: he is wearing one of my nightcaps, he is in his shirtsleeves because he took his coat off ... his shirt is undone and he has his sleeves rolled up ... he was trying something on.... My Lord! Spare him he is only a child! I never should forgive myself if I had been the cause ...

COUNT: Your terror only serves to aggravate his crime!

COUNTESS: It's not his fault. He was about to leave: it was I that had him sent for!

COUNT: Get up, and get out of my way! You have the audacity to kneel in front of me, pleading for another man!

COUNTESS: Very well, Sir. I will get up. I will get out of your way. I will even give you the key to the closet: but if you love me . . .

COUNT: Love you, you unfaithful woman?

The COUNTESS *collapses into an armchair, hiding her face in a handkerchief.*

Sc.17   COUNTESS: Oh heavens! He'll be murdered.

The COUNT *unlocks the door and opens it:* SUZANNE *comes out.*

COUNT: It's Suzanne!

SUZANNE: 'I'll kill him!' 'I'll kill him!' Well, kill the wicked page-boy then!

COUNT: (*aside*) What a fiasco! (*Aloud*) And you pretend to be amazed as well! But perhaps she's not the only one in there!

Sc.18   *The* COUNT *goes into the closet:* SUZANNE *runs to the* COUNTESS.

SUZANNE: Calm yourself, my Lady. He's well away. You should have seen him jump!

COUNTESS: Oh, Suzette, I am dead!

Sc.19   *The* COUNT *comes out of the closet.*

COUNT: There's no one there. On this occasion I was wrong. Madam, you are a most accomplished actress.

SUZANNE: And me, Your Lordship?

The COUNTESS *keeps her handkerchief to her mouth, still recovering.*

COUNT: What, Madam, are you laughing?

COUNTESS: Why not, Sir?

COUNT: What a ghastly joke! And what conceivable reason could you have for doing a thing like that?

COUNTESS: Are we to feel pity for your lunancy?

COUNT: Do you call that lunacy? My honour was at stake!

COUNTESS: Am I to be eternally the victim either of neglect or jealousy, with you the only one allowed to say when we are to be reconciled?

COUNT: Oh Madam, that is harshly spoken . . .

SUZANNE: Her Ladyship could easily have let you call the servants!

COUNT: You are quite right. I should be ashamed of myself. Forgive me, I am so confused . . .

COUNTESS: No, Sir. An insult of that kind is inexcusable. I shall retire to the Ursulines.* I can see I should have done so long ago.

COUNT: Could you do that . . . without . . . some regrets?

SUZANNE: I'm sure there would be tears afterwards . . .

COUNTESS: Even so, Suzanne, I'd rather mourn him than stoop so low as to forgive him: he has offended me too much.

COUNT: Rosine!

COUNTESS: I am no longer the Rosine you so passionately pursued. I am poor Countess Almaviva, the sad, abandoned wife that you no longer love.

SUZANNE: Madam!

COUNT: Have pity on me . . . !

COUNTESS: You had none for me.

COUNT: But there was the letter too: it made my blood boil . . .

COUNTESS: I did not consent to its being written.

COUNT: You knew about it?

COUNTESS: It was that foolish Figaro.

COUNT: So he was in it!!

SUZANNE: Madam!

COUNTESS: He gave it to Bazile . . .

COUNT: Who told me that he'd had it from a peasant. Oh, the perfidious minstrel! The two-faced traitor! He'll pay for this!!!

COUNTESS: You expect to be forgiven yourself, and you have never once forgiven anybody else: how like a man! Oh, if ever I consented to forgive you in view of the confusion the letter may have thrown you into, I should at least demand the amnesty be general!

COUNT: Well, granted: with all my heart, Countess! But how can I atone for so humiliating a mistake?

COUNTESS: It was humiliating for us both.

COUNT: Oh say for me alone! But I am still wholly at a loss to know how women are so quick to assume precisely the right voice and tone to suit the circumstances: you blushed, you wept, your face was drawn – upon my honour, it still is!

COUNTESS: I was blushing . . . with resentment at your insinuations. As if any man had the sensitivity to distinguish between the indignation of an honest woman that has been humiliated and the confusion born of a deserved reproach . . .

COUNT: And the page half-undressed, in his shirtsleeves, practically naked?

COUNTESS: You see him, standing there before you. Are you not happier to have found him than the other? In general you don't find meeting him particularly hateful . . .

COUNT: And all the pleading and the simulated tears?

COUNTESS: You make me laugh, and I have very little inclination to . . .

COUNT: We think we're all so skilled in politics, and we are as innocent as children. It is you, Madam, that the King should send as Ambassador to London. You women must have made a very thorough study of the art of self-control to be so deuced successful at it.

COUNTESS: It's always you that force us to it.

SUZANNE: Allow us to be prisoners on parole, and you'll see if you can trust our sense of honour or not.

COUNTESS: Let's call a halt, my Lord: perhaps I went too far. But if I am prepared to be indulgent in just as grave a case, it must at least mean you will treat me similarly. . . . Oh Suzanne, I'm so feeble! I set such a bad example to you! No one will believe we're truly angry ever again!

> *She holds out her hands to the* COUNT, *who kisses them*
> *passionately.*

SUZANNE: Good ! Madam, with them it seems it always has to come to this.

Sc.20   *Enter* FIGARO, *out of breath.*

FIGARO: They told me Madam wasn't well. I came as quickly as I could. I'm very glad to see that everything's in order.

COUNT: You are most attentive.

FIGARO: That is what I am here for, Sir. But as everything's in order, Your Lordship, all your young serfs, boys and girls, are down below with the fiddles and bagpipes, waiting to accompany me the moment you permit me to bring in the bride . . .

COUNT: And who will be looking after Her Ladyship in the house?

FIGARO: Looking after her? She's not ill.

COUNT: No, but the man who isn't here who is supposed to have an assignation with her.

FIGARO: Man that isn't here?

COUNT: The man in the letter you handed to Bazile.

FIGARO: Who says I did?

COUNT: Even if I didn't know it from other sources, you dishonest person, you are betrayed by your physiognomy which tells me instantly that you are lying!

FIGARO: Well, if that's what it is, it isn't me that's lying, it's my physiognomy . . .

SUZANNE: It's no good, my poor Figaro, don't waste your breath when you're beaten: We've told him everything.

FIGARO: Told him what? You're treating me as if I was Bazile . . .

SUZANNE: That you wrote the letter earlier on to make His Lordship think, when he came back, that the little page was in the closet when I was in there with the door locked.

FIGARO: If Madam says I did, if Suzanne says I did, if Your Excellency says I did – then who am I to say I didn't? But I'll be truthful with you, Sir: if I was you, I wouldn't believe a word of what we're telling you.

COUNT: All the evidence against you, and you persist in lying! Over the years I begin to find that irritating!

COUNTESS: Oh, the poor man! Tell the truth indeed! Why ask him to break the habit of a lifetime?

FIGARO: (aside) I've warned him.

SUZANNE: (aside) Have you seen the page?

FIGARO: (aside) Still a little bruised.

SUZANNE: (aside) Poor lamb!

COUNTESS: Come, Sir, they're desperate to be married: it's very natural they should be impatient: let's go in and begin the ceremony.

COUNT: (aside) Marceline, Marceline!! (Aloud) I would like . . . to be . . . dressed at least.

COUNTESS: For our own people? Am I?

Enter ANTONIO, *drunk and carrying a flowerpot.*   Sc.21

ANTONIO: Your Lordship! Your Lordship!

COUNT: What do you want, Antonio?

ANTONIO: Have bars put on the windows as overlooks my flowerbeds, will you? All sorts of things they throws out of those windows, and just a moment ago they throw'd a man out!

COUNT: Out of that window?

ANTONIO: Look what they gone and did to my gillyflowers!!

SUZANNE: (aside) Look out, Figaro, look out!!!

FIGARO: Your Lordship, he's been drunk since breakfast time.

ANTONIO: That's where you're wrong, young fellow, my lad! I'm still drunk from last night – that's what comes of jumping to conclusions.

COUNT: This man! This man! Where is he?

ANTONIO: Where is he?

COUNT: Yes.

ANTONIO: That's what I'm saying. . . . I want you to find him, you see: I am your servant: there's no one else excepting me as takes care of your garden. A man falling in it, and you'll agree my reputation's seriously damaged . . .

SUZANNE: *(aside)* Distract him, distract him!

FIGARO: You're still drinking, then?

ANTONIO: Oh, if I didn't drink I'd be a lunatic.

COUNTESS: But taking drink like that when there's really no need for it . . .

ANTONIO: Drinking when we are not thirsty, making love in season, out of season, that's all there is as separates us from the other animals.

COUNT: Answer me or I will have you sacked!!

ANTONIO: But would I go, though?

COUNT: What did you say???

ANTONIO: If you hain't got enough up there . . .

(He taps his forehead)

. . . to keep a good servant when you see one, I am not stupid enough, I'm not, to dismiss a master as good as you are . . .

COUNT: You said that someone threw a man out of those windows . . .

ANTONIO: Yes, My Excellency. Just a moment ago. In a white waistcoat, and he was away, Lord love us, running . . .

COUNT: Then what happened?

ANTONIO: I wanted to run after him, but I give myself such a great thump on the fist against the gatepost, I couldn't move hand nor foot all up this little finger.

He shows the COUNT *his finger.*

COUNT: At least you'd recognise the man?

ANTONIO: Oh yes, righty-ho I would. If I'd seen him, though . . .

SUZANNE: *(aside)* He didn't see him!

FIGARO: Well, what a song and dance about a flowerpot! How much longer are you going on about a gillyflower, you old whiner? There's no use looking any further, Your Lordship; it was me that jumped.

COUNT: What?? You??

ANTONIO: Your body must have grown a lot since then; because I thought you were a big bit littler and more skinnier.

FIGARO: Certainly! When you jump you roll yourself up in a ball.

ANTONIO: I reckon it were more like, who could say, that little weedy page-boy.

COUNT: You mean Chérubin?

FIGARO: Oh yes, come back on purpose with his horse all the way from the gates of Seville, which is where he more than likely is by now.

ANTONIO: Oh no, I don't say that, I don't say that: I never saw no horse jump out, else I'd have said so.

COUNT: Patience!!!

ANTONIO: Well, seeing as it was you, it's only right as I should give you back this titchy bit of paper as come out of your waistcoat pocket when you fell . . .

COUNT: Give it to me!

FIGARO: (aside) He's caught me!

COUNT: Your terror will not have driven from your mind entirely the contents of this paper, nor how it came to find its way into your pocket . . . ?

FIGARO: No, I'm sure it hasn't. . . . It's just I've got so many of them. There's always something that needs answering, isn't there? What about this one? No, that's a letter from Marceline, four pages of it. Beautiful. It wouldn't be the appeal from the poor poacher that's in prison? No, here it is! I had the inventory of furniture for the manor house in the other pocket . . .

COUNTESS: (aside) Oh God, Suzette, it's Chérubin's Commission.

SUZANNE: (aside) We've lost: he's got us: it's the Commission.

COUNT: Well, you're the famous improvisor, you can't guess?

ANTONIO: His Lordship says if you can't guess.

FIGARO: Phew, you horrible old man, there's no need to talk so near my face!

COUNT: You don't recall at all what this can be?

FIGARO: Oh! Oh! Oh! Poverino! It must be that poor child's Commission! He gave it me and I forgot to give it back. Oh! Oh! Oh! I'm such a scatterbrain! What will he do without his Commission? I must run after him . . .

COUNT: And why would he have given it to you?

FIGARO: He wanted me to . . . do something to it.

COUNTESS: (aside) There's no seal on it.

SUZANNE: (aside) The seal!

COUNT: You don't answer?

FIGARO: Because . . . there's something missing. . . . He says it's customary . . .

COUNT: Customary? Customary? What do you mean, it's customary?

FIGARO: To put your coat of arms on it in sealing wax. I expect you thought it wasn't worth the trouble!

The COUNT *crumples the Commission up in a rage.*

COUNT: So! Fate has decreed. I am to be for ever hoodwinked, am I? (*Aside*) Figaro is telling them precisely what to do and I shall never be revenged.

FIGARO: You won't go without giving orders for the wedding?

Sc.22   *Enter* BAZILE, BARTHOLO, MARCELINE, GRIPE-SOLEIL, *valets and tenants.*

MARCELINE: Do no such thing, Your Lordship! Our claims have preference to his: you owe us justice! He is contractually engaged to me!

COUNT: (*aside*) Revenge at last!!

FIGARO: Engaged? What do you mean, engaged? Explain yourself!

MARCELINE: Yes, I'll explain, dishonest man!

COUNT: What is this, Marceline?

MARCELINE: An engagement to be married.

FIGARO: A letter of agreement, that was all, about some money that you lent me.

MARCELINE: Upon condition he would marry me. You are a great Lord, the most powerful justice in the province . . .

COUNT: Present yourselves before the Court, and I will hear any case that's brought before me . . .

BAZILE: Then, Your Eminence will permit me to press my own claims on Marceline . . . ?

COUNT: (*aside*) Aha, the villain with the letter! (*Aloud*) Your claims? Your claims? How dare you open your mouth in front of me, you great blockhead!!

ANTONIO: Got him with first shot! That's him all right!

COUNT: Marceline, everything will be postponed until we have examined your claims, which will be done publicly in the great audience chamber. Bazile, my wonderfully honest, good and faithful servant, you will go to the village and summon the magistrates.

BAZILE: To hear her case?

COUNT: And you will also bring me the peasant who gave you that letter.

BAZILE: How could I know which one it was?

COUNT: Do you refuse?

BAZILE: I did not come to this castle to be the errand-boy.

COUNT: What do you say?

BAZILE: As a gifted performer on the village organ, I am employed to instruct Her Ladyship in the clavichord, the women in singing, the pages in the mandoline, and principally to entertain the members of your household with my guitar, whenever it may please you to command.

GRIPE-SOLEIL: I'll go, Your Lordship, if it please you, Sir.

COUNT: What is your name and your employment?

GRIPE-SOLEIL: I am Gripe-Soleil, Your Good Lorship: the little goatherd, what am commanded to be assisting with the firey-works. I knows where to find all the judges.

COUNT: I like your zeal. You may go. (*To* BAZILE) But you will accompany this gentleman, playing your guitar and singing to entertain him on the road. He is a member of my household.

GRIPE-SOLEIL: Oh, I'm a member of the household!!!

SUZANNE *tries to calm him.*

BAZILE: I am to accompany the goatherd, playing?

COUNT: That is what you are employed to do! Go, or I shall have you sacked!!

[*Exit the* COUNT]   Sc.23

BAZILE: (*aside*) I should not consort together with an iron cauldron: I am but a fragile . . .

FIGARO: . . . Little pitcher. With great big ears and nothing in between!

BAZILE: I'm not going to help *them* get married. I'm going to be sure I am married to Marceline. (*Aloud to* FIGARO) Promise me you will not settle until I return!

He takes up his guitar from a chair.

FIGARO: Settle! Oh no fear, no, not even if you never come back ever. You don't seem in a very tuneful mood: would you like me to begin, then? Come on, cheer up, la-la-la-la, for the girl I'm going to marry!

(FIGARO *begins to lead them off-stage, dancing a seguidilla, and moving backwards towards the door,* BAZILE *playing the guitar.*
FIGARO *sings:*)

I can't describe the pleasure
She's a treasure
She's my Suzanne
Zanne zanne zanne
Zanne zanne zanne
Zanne zanne zanne
Zanne zanne zanne!

She, more than any riches
Bewitches
All my reason
Zon zon zon
Zon zon zon
Zon zon zon
Zon zon zon.

Sc.24   [*Exit all except the* COUNTESS *and* SUZANNE]

COUNTESS: You see, Suzanne, the pretty pickle your lunatic companion got into with his letter?

SUZANNE: Oh Madam, when I came out of that closet, you should have seen your face! First of all it went completely blank: but that was only like a cloud passing over it, and then it came out, bright, bright, bright red!!

COUNTESS: Oh, that dreadful gardener! It all confused me so much I couldn't think of anything at all!

SUZANNE: Oh Madam, that's not true at all! It made me realise that if you know how to behave in polite society, a proper lady has the confidence to lie herself blue in the face and never bat an eyelid.

COUNTESS: Do you think the Count believes it? What happens if he finds that child in the house?

SUZANNE: I'll go and tell them to make sure they hide him properly!

COUNTESS: He must go. After what has happened, you can understand that I'm not particularly anxious to send him to the garden in your place . . .

SUZANNE: One thing's certain is that I'm not going. So once again my wedding . . .

COUNTESS: Wait. . . . What if I went myself . . . ?

SUZANNE: You, My Lady?

COUNTESS: Then there'd be no risk to anyone . . . he would not be able to deny it . . . I could punish him for being jealous . . . prove to him that he's unfaithful, and then. . . . Let's do it: we have been fortunate the first time, taking chances: it makes me want to try again. . . . Let him know immediately you will be in the garden. . . . But whatever happens, nobody . . .

SUZANNE: Oh Figaro!

COUNTESS: No, no. He would only want to complicate it. . . . Find me my velvet mask and my stick so I can go and muse upon it on the terrace.

Sc.25   SUZANNE *goes into the closet.*

Oh, the ribbon, my pretty ribbon, I'd forgotten all about you.

(*She finds the ribbon in the armchair and rolls it up*)

I'm going to keep you with me always! You will remind me of the time that poor child. . . . Oh my dear husband, what have you done? And what am I doing at this moment?

SUZANNE *comes back, the* COUNTESS *hiding the ribbon down the*   Sc.26
front of her dress.

SUZANNE: Here's the stick and your mask.

COUNTESS: Remember, I said you're not to mention a word of this to Figaro . . .

SUZANNE: My Lady, it's perfect, your plan. I've just been thinking about it. It ties up everything, puts an end to everything and solves everything: and whatever else may happen I shall definitely be married!

She kisses the COUNTESS*'s hand and they go off. During the entr'acte,* VALETS *reset the stage for Act III. They bring in two benches with backs for the lawyers, which they place stage left and stage right, leaving sufficient room for people to pass behind them. They put a rostrum with two steps up to it in the centre upstage, on which they place the* COUNT*'s chair. The* CLERK OF THE COURT*'s table and stool are downstage and to one side, and the chairs for* BRID'OISON *and the other magistrates are on either side of the rostrum.*

ACT III

Sc.1   *The Throne Room in the Castle, used as a court room: upstage left a canopied throne on a dais, with a portrait of the King above the throne. The* COUNT *in conversation with* PEDRILLO, *in his shirt-sleeves and riding boots, with a sealed envelope in his hand.*

COUNT: So that is understood?
PEDRILLO: Your Excellency, Yes, Sir.

Sc.2   [*Exit* PEDRILLO]

COUNT: Pedrillo!

Sc.3   *Re-enter* PEDRILLO

PEDRILLO: Your Excellency?
COUNT: No one's seen you?
PEDRILLO: Not a soul, Sir.
COUNT: Take the Arab stallion.
PEDRILLO: Already saddled, Sir. At the garden gate.
COUNT: Like the blazes, straight to Seville.
PEDRILLO: Can't be more than twenty miles, Sir. Good road.
COUNT: Dismount, find out if the boy is there.
PEDRILLO: At the house, Sir?
COUNT: Yes. And most important, when he arrived.
PEDRILLO: Sir.
COUNT: Hand him his Commission, and come back as fast as possible.
PEDRILLO: And if he isn't there, Sir?
COUNT: Come back even faster and inform me! Go on!

                                                      [*Exit* PEDRILLO]

Sc.4   (*The* COUNT *paces up and down, deep in thought*)

It was foolish of me, sending Bazile away! . . . Being angry serves no purpose whatsoever. A man jumps out of the window, and then another man confesses or pretends that it was him. I can't follow it . . . it's all so confusing! . . . Taking liberties with the lower classes on

one's estate is one thing, what difference can it make to anyone of
that sort? But my wife, the Countess! If some insolent swine ever
dared. . . . What am I thinking of? It's true, when one is roused the
most restrained imagination runs riot, like a nightmare! Surely she
has some self-respect! What about mine? What the devil do I look
like? On the other hand, what am I doing? I wonder if Suzanne's
been indiscreet about my intimate attentions. She hasn't even had
them yet. Whose fault is it I've become entangled in this madness? I
have tried to free myself from it, scores of times. . . . It's the curious
effect of indecision: if I was absolutely certain that I wanted her, I'd
find her a great deal less desirable. Figaro certainly believes in keep-
ing people waiting. I must be very skilful in the questions that I ask
him . . .

    (*Enter* FIGARO *upstage: he stops and listens*)

. . . and try, in the course of conversation, to discover in the subtlest
way imaginable whether he knows that I am in love with Suzanne . . .   *Sc.5*

FIGARO: (*aside*) So there we have it!

COUNT: If she's as much as breathed a word about it to him . . .

FIGARO: (*aside*) As I thought.

COUNT: I'll make him marry the old one.

FIGARO: (*aside*) And break poor Bazile's heart!

COUNT: And then we'll see what can be done with the young one . . .

FIGARO: (*aside*) My wife, if you please!

The COUNT *turns round.*

COUNT: What? Yes? What is it?

FIGARO: Me, Sir. I believe you sent for me.

COUNT: And why that observation?

FIGARO: I said nothing, Sir.

COUNT: 'My wife, if you please!'

FIGARO: It was . . . the end of a sentence. I was saying 'Go and tell my
wife, if you please . . .'

COUNT: Your wife!

(*The* COUNT *paces up and down*)

Perhaps you could tell me, Sir, what can have kept you when I had you
called?

FIGARO *pretends to straighten his clothes.*

FIGARO: My clothes were all muddy from falling in the flowerbed: I
was changing.

COUNT: Does that take an hour?

FIGARO: It takes time.

COUNT: The servants in this house . . . take longer to dress than their masters!

FIGARO: That's because they haven't got servants to assist them.

COUNT: I did not wholly understand just now what it was that made you run yourself to the unnecessary risk of hurling yourself . . .

FIGARO: Risk!! You'd think I'd been jumping to my death in the bottomless pit . . .

COUNT: Don't try to throw me off the scent by pretending that you're following me when you're not, you devious valet! You know very well it's not the risk that I find disquieting, it's why you did it!

FIGARO: You believe an untrue story, you come in in a rage, you turn everything upside down like some great roaring cataract in the Sierras: you are looking for a man, you have to have one or you are going to break down doors, smash holes in walls. . . . It so happens I am there: now who knows, when you're in a rage . . .

COUNT: You could have gone down the stairs.

FIGARO: And have you catch me in the corridor?

COUNT: The corridor!!! (*Aside*) I am losing my temper and damaging my chances of discovering what I want to know.

FIGARO: (*aside*) Let him come on and play it very close!

COUNT: That is not what I intended to say . . . we will not mention it again . . . I . . . yes, I had had some thought of taking you to London, my Official Runner at the Embassy, but I have considered it, and . . .

FIGARO: Your Lordship's changed his mind . . . ?

COUNT: Well, first of all, you don't know any English.

FIGARO: I know 'God damn'.

COUNT: I do not understand.

FIGARO: I said I know 'God damn'.

COUNT: Well?

FIGARO: Well, English is a beautiful language! A little takes you a long way. If you can say 'God damn' in England you won't go short of anything, no matter where you go. Say you want a good plump chicken for dinner. Go into an inn, and make this gesture to the serving man . . .

(*He mimes turning a spit*)

God damn! They bring you calf's foot soaked in brine with no bread. It's splendid. You like a glass of excellent burgundy or claret, no more than this . . .

(*He pops an imaginary cork from a bottle*)

God damn! And they serve you with a mug of beer in a pewter tankard with froth on top. What satisfaction! You meet one of those pretty creatures that go mincing along, eyes down, elbows back, wriggling their hips a little? You put all your fingers very elegantly to your lips like this. Ooooh, God damn!! And they give you a clout that would fell an ox, to show they understand. The English, it's true, do add here and there some other phrases when they're talking to each other, but it's obvious God damns the root of the national tongue. And if Your Lordship hasn't any other cause for leaving me in Spain . . .

COUNT: (aside) He wants to come to London. She has not said anything.

FIGARO: (aside) He thinks that I know nothing: I'll play him a little longer, his way . . .

COUNT: What possible reason could my wife have had for playing me a trick like that?

FIGARO: Goodness me, Your Lordship, you must know that better than I do.

COUNT: I am very considerate, I deluge her with presents.

FIGARO: You give her things, but you're unfaithful. No one's going to thank you for the trimmings if you're starving them . . .

COUNT: There was a time you told me everything.

FIGARO: There's nothing that I'm keeping from you now.

COUNT: How much did the Countess give you for that amusing little plot?

FIGARO: How much did you give me for dragging her out of the clutches of that Doctor? Come, my Lord, don't abuse a man that's useful to you: you might turn him into a bad servant . . .

COUNT: The number of times I've seen you on the way to make your fortune, and you have never once gone straight.

FIGARO: How do you expect me to? A great struggling mob: everybody trying to get on faster than the next man, pushing, elbowing, knocking each other down: it's every man for himself and anybody else gets trampled on. That's how it's done. As far as I'm concerned, I've had enough.

COUNT: With your originality and intelligence you might well be promoted to some important public office one day . . .

FIGARO: Promoted? For intelligence? You're laughing at me, Sir. If you're mediocre and prepared to crawl, I agree, you can get anywhere.

COUNT: You'd only have to let me give you some instruction in politics . . .

FIGARO: I know all about politics.

COUNT: Like English. The root of the tongue . . .

FIGARO: Yes. If it was anything to boast about. . . . Having to pretend you don't know what you do know, and do know what you don't know: that you're listening when you can't understand a word, and not listening when you can: but most of all that you're more powerful than you really are. As often as not the biggest secret that you have to keep is that there isn't one: going to your office to sharpen pens, having to appear immensely wise when you are, as the saying is, a drivelling idiot: always playing a part, convincingly or otherwise: spreading spies and paying traitors: steaming open secret documents, intercepting letters, trying to dignify the squalor of the means by the importance of the ends: that's politics, or I'm a dead man!

COUNT: Oh, but that is dishonesty behind the scenes you're talking about . . .

FIGARO: Politics, dishonesty in high places, call it what you please, I do not believe they're wholly unrelated; make what you like of it . . . 'I'd sooner have my love, oh joy . . .' as the good old king says in his song . . .*

COUNT: (aside) He doesn't want to go. I see . . . Suzanne has betrayed me.

FIGARO: (aside) I'm only leading him on to get my own back!

COUNT: So you hope you're going to win your case against Marceline?

FIGARO: Your Excellency – how can you think it is a crime for me to jib at an old maid when you allow yourself the liberty of making off with all the young ones?

COUNT: (ironically) In court, a magistrate forgets himself and fixes his attention on the letter of the law.

FIGARO: Easy on the powerful and savage on the weak!

COUNT: Do you think I am joking?

FIGARO: Well, who knows, Your Lordship? *Tempo é galant' uomo*, time is a gallant man, as the Italian has it: time always tells, and time will tell who's for me and who's against.

COUNT: I can see she's told him everything. He'll have to marry the old governess.

FIGARO: (aside) He's playing a very cautious game: I wonder how much he's found out?

Sc.6   *Enter a* LACKEY.

LACKEY: His Worship, Mr Gusman Brid'oison, Sir.

COUNT: Brid'oison?

FIGARO: That's right, Sir. The local justice, the presiding magistrate, your lawyer.

COUNT: Tell him to wait.

[*Exit the* LACKEY]

FIGARO *hesitates, watching the* COUNT *who seems to be thinking*   Sc.7
of something else.

FIGARO: Is this as you wanted it, Your Lordship?

COUNT: What? . . . I told them to prepare this chamber for the public hearing.

FIGARO: Well, what isn't here? The big armchair for you, good chairs for all the lawyers, the stool for the Clerk of the Court, two benches for the barristers, the floor for the *beau monde* and then the rabble at the back. I'll go and get the men to wax the floor.

[*Exit* FIGARO]   Sc.8

COUNT: (*stands*) The shifty menial. He had me seriously embarrassed. Whenever there's an argument he immediately seizes the advantage, catches one in a stranglehold and then proceeds to tie one up in knots. So you are in league to make a fool of me, are you, you pair of jailbirds? Be friends, be lovers, be whatever you please and I consent, but God Almighty, married . . . !

Enter SUZANNE.   Sc.9

SUZANNE: (*out of breath*) Your Lordship. . . . Pardon me, Your Lordship . . .

COUNT: Yes? What is it, Suzanne?

SUZANNE: You're very angry?

COUNT: It would appear that there is something that you want . . .

SUZANNE: My mistress is having her vapours: I came to ask you if you could lend us your bottle of sal volatile. I'd bring it back immediately.

The COUNT *gives her the bottle.*

COUNT: No, no, you can keep it. You'll be needing it yourself before very long.

SUZANNE: I never knew women like me could have the vapours. It's a society complaint: you can only catch it in a boudoir . . .

COUNT: Nevertheless, a girl that is engaged and very much in love, who suddenly loses her future husband.

SUZANNE: If I pay Marceline with the money that you promised me . . .

COUNT: *I* promised you?

SUZANNE: I had understood you to have done so, Sir!

COUNT: Yes . . . if you agreed to be more reasonable.

SUZANNE: I thought it was my duty to comply with all your wishes, isn't it, Your Excellency?

COUNT: You cruel girl! Why didn't you say all this before?

SUZANNE: It's never too late to tell the truth, Sir, is it?

COUNT: Would you . . . come at twilight . . . to the garden?

SUZANNE: I go there every evening for a walk, Sir, don't I?

COUNT: You were so severe this morning . . .

SUZANNE: This morning? What about the page behind the chair?

COUNT: She's right. I had forgotten! But why have you always refused when Bazile's told you . . .

SUZANNE: Why do we need a Bazile?

COUNT: She's always right. However, there is a certain person by the name of Figaro I am very much afraid you have told everything.

SUZANNE: Oh yes, I tell him everything all right. Except for what he doesn't need to know.

COUNT: Oh you delicious girl! You promise me? And if you weren't to keep your word; let it be clearly understood, my sweetheart: no rendezvous this evening, no money and no marriage.

SUZANNE: But on the other hand, Your Lordship, no marriage and no *droit de seigneur*.

COUNT: Where does she get it from? God, she'll drive me mad all over again! . . . But your mistress will be waiting for the bottle . . .

SUZANNE: I needed some excuse to talk to you, didn't I?

She gives him back the sal volatile bottle. The COUNT *tries to kiss her.*

COUNT: You adorable creature!

SUZANNE: There's someone coming!

COUNT: (*aside*) She's mine!

The COUNT *himself runs off, leaving* SUZANNE *alone.*

SUZANNE: I'll go straightaway and tell Her Ladyship.

Sc.10   *Enter* FIGARO.

FIGARO: Suzanne! Suzanne! Where are you running to? You've been with His Lordship!

SUZANNE: You can go to court now, if you want. You've just won your case!

[*Exit* SUZANNE, *running off*]

FIGARO: Hey! But . . .

[*Exit* FIGARO, *following her*]   *Sc.11*

Re-enter the COUNT.

COUNT: 'You've just won your case!' A fine trap I was about to blunder into. The dear creatures. The insolence of it!! I'll punish them, though. An irreversible decision in court, entirely in accordance with the law – What if he were to pay the old woman? What could he pay her with? If he were to pay. . . . Aha! There's always noble old Antonio: he's so proud of his ancestry he despises Figaro and thinks his niece is marrying beneath her. If I encourage him in his insanity. . . . Why not? In the vast field of intrigue, one must know how to cultivate everything – even the vanity of an idiot! Antonio!

Enter MARCELINE, *followed by* BRID'OISON *and* BARTHOLO.   *Sc.12*
As he sees her coming on, the COUNT *sneaks off.*

MARCELINE: Sir, if you could listen to my side of the case . . .
BRID'OISON: Ve-very well, let's ta-talk about it verbally.
BARTHOLO: There is a promise of marriage . . .
MARCELINE: Which was accompanied by an advance . . . of money.
BRID'OISON: I understand. Et cetera. And all tha-tha-that that entails.
MARCELINE: Certainly not, Sir. There was no et cetera.
BRID'OISON: I understand. Have you the mo-mo-money to pay?
MARCELINE: No, Sir. I was the one that lent it.
BRID'OISON: I understand. And you're de-de-de-demanding that the mo-money be repaid?
MARCELINE: No, Sir, I am demanding that he marry me.
BRID'OISON: Aha. Indeed. I understand it now, entirely. And does he wa-wa-want to marry *you*?
MARCELINE: No, Sir. That is what the case is all about!
BRID'OISON: Are you suggesting I don't understand the case?
MARCELINE: No, Sir. (*To* BARTHOLO) Am I making any progress whatsoever? (*To* BRID'OISON) Are you quite sure that you'll be trying the case?
BRID'OISON: Would I have bou-bou-bought my sacred trust for any other purpose?
MARCELINE: I think it's wicked to sell positions like that!

BRID'OISON: So do I. They'd do far better if they gave them us for nothing. Against whom do you bring this case?

Sc.13   Enter FIGARO, *rubbing his hands.*

MARCELINE: Sir, against that dishonest individual there.

FIGARO: Perhaps I am embarrassing you. . . . His Lordship will be back in just a moment, Your Worship.

BRID'OISON: I've seen that man be-be-be-before somewhere.

FIGARO: Serving your wife in Seville, Your Worship.

BRID'OISON: Whe-when was that?

FIGARO: A little under a year before Your Worship's youngest son was born, Sir, the young master. A very pretty child, I think I can say without boasting.

BRID'OISON: Oh yes, very pretty. The prettiest of them all. I am told you are in some ta-ta-ta-trouble here . . .

FIGARO: Very good of you, Your Worship. But it's nothing to speak of . . .

BRID'OISON: A pa-pa-pa-promise of marriage! Oh, the poor f-fool!

FIGARO: Your Worship . . .

BRID'OISON: There's a good lad, have you seen my private secretary?

FIGARO: Isn't that the Clerk of the Court?

BRID'OISON: Yes, he fills both offices si-si-simultaneously.

FIGARO: I guarantee he fills his pockets. Oh yes, I saw him for the deposition, then the supplementary deposition, as is the common practice . . .

BRID'OISON: Oh yes, one must observe the proper forms.

FIGARO: Oh certainly, Your Worship: in court it is the public that provides the funds, the lawyers supply the forms.

BRID'OISON: The boy is not the fool I took him for. . . . Well, my friend, since you seem to be so well infor-informed, I'll take a special interest in your case, I promise you . . .

FIGARO: I hope you will, Your Worship. I rely on your sense of equity, even though you are our justice.

BRID'OISON: What? Yes, I'm your justice. But what do you expect if you owe someone money and you do-do not pay?

FIGARO: Well, you see, Your Worship, then it's as if I hadn't owed it in the first place . . .

BRID'OISON: Exactly. What? What did you say?

Sc.14   Enter the COUNT, *preceded by an* USHER.

USHER: Gentlemen, His Lordship.

COUNT: You should not have taken the trouble to robe, Mr Brid'oison! Not here: this is a domestic matter. Your town clothes would have been more than good enough ...

BRID'OISON: You are mo-more than good enough, Your Lordship. But I ne-never go without them, for the form's sake. ... You will find that there are those who will roar with laughter in a judge's face if he appears in ordinary clothes, and yet will tremble at the sight of the humblest lawyer with his robes on. The fo-fo-forms, you see, the forms ...

COUNT: (to the USHER) Declare the hearing open.

The USHER opens the doors and barks the announcement:

USHER: Public hearing open!!

Enter ANTONIO, SERVANTS, PEASANTS and their wives all wearing   Sc.15
their best clothes. The COUNT goes to sit on the throne,
BRID'OISON in a chair to one side of him: DOUBLE-MAIN takes
his place on the stool behind the table. The magistrates and
barristers on the benches: MARCELINE beside BARTHOLO, FIGARO
sits on the other bench. The SERVANTS and PEASANTS stand at the
back.

BRID'OISON: (to DOUBLE-MAIN) Mr Double-main. C-c-call the cases!

DOUBLE-MAIN: (reading) 'The most noble, very noble, infinitely noble Lord Pedro Jorge, hidalgo, Baron of Los Altos and Montes Fieros and Otros Montes: against Alonzo Calderon,* a young dramatist.' It is a case of an abortive comedy, each party disowns it and blames the other.

COUNT: They are both entirely right to do so. Case dismissed. If they collaborate on any further work, so that it have some success, be it ordered that the nobleman shall provide his name and the dramatist his talent.

DOUBLE-MAIN: 'Barbe - Agar - Raab - Madeleine - Nicole - Marceline de Verte-Allure, being a woman of mature years, against Figaro ...' Baptismal name blank.

FIGARO: Anonymous.

BRID'OISON: Anonymous! Is that a pa-patron saint?

FIGARO: Yes. Mine.

DOUBLE-MAIN: (writing) Against Anonymous Figaro. Rank or title?

FIGARO: Gentleman.

COUNT: You, a gentleman?

The Clerk, DOUBLE-MAIN, *writes again.*

FIGARO: If Heaven had so intended I would be a member of the Royal Family.

COUNT: (*to* DOUBLE-MAIN) Proceed.

USHER: (*barking*) Silence! If you please!

DOUBLE-MAIN: In the case of an objection lodged against the marriage of the said Figaro by the said party, Marceline de Verte-Allure. Doctor Bartholo for the plaintiff, the said Figaro for himself, if the Court permits it, contrary to established legal use in this province.

FIGARO: Use, Mr Clerk of the Court? Abuse more often. Any layman with a little instruction is always more familiar with his own case than some cringing, bawling barrister who knows everything there is to know except the facts and thinks ruining his client no more embarrassing than boring everyone in court or sending Your Worships off to sleep: I myself will put the facts in a few well-chosen words. Your Worships . . .

DOUBLE-MAIN: Those you have already uttered are redundant as you are not the plaintiff. You are permitted only to defend yourself. Doctor, step forward please, and read the agreement . . .

FIGARO: Yes, an agreement.

BARTHOLO: It is very clear.

BRID'OISON: That remains to be-be seen.

DOUBLE-MAIN: Quiet, if you please!

USHER: Silence!

LACKEY: Silence!

BARTHOLO: (*reading*) 'I, the undersigned, acknowledge receipt from Mistress etcetera etcetera Marceline de Verte-Allure at the Castle of Aguas Frescas, of the sum of two thousand old, milled-edged piastres: which sum I will restore to her on her requiring it, and will marry her in the castle in recognition of her generosity and etc.' Signed simply Figaro. My submission is for payment of the sum demanded and execution of the promise. With costs.

(*He turns to the Court as a whole*)

Your Worships, no more absorbing case has ever been submitted to the judgement of a court: and since the case of the lovely Thalestris versus Alexander the Great . . .*

COUNT: Before we go back any further, Counsel, are we agreed the document is valid?

BRID'OISON: (*to* FIGARO) Have you any objection to make to what has been read out?

FIGARO: Yes, Your Worships, I submit that there was malice, error and malfeasance in the manner in which the evidence was read: because it is not stated in the manuscript 'which sum I will restore to her *and* marry her': but 'which sum I will restore to her *or* marry her', which is entirely different.

COUNT: Is it an 'and' in the deed or an 'or'?

BARTHOLO: In my submission, Sir, it is the copulative conjunction 'and', binding together the correlative members of the sentence: I will pay the young lady, *and* I will marry her . . .

FIGARO: In my submission, Sir, it is the disjunctive 'or' separating the said members. I will pay the damosel *or* I will marry her. I can out-pedant pedants any time: if he decides to talk in Latin I shall go on in Greek: I am going to exterminate . . .

COUNT: How is one to give judgement in a case like this?

BRID'OISON *attempts to rise to speak.*

BARTHOLO: If I may cut the Gordian knot,* Your Worships, and not quibble any longer over a word, we will concede that it is 'or'.

FIGARO: I demand to have that in writing!

BARTHOLO: And we will keep to it. A shoddy refuge where the guilty man will find scant comfort. Let us examine the deed again in this sense. 'Which sum I will restore to her or marry her in the castle. . . .' It is a matter, Your Worships, only of place. As one might say 'Apply the leeches here, *or* in bed'. One place or the other. 'Take two grains of rhubarb in warm water *or* with a little tamarind.'* Where is immaterial. Thus 'or marry her in the castle instead of in the village'.

FIGARO: Not at all. The sense is as in the example 'Either the illness will kill you, *or* the Doctor will'. Or else the Doctor. Another example. 'Either you will never write anything successful, or fools will be disparaging about your work!' Or else . . . fools. The sense is perfectly clear. In the case I quoted, fools or villains govern the subject, you. Is Counsel for the prosecution suggesting I have forgotten my syntax? Thus, I will pay her or I will marry her, comma, in the castle.

BARTHOLO: Without the comma.

FIGARO: It is there. It is marry her, comma, Your Worships, in the castle.

BARTHOLO: Without the comma, Your Worships.

FIGARO: It was there, Your Worships. Besides, can a man be made to make entire restitution to his wife on his wedding day?

BARTHOLO: Yes. A marriage is deemed to exist goods and chattels apart.

FIGARO: Then in our case bodies apart: if marrying her doesn't mean I'm quits.

The magistrates get up and discuss this in whispers.

BARTHOLO: A curious way of settling your accounts.

DOUBLE-MAIN: Quiet, if you please.

USHER: (*barking*) Silence!

LACKEY: Silence!

DOUBLE-MAN: Silence!

USHER: Silence!

LACKEY: Silence!

BARTHOLO: That is what the swine calls working off his debts!

FIGARO: Is this your case you're arguing, my learned friend?

BARTHOLO: I am defending this young lady.

FIGARO: Well, continue with your ravings by all means, but there is no need to be insulting. When the courts originally allowed lawyers to speak on behalf of litigants they did not give them a licence to insult the public. It degrades a noble institution.

The magistrates continue to confer in whispers.

DOUBLE-MAIN: Quiet, if you please.

USHER: (*barking*) Silence!

COUNT: How does the defendant answer: that he wishes to remain single. Very well, he may . . .

FIGARO: I've won!

COUNT: . . . But as the document says 'which sum I will restore to her on her requiring it or else marry her, etc. etc.', this Court orders the defendant to pay two thousand old piastres to the plaintiff, or else marry her before the day is out.

FIGARO: I've lost!

ANTONIO: A superb decision!

FIGARO: Why is it superb?

ANTONIO: Because you hain't my nephew, any more, that's why! My humble thanks, Your Lordship.

USHER: The Court will be upstanding.

The SERVANTS, PEASANTS, etc. leave.

ANTONIO: I am going to tell my niece what's happened.

[*Exit* ANTONIO]   *Sc.16*

MARCELINE: Ah, I breathe again.

FIGARO: And I am choking!

COUNT: (*aside*) At least I am revenged, and that's a consolation.

FIGARO: (*aside*) So much for Bazile objecting to Marceline's marriage! I might have known he wouldn't come back!

He sees the COUNT *about to go.*

You're leaving us, Your Lordship?

COUNT: You have the verdict.

FIGARO: (*to* BRID'OISON) It's all your fault, you blithering old windbag!

BRID'OISON: Me, a b-b-blithering old . . .

FIGARO: Yes. And I am not going to marry her. I am a gentleman, damn it!

The COUNT *stops.*

BARTHOLO: You will marry her.

FIGARO: Without obtaining the consent of my illustrious parents.

BARTHOLO: Tell us what they're called! Produce them!

FIGARO: All I ask for is a little time: I'm very near to seeing them again. Fifteen years I've been looking for them . . .

BARTHOLO: Conceited fool! Found on a doorstep, I imagine.

FIGARO: Not found, Doctor. Lost. Or rather stolen.

The COUNT *comes back.*

COUNT: Stolen? Lost? What proof have you? He'd only complain that we were doing him some injustice . . .

FIGARO: Your Lordship. If the lace swaddling clothes, the embroidered coverlets and jewels set in gold that were with me when the robbers found me were not sufficient evidence that I was nobly born, the trouble that my parents had taken to provide me with a distinctive mark would be proof enough of what a precious little boy I was: this hieroglyph here on my arm . . .

He begins to roll up his sleeve on his right arm. MARCELINE *gets up, very excited.*

MARCELINE: A doctor's spatula? On your right arm?

FIGARO: How did you know that?

MARCELINE: God! It's him!

FIGARO: Yes, it's me!

BARTHOLO: Who?

MARCELINE: It is Emmanuel!

BARTHOLO: Were you carried off by gypsies?

FIGARO: From near a castle. Doctor, if you are able to restore me to my noble family, name the price! Heaps of gold are nothing to my parents, they're . . .

BARTHOLO: This is your mother.

FIGARO: My nursemaid . . .

BARTHOLO: Your own mother!

COUNT: His mother?

FIGARO: Explain yourself!

MARCELINE: This is your father.

FIGARO: Oh! Oh! Oh! Mercy on us!

MARCELINE: Has not nature told you so a thousand times?

FIGARO: No. Never.

COUNT: (aside) His mother!

BRID'OISON: It's c-clear he will not marry her.

BARTHOLO: And nor will I!

MARCELINE: And nor will you? What of your son? You swore to me . . .

BARTHOLO: I was mad. If memories like that were binding, one would have to marry everybody.

BRID'OISON: And if you thought about it for as l-l-l-long as that, nobody would ever marry anyone.

BARTHOLO: Such notorious misdemeanours! Your lamentable youth!

MARCELINE: Yes, lamentable: and more so than you think. I don't deny I made mistakes! What has come to light today is more than proof enough of that. But it's very hard to have to expiate them after thirty years of leading a blameless life. From birth it was my nature to be virtuous, and I became so as soon as they permitted me to use my reason. . . . But at that age, when we have our illusions, our innocence and almost nothing else, when seducers are besieging us and we feel most keenly the cruel edge of poverty, what can a child do against so many enemies in league with one another? And yet some here condemn us most severely that may themselves have made a dozen women miserable.

FIGARO: Those that are most guilty are least generous: that's always true.

MARCELINE: It's more than ingratitude in men: it's scorn, wanting to destroy the toys you played with in your lust: your victims! It's you that should be punished for the errors of our youth! You and your magistrates, so proud at being able to condemn us. You're guilty of culpable neglect: you let them take from us every honest means of earning a livelihood. Is there a single occupation open to women, the wretched creatures? We had a natural right to work as dressmakers and yet they're training men to do it by their thousands.

FIGARO: They even make soldiers sew on their own buttons.

MARCELINE: Even in the most exalted circles, women only receive the most contemptible treatment, trapped with the appearance of respect and love into a slavery that's all too real! Treated as children in property, punished as adults for our faults. However you consider it, your behaviour towards us can only inspire loathing, or else pity.

FIGARO: It's true.

COUNT: (aside) Too true.

BRID'OISON: My G-G-G-God, it's true!

MARCELINE: But what is it to us, my son, to be rejected by an unjust man? Do not consider where you came from, look where you are going. That is all that matters to any of us. In a few months your bride will be dependent on no one but herself. She'll marry you, I vouch for that. Live here with a loving wife and a loving mother and we shall only ever quarrel as to who does most to cherish you. Be indulgent with us, happy for yourself, my son: be cheerful and generous and good to everyone, and your mother will have nothing more to ask.

FIGARO: Everything you say is solid gold, mother, and I will follow your advice. What fools we are though! Thousands and thousands of years the earth's been turning, and in all that ocean of time, of which I happen to have scooped up thirty paltry years I'll never see again, I was torturing myself to find out who I owed them to! I pity anyone who lets it worry them. To spend a lifetime fretting, chafing endlessly against the yoke, like a poor old horse on the towpath, dragging against the stream, that can never rest even when they stop he goes on pulling although he has come to a standstill. We'll wait! ... Father, you have my apologies ... and you, mother, embrace me ... as maternally as you can.

MARCELINE *throws her arms round his neck. Enter* SUZANNE   Sc.17
with a purse in her hand.

SUZANNE: Your Lordship, stop! Don't marry them! I've come to pay this lady with the dowry that my mistress has given to me.

COUNT: (aside) Confound her mistress! It seems everything is conspiring ...

Sc.18   *Enter* ANTONIO, *seeing* FIGARO *embracing* MARCELINE.

ANTONIO: Oh, ho! Fancy that now!
SUZANNE: I see. Come, Uncle!

(SUZANNE *tries to go, but* FIGARO *pulls her back. She slaps
his face*)

You've got a cheek, you have! How dare you hold on to me?
FIGARO: Now, is that love? Before you leave us, I beseech you to look
into this dear woman's face!
SUZANNE: I am looking at it . . .
FIGARO: And what do you think?
SUZANNE: I think she's horrible!
FIGARO: Long live jealousy! She's not in competition with you!
MARCELINE: Come kiss your mother, my pretty Suzette.
SUZANNE: You!
MARCELINE: That wicked man that's teasing you is my son.
SUZANNE: His mother!!!
COUNT: What a vexing episode.
MARCELINE: No, no, my heart was powerfully drawn to him: 'twas but
deceived as to its motive. It was the common bond of blood that must
have prompted me . . .
FIGARO: And common sense that prompted me, mother, it made me
think instinctively I shouldn't marry you: I was very far from ever
hating you . . . witness the money.
MARCELINE: It's yours.
                    She gives him back the written agreement.
Take back your bond. It is your dowry!
SUZANNE: Take this one too.

SUZANNE *throws him the purse.*

FIGARO: My very deepest gratitude!
MARCELINE: I was never happy as a girl, and I seemed doomed to be
the most miserable of women, and now I am the most fortunate of
mothers! Kiss me, my two children. All my tenderest love is shared
between you. Now that I am as happy as it's possible for me to be,
children, how well I shall love . . .
FIGARO: Stop it, dear mother, stop! Do you want to see me weeping
for the first time in my life? At least I'm crying out of happiness. How
foolish! I almost feel ashamed of it. I can feel the tears running
through my fingers. . . . Look! (*He spreads his fingers*) And I was

trying to hold them back, like a fool. . . . Why should I be ashamed of it? I want to laugh and cry at the same time: I shall never feel like this again . . .

He puts his arm round his mother on one side, and SUZANNE *on the other.*

MARCELINE: Oh my love . . .

SUZANNE: My dear love . . .

BRID'OISON: Well, I must be f-f-foolish too . . .

FIGARO: Now I can defy despair! Attack me if you dare, with these two precious women to protect me!

ANTONIO: Not so much of the love-talk, if you please! When it comes to being married into a family, 'taint no bad thing, if the parents are first, if you take my meaning . . . (*to* MARCELINE) You've had his hand in marriage, I presume?

BARTHOLO: My hand! I'd sooner that it withered and dropped off than give it to the mother of a clown like that!

ANTONIO: So you're only a cruel stepfather, are you? (*To* FIGARO) In that case, Romeo my lad, I won't hear of it.

SUZANNE: Oh Uncle!

ANTONIO: Am I going to be giving my sister's child to summat as bain't be no one's?

BRID'OISON: How could he p-p-p-possibly be no one's child, you imbecile. Everyone is someone's child . . .

ANTONIO: Tarah!!! He's not having her!

[*Exit* ANTONIO]   *Sc.19*

COUNT: Court dismissed.

BARTHOLO: (*to* FIGARO) And now you'd best find someone to adopt you . . .

He is about to go when MARCELINE *runs and drags him back.*

MARCELINE: Stop, Doctor, do not go!

FIGARO: (*aside*) Oh, every fool in Andalusia's been let loose to prevent me being married!

SUZANNE: Poor dear Papa, he is your son . . .

MARCELINE: Witty, talented, handsome . . .

FIGARO: And never cost you a farthing!

BARTHOLO: What about the hundred crowns you stole from me?

MARCELINE: We'll take such good care of you, Papa!

SUZANNE: And love you so much, dear Papa . . .

BARTHOLO: Papa! Papa! Poor dear Papa! I let myself be taken like a child.

(MARCELINE, *and* SUZANNE *kiss him*)

Oh no, I have not said yes. Where is His Lordship?

FIGARO: Let's all run and find him! Let's force him to decide! If he's concocting some new plot we'd have to start all over again!

ALL: Run! Run!

Sc.20

[*Exit all except* BRID'OISON]

BRID'OISON: Even more f-f-foolish than His Worship! It is permissible to say such things to oneself . . . but. . . . They're not at all polite in these pa-pa-parts, I must say . . .

[*Exit* BRID'OISON]

ACT IV

A gallery, decorated with candelabra and chandeliers, flowers and garlands, ready for the celebrations: downstage right a table with an inkstand, upstage an armchair.

FIGARO: Well, love are you happy? My mother's silver tongue has finally convinced the Doctor. He may find her repulsive but he's marrying her.

SUZANNE: But there's not one of all the things you'd planned, and we were expecting, has happened, all the same!

FIGARO: Blind chance has done better than all the rest of us together, little one! That's the way the world goes: we can work and plan and scheme on one side: blind chance decides the outcome. And all of us from the half-starved conquerer that dreams of swallowing the entire earth to the peaceable blind man allowing himself to be led by his dog, we're all toys for chance to play with as the whim may take it ... and the blind beggar with the dog is often better advised and less deceived in what he sees than the other poor blind fool with all his powers about him. And as for the dear blind God of love ...

(He puts his arms round her waist.)

... allow me, if I may go on talking nonsense, to be the good dog that leads him to your pretty little door and we'll live there happily ever after ...

SUZANNE: Love and you?

FIGARO: Me and love.

SUZANNE: And you won't both go roaming off to find another home?

FIGARO: If you catch me at it, I hope a thousand million men ...

SUZANNE: You're going to exaggerate: tell me the honest truth.

FIGARO: I'm telling you the most honest truth there is ...

SUZANNE: Go on, you liar! You mean there's more than one?

FIGARO: Oh yes. Ever since they found that with the passage of time, old folly can become accepted wisdom, and ancient little lies, however badly they were planted, have grown into enormous truths, there have been hundreds of them . . . all the different species: those you know and never dare confess: because not every truth is good to talk about: and those you may profess without attaching any faith to them, because not every truth is good to believe in, and passionate oaths, and mothers' threats, and things a man may promise when he's drunk, or in power, a merchant's final offer. . . there's no end of them. Only my love for Suzette is the genuine truth.

SUZANNE: I don't know about fancy talk like that: all I know is I'm only going to love my husband.

FIGARO: You keep to that and you will be an exception to the rule . . .

Sc.2   *He tries to kiss her. Enter the* COUNTESS.

COUNTESS: Ah, so I was right. I said wherever they are, you can be sure, they'll be together. You're wanted, rather urgently, I think . . .

FIGARO: It's true, Your Ladyship . . . I was forgetting myself. I'll go and offer my excuses.

He tries to take SUZANNE *with him: the* COUNTESS *stops her going.*

COUNTESS: She'll come in a moment.

Sc.3   [*Exit* FIGARO]

Have you everything we need for changing clothes?

SUZANNE: We shan't be needing anything, Your Ladyship.

COUNTESS: You're not telling me the truth . . .

SUZANNE: I swear to God. . . . But . . . Oh . . . what can you be thinking then, Your Ladyship . . . ?

COUNTESS: Simply that you are in league with the Count, and beginning to regret that you confided in me as to what your plans were. I know you through and through. Both of you. Leave me . . .

She tries to go. SUZANNE *throws herself at her feet.*

SUZANNE: In the name of Heaven, you are the only hope that any of us has. Your Ladyship, you don't know how you hurt me. . . . After you've always been so kind to me . . . and the dowry that you gave me . . .

COUNTESS: Oh, I'm sorry . . . I don't know what I'm saying. If we change places in the garden, sweetheart, you will be in no danger. You'll keep your promise to your husband and help me to bring back mine . . .

SUZANNE: You've made me so unhappy . . .

COUNTESS: I am a very foolish woman, that is all . . .
  (*She kisses* SUZANNE *on the forehead*)
Where did you agree to meet?

SUZANNE *kisses the* COUNTESS*'s hand.*

SUZANNE: Garden was the only word I heard . . .
COUNTESS: Take this pen and we'll arrange a place.
SUZANNE: Write to him?
COUNTESS: We must.
SUZANNE: Your Ladyship. At least it should be you that . . .
COUNTESS: I take the entire responsibility . . .
  (SUZANNE *sits down at the table and the* COUNTESS *dictates*)
New words to the old song 'How sweetly falls the twilight within the
chestnut grove'.
SUZANNE: Within the chestnut grove?
COUNTESS: 'How sweetly falls the twilight within the . . .'
SUZANNE and COUNTESS: 'Chestnut grove'.
SUZANNE: It's perfect.
  (*She folds the paper*)
What shall I seal it with?
COUNTESS: A pin. Quickly! It will do as a reply. Write on the back
'Return the pin . . .'

Enter a YOUNG SHEPHERDESS, CHERUBIN *disguised as a girl,*   Sc.4
FANCHETTE *and other little maids dressed in the same style, with*
bunches of flowers.

FANCHETTE: Madam, they are from the village, coming to present you
with bouquets . . .
COUNTESS: They are charming. . . . Pretty little girls. I feel very guilty
that I don't know all of you: who is that sweet child that looks so
shy?
YOUNG SHEPHERDESS: A cousin of mine, Your Ladyship, she has come
for the wedding . . .
COUNTESS: She is pretty. And as I cannot carry all these posies, let us
give the honour to our little visitor.
  (*She accepts* CHERUBIN*'s bouquet and kisses him on the forehead*)
She's blushing. Suzanne, don't you think she looks like someone . . . ?
SUZANNE: You could mistake her for him, it's true!

CHERUBIN *lays one hand on his heart.*

CHERUBIN: Oh, that kiss went to my heart!

Sc.5   *Enter* ANTONIO *and the* COUNT.

ANTONIO: And I'm a-telling you, Your Lordship, that he's here! The
girls dressed him in my daughter's room: all his things are there, and
here's his regimental hat as what I pulled from out of the bundle . . .

He goes forward, looking at all the little girls, and recognises
CHERUBIN. *He pulls off his bonnet, letting his long ringlets fall to*
his shoulders: he puts the regimental hat on his head.

ANTONIO: Well, dang me! There's your officer.

COUNTESS: Oh heavens!

SUZANNE: You little terror!

ANTONIO: I said upstairs as it was him.

COUNT: Well, Madam?

COUNTESS: Well, Sir? As you see I am more surprised than you are,
and certainly as angry.

COUNT: I am going to punish you for disobedience.

FANCHETTE: Oh Your Lordship! Listen, please! Every time you come
and kiss me, you know you always say 'If you'll love me, Fanchette,
I'll give you whatever you want . . .'

COUNT: Me? I said that?

FANCHETTE: Yes, Your Lordship. Instead of punishing Chérubin, give
him to me for my husband and I'll love you to distraction.

COUNT: Fancy being fascinated by a page-boy!!! (*Aside*) There is some
evil genius here seems bent on thwarting me . . .

Sc.6   *Enter* FIGARO.

FIGARO: Your Lordship, if you won't let our little girls here go, we'll
never be able to start the celebrations or the dancing . . .

COUNT: Dancing? You? You mustn't think of it! Not after the fall you
had this morning. You were particularly fortunate the flowerbeds
were of such soft compost . . .

He spins FIGARO *round.*

FIGARO: Very fortunate, no doubt about it, or else I'd . . .

ANTONIO *spins him round.*

ANTONIO: Then he rolled hisself up in a ball and fell all the way down
to the bottom . . .

FIGARO: Someone more nimble would have remained in the air, is that it? Come along then, little girls!

ANTONIO *drags* CHERUBIN *out by the arm.*

ANTONIO: Well, here's one little girl at least as says my future son-in-law's a liar!

FIGARO: Chérubin! (*Aside*) God rot him! Little namby-pamby.

ANTONIO: You've got there, have you?

FIGARO: I'm there all right, I'm there.... Well, what have you been squealing about?

COUNT: He doesn't squeal: he talks. And he says that it was he who jumped into the gillyflowers.

FIGARO: Why not? The leaping fever may be catching. Look at the Gadarene Swine!! And when you're in a rage there's nobody who wouldn't rather risk ...

COUNT: What? Two at once?

FIGARO: There could have been two dozen of us jumped. What does it matter, Your Lordship, as long as nobody was hurt? Oh for Heaven's sake, are you coming or are you not?

COUNT: What is this, a farce?

A fanfare off-stage.

FIGARO: There's the signal for the march. Take your places, my beauties.... Come, Suzanne, give me your arm ...

They all run off, except the COUNT, *the* COUNTESS *and*   Sc.7
CHERUBIN, *hanging his head.*

COUNT: Did you ever see such impertinence? And as for you, my artful little man, pretending to be ashamed of yourself: go and put your clothes on again at once, and don't let me catch you anywhere again tonight!

COUNTESS: He'll be so bored!

CHERUBIN: Bored! What I bear upon my forehead would keep me happy for a hundred years in prison, and more!

They watch him run off, putting on his hat.   Sc.8

COUNT: What has he on his forehead he's so happy about?

The COUNTESS *walks up and down, fanning herself vigorously.*

COUNTESS: His ... his first regimental hat, I suppose: to children, everything's a game ...

She is about to go.

COUNT: Won't you stay, Madam?

COUNTESS: You know I am not well.

COUNT: Suzanne is your protégée. Stay a moment or I should think you angry.

COUNTESS: Here they come now, both the wedding parties: let us sit down and receive them.

COUNT: The wedding! Ah well, what we are powerless to prevent I suppose we must suffer in silence . . .

Sc.9   *The march 'Spanish Follies'. Gamekeepers with guns on their shoulders, the police superintendent, the magistrates, BRID'OISON, PEASANTS and their wives in their best clothes, lead in the march. Then two bridesmaids with virgin head-dress of white plumes, two bridesmaids with the white veil, two bridesmaids with white gloves and the bouquet. SUZANNE on ANTONIO's arm, six bridesmaids carrying the head-dress, veil and gloves in the same way for MARCELINE. MARCELINE on FIGARO's arm. BARTHOLO bringing up the rear with a large bouquet of flowers. The bridesmaids pass in front of the COUNT, giving the brides' head-dresses and veils to the COUNT's footmen. The PEASANTS and their wives form two ranks on either side of the room, and there is a Fandango danced with castanets. Then a Ritornello is played as ANTONIO leads SUZANNE up to the COUNT and she kneels in front of him. While he is putting the head-dress on her head, then the veil, and is giving her the gloves and the bouquets, two bridesmaids sing:*

> Young bride, Oh delight in a blessing so glorious
> A master that grants you your freedom again
> Preferring to pleasure a virtue victorious
> Conveying you chaste to the arms of your swain.

During the last line of the song, SUZANNE who is kneeling in front of the COUNT tugs at his coat and shows him the note she is holding: then, as the COUNT pretends to be putting the head-dress straight, she raises her hand and gives it to him. The COUNT slips it discreetly into his breast pocket: the song ends: SUZANNE rises and drops a low curtsey. FIGARO comes forward to receive her from the COUNT, and withdraws with her to the other side, where he stands beside MARCELINE. A second Fandango. Impatient to read the note, the COUNT comes downstage and takes out the

paper: as he does so he pricks his finger on the pin, shaking it,
squeezing it and then putting it in his mouth: then he unfolds the
paper. The orchestra plays more softly.

COUNT: Damn all women! They will stick pins in everything!

He throws the pin away, then reads the letter and kisses it:
FIGARO *is watching him, standing with* MARCELINE *and*
SUZANNE.

FIGARO: It's a love-letter one of the little maids must have slipped into
his hand as she was going past. It was fastened with a pin and he's
pricked his finger terribly!

(The dance begins again: the COUNT *puts the letter away and*
starts looking for the pin: he finds it and sticks it in his sleeve)

Everything the beloved has touched is precious to him! He's even
picking up the pin! Oh, he's a comical man!

SUZANNE *exchanges nods with the* COUNTESS: *the dance comes to*
an end: the Ritornello *is played through again, and* FIGARO *leads*
MARCELINE *forward to kneel in front of the* COUNT. *The* COUNT
raises the head-dress to put it on her head, when there is a sudden
interruption.

USHER: Stop if you please. You can't all come in. Guards, here.
Guards!!

COUNT: What is it?

USHER: Your Lordship, it is Señor Bazile, with half of the village after
him on account of him singing as he goes along.

COUNT: He may come in alone.

COUNTESS: Tell me I may go now.

COUNT: I shall not forget your generosity . . .

COUNTESS: Suzanne! She will return directly. . . . *(Aside)* We must go
and change our clothes . . .

She goes off with SUZANNE.

MARCELINE: He never comes into this house without bringing trouble
with him!

FIGARO: Oh, I'll go and take him down a peg or two . . .

Enter BAZILE *with his guitar, followed by* GRIPE-SOLEIL. BAZILE   *Sc.10*
is singing:

BAZILE:

> Loving hearts that never waver
> Blame not loves that swiftly flower
> Is it sin to sip and savour
> Crime to change with ev'ry hour?
> What hath Cupid wings, Oh say, for
> But to flit from bower to bower
> But to flit from bower to bower
> But to flit from bower to bower?

FIGARO: Yes, that is precisely why he has the wings on his back. Tell me, friend, what do you mean by all this singing?

BAZILE: I am giving proof of my allegiance to His Lordship by entertaining this gentleman, who is a member of his household, so that I may have my turn at demanding justice.

GRIPE-SOLEIL: Bah, m'lud! I don't find it very entertaining: all that there string-plucking and a-caterwauling.

COUNT: Once and for all, Bazile, what is it you are demanding?

BAZILE: What is mine by rights, my Lord: the hand of Marceline; and I have come to lodge the strongest possible objection . . .

FIGARO: How long is it, Sir, since you beheld the visage of a lunatic?

BAZILE: I am looking at one at this very moment, Sir!

FIGARO: Well, since my eyes appear to furnish you with such an excellent reflection, perhaps you'd care to observe the effect of what I am about to prophesy. If you as much as give a hint of entering this lady's proximity . . .

BARTHOLO: Ha ha! Why? Let him speak!

BRID'OISON *steps between them.*

BRID'OISON: Is it ne-ne-necessary for two f-f-friends . . .

FIGARO: Us? Friends?

BAZILE: What an erroneous assumption!

FIGARO: Because he writes his turgid miserable dirges?

BAZILE: Better than your awful doggerel!

FIGARO: Organ-grinder!

BAZILE: Inky-fingered hack!

FIGARO: Oratorio scribbler!

BAZILE: Cocky little diplomatic jockey!

COUNT: You are both most impertinent!

BAZILE: Did you promise, yes or no, that if you were not provided for within four years, I would have the first refusal?

MARCELINE: On what condition did I make that promise?

BAZILE: That if you were to find some son you'd lost, I would oblige you by adopting him.

ALL: He's found!!

BAZILE: That is as may be.

ALL: And here he is!!

As they point to FIGARO, BAZILE *shrinks back in horror.*

BAZILE: I have seen the Devil!

BRID'OISON: And you re-re-nounce all claims on his d-dear mother?

BAZILE: What could be more vexing than to be thought to be the father of a nincompoop?

FIGARO: Being thought to be the son of one: you're making fun of me!

BAZILE: If this gentleman is to be of any consequence here, I can see no further purpose in my staying . . .

[*Exit* BAZILE]   *Sc.11*

COUNT: Draw up both the contracts: I will sign them.

ALL: Three cheers for His Lordship! Hip-hip! Hooray!!!

They go out. The COUNT *begins to follow them.*   *Sc.12*

COUNT: I must have an hour or so alone.

GRIPE-SOLEIL: And I must go and help with setting up the fireworks under them chestnuts like as I was told to . . .

COUNT: What fool told you to do a thing like that?

FIGARO: What harm is there in that?

COUNT: When my wife is indisposed! How will she be able to see the fireworks? On the terrace is the place to put them, opposite her rooms.

FIGARO: You understand, Goatherd? On the terrace.

COUNT: Under the chestnuts! (*Aside, as he is going off*) They were going to incinerate my love-nest!

FIGARO: Very concerned about his wife!

He is about to go off, but MARCELINE *stops him.*   *Sc.13*

MARCELINE: A word with you, my son. I would like to think that things were straight between us . . . my misguided love has made me in the past unjust towards your charming wife: I imagined she was in collusion with His Lordship, even though Bazile assured me to the contrary.

FIGARO: You don't know much about your son if you think I am going to be upset by any woman's instinct! However clever you all are you won't persuade me to believe in that.

MARCELINE: It always is more comforting to think so, son: jealousy ...

FIGARO: Jealousy is the result of idiotic pride, or else a kind of madness. Oh, as to that, mother, my philosophy is solid as a rock ... and if Suzanne has to be unfaithful to me one day, I forgive her in advance ... she isn't going to find it easy ...

Sc.14

(*He turns round:* FANCHETTE *has come in and is searching for someone*)

Aha! My little cousin. You were listening!

FANCHETTE: No, I wasn't! I was told that listening was naughty!

FIGARO: Well, it's true. But as it has its uses, we usually overlook that.

FANCHETTE: I was looking to see if somebody was here ...

FIGARO: Already telling lies, you wicked little girl! You know he couldn't possibly be here ...

FANCHETTE: Who couldn't?

FIGARO: Chérubin.

FANCHETTE: It isn't him I'm looking for. I know where he is: it's my cousin Suzanne.

FIGARO: And what do you want her for, my dear cousin?

FANCHETTE: Well as it's you, my dear cousin, I'll tell you. It's ... it's just a pin I want to give her back.

FIGARO: A pin! A pin! Who from, you little minx? At your age, doing ...

(*He makes an effort to control himself*)

Doing whatever you turn your hand to wonderfully, Fanchette: and you're such an obliging little girl, you'll do anything for anybody ...

FANCHETTE: Why are you so cross with me? I'm going ...

FIGARO: No, no, I'm only teasing you: I know that pin you've got is the one His Lordship said you were to give to Suzanne, the one that was stuck in the letter that he had: there, you see, I know all about it.

FANCHETTE: Well why ask, if you knew?

FIGARO: Because it's rather amusing to find out what his Lordship told you to do ...

FANCHETTE: Well, it was just as you said: 'Here, Fanchette, give your pretty cousin this pin and you can tell her it's the answer to the chestnuts.'

FIGARO: The chest ...

FANCHETTE: ... The chestnuts. He did say something else as well. He said 'Be careful no one sees you ...'

FIGARO: You must do as he says: fortunately nobody *has* seen you, so run your errand like a good little girl, and don't say any more to Suzanne than what His Lordship told you ...

FANCHETTE: And why would I do that? Cousin, you must think I'm a child ...

FANCHETTE skips off.   Sc.15

FIGARO: Well, mother?

MARCELINE: Well, son?

FIGARO: Well, that's.... Really there are some things ...

MARCELINE: There are some things! Oh, what's the matter?

FIGARO: What I just heard, mother. It hit me like a bullet, here.

MARCELINE: So the heart full of confidence was just a balloon filled with hot air: one pin and it's all gone ...

FIGARO: But that pin, mother, it was the one that he picked up!

MARCELINE: 'Jealousy! Oh, as to that, mother, my philosophy is solid as a rock ... and if Suzanne has to be unfaithful to me one day, I forgive her in advance ...'

FIGARO: Oh mother, you talk as you feel: you set the most stony-hearted judge to plead his own defence, and watch him talk about the law. No wonder he was so incensed about the fireworks! As for that charmer with her pretty pins, she isn't quite as clever as she thinks she's being with her chestnuts! I may be married enough to make my rage legitimate, but not enough to mean that I can't marry someone else and then abandon her.

MARCELINE: Yes, that's right! Go and ruin everything for one suspicion! What proof have you, just tell me, that it's you she's trying to deceive, and not His Lordship? Have you seen the evidence before you condemn her out of court like this? Do you know that she will be there underneath the trees? What her reason is for going there? What she will say, what she will do? I took you for a better judge than that!

FIGARO: You're right, Mother, always right.... Reason, reason, reason. But, mother, let's give human nature its due ... we'll be the better for it afterwards. Let's see the evidence as you say before we make the accusations or do anything. I know the place where they are to meet. Goodbye, mother!

[Exit FIGARO]   Sc.16

MARCELINE: Goodbye. And so do I. Now I've prevented him from doing anything impetuous I'll see what Suzanne's doing, or better still I'll warn her. She's such a pretty creature. Oh, when rivalry doesn't keep us in a state of civil war, we poor oppressed women instinctively defend ourselves against those proud, terrifying, and yet somehow . . . rather stupid men.

ACT V

An avenue of chestnuts in a park: stage left and right, two   Sc.1
pavilions, kiosks or temples. Upstage a glade with decorations:
downstage a marble seat. The stage is in almost complete
darkness. Enter FANCHETTE, *with two biscuits and an orange, and*
an illuminated paper lantern.

FANCHETTE: In the pavilion on the left, he said. That's this one. What
if he went and never came, now? Those mean people in the pantry,
they'd only give me an orange and two biscuits. 'Who is it for, young
Miss?' 'Well, Sir, it's for someone.' 'Oh, we know!' What if it is for
him? Just because His Lordship doesn't want to see him is he meant
to starve to death? But they cost me a great smacking kiss on the
cheek. Who knows, perhaps he'll pay me back. . . . Oh!

She sees FIGARO *looking at her, and runs into the pavilion stage*   Sc.2
left. FIGARO *comes in with a greatcoat over his shoulders, and a*
broad-brimmed hat pulled down low over his eyes.

FIGARO: Fanchette!

(*Enter* BAZILE, ANTONIO, BARTHOLO, BRID'OISON, GRIPE-
SOLEIL, *servants and workmen.* FIGARO *peers at them as they*
arrive, then addresses them in a gruff, military tone)

Good-day to you, gentlemen. Good evening. All present? When you
hear me call, come running, all of you, and say whatever you please
about me if I don't show you something good.
BAZILE: (*aside*) So His Lordship and his Suzanne have come to
arrangement without me, have they? I'm very glad they're going to be
ambushed!
FIGARO: And now, you louts, I've given you your orders, out of my
light! I may wish I was dead, but if I catch one of you . . .

He grips GRIPE-SOLEIL *by the arm.*

GRIPE-SOLEIL: Ow! Ow! Oh! Oh! You cruel devil!

BAZILE: Since you *are* the bridegroom, Heaven grant you'll always be as happy as you are today! Ha! Ha!

Sc.3   [*Exit all except* FIGARO]

FIGARO: Oh woman, woman, woman! Such a weak, deceitful creature! No animal in creation can disobey its instinct, is yours to be unfaithful? No, Your Lordship, you will not have her, you will not have her! Just because you're a great nobleman, you think you're a great genius! Being an aristocrat, having money, a position in society, holding public office – all that makes a man so arrogant! What have you ever done for all this wealth? You took the trouble to be born and nothing else! Apart from that you're rather an ordinary man. And me, God damn it, a nobody, one of the crowd, and I've had to use more skill and ingenuity simply to stay alive than they've expended in a hundred years in governing the whole of Spain! And you dare challenge me! There's someone coming ... it's her ... it's nobody! ... The night's as dark as hell and here am I, playing husbands, of all the stupid occupations and I'm not half married yet!

                        (*He sits down on the seat*)

Could there be anything stranger than my fate? Son of ... I don't know who, carried off by bandits, brought up with their morals, I come to be disgusted by them, despise them and want to earn an honest living: everywhere I go they throw me out. I study chemistry, pharmacy, surgery, and with all the influence of a noble lord behind me, the only thing they'll let me practise on is horses. Tired of making poor sick creatures miserable and wanting to do something entirely different, I throw myself with great enthusiasm into the theatre. I wish I'd tied a boulder round my neck! I knock together a comedy of manners, set in a harem, thinking, as a Spanish author, I can ridicule Mohammed in it with impunity. Immediately, some ambassador from God knows where complains my couplets are offensive to the Ottoman Empire, Persia, part of the Indian peninsula, all of Egypt, the kingdoms of Cyrenacia, Tripoli, Tunis, Algiers and Morocco: and so my play goes up in smoke to satisfy the Muslim Pashas, when there isn't one of them can read and when they go on skinning us alive and call us Christian Dogs. When they see the spirit will not bend, they persecute it simply from vindictiveness. My cheeks were falling in, my credit had run out: I saw the awful bailiff coming with his quill stuck in his wig. ... Trembling with terror, I bend to fresh exertions. There's a debate begins about the nature of wealth, and since it isn't necessary to touch a thing in order to discuss it, I set out, stony broke, to write about the value of money and net profits. No sooner have I done so, than I observe, from the floor of a hired carriage, a drawbridge being lowered for me, belonging to a fortress, on entering which I abandoned hope and liberty.

(He gets up)

I'd like to get my hands on one of those fly-by-night tyrants. I'd tell him . . . that insults in print are of no importance to anyone except to those who are trying to suppress them: that without the liberty to criticise no praise has any value: and that only little men are scared of little jokes.

(He sits down again)

Tired of feeding a prisoner they've never heard of – they throw me into the street. And since a man has to have his dinner, even when he's not in prison, I sharpen my pen again and ask everybody what the great debate is now. They tell me that during my period of economic restraint a new free system's been established in Madrid, governing the sale of products, including products of the printing press: and that providing I don't write about the authorities, or the church, or politics, or morals, or anybody holding public office, or influential corporations, or the Opera, or the other theatres, or mention anyone with any opinion at all, I am at liberty to print anything subject to it being inspected by two or three censors. Wishing to take advantage of this glorious liberty, I advertise that I am starting a new paper. I call it *The Useless News*, thinking I'm not trespassing on anyone else's preserves – whew! – thousands of poor miserable hacks all up in arms against me for plagiarism. I'm suppressed and there I am, once more without employment. . . . Despair was very near to laying hold of me. They consider me for a post in Government Service, but as bad luck would have it, I was suitable: they needed a schemer so a ballet-dancer got it. All that was left for me was thieving. I set up as a croupier at Pharoah: then, my dear, good people! I'm asked to dinner everywhere, everyone in what's called good society very politely opens their doors to me as long as they can keep three-quarters of the profit. I would have made a fortune: but as everyone was looting and pillaging all round me and demanding that I should be honest, I was doomed to fail again. For a while I was going to end it all and then the Good Lord calls me back to where I first began. I pack my razors and my strop, and leaving the dreams to the fools that live on them, I go lathering from town to town and live at last without a care in the world. A nobleman is in Seville, he recognises me, I find him a wife, and as a reward for having *his*, entirely thanks to my exertions, he tries to sail away with *mine*. . . . What an amazing sequence of events. How did all that happen to me? Why those things and not others? Who was it said it must be me? Forced to travel a road I came upon without knowing it, that I shall have to leave without wanting to, I've scattered as many rosebuds as my natural optimism has permitted. There again, I say my natural optimism without knowing if it's mine any more than any of the rest is . . . nor even what this *me* is that I'm so concerned about: a little shapeless bundle of undiscovered mysteries, then a poor little imbecile of a creature, a little playful animal, a young man who'll do anything for pleasure, with every appetite to enjoy, doing any work to live: a master here, a servant there, as blind chance decides: ambitious, out of vanity, hard-working of necessity but idle with the greatest pleasure: an orator, depending on the danger, a poet for recreation, a musician on occasion, a lover in moments of madness: I've seen everything, done everything, exhausted everything: then the illusion was destroyed and I was too disheartened . . . disheartened . . . Suzanne! Suzanne! Suzanne! How you make me suffer! I hear footsteps. . . . There's someone coming. . . . This is the moment of the crisis!

Sc.4   *Enter the* COUNTESS *in* SUZANNE's *clothes,* SUZANNE *in the*
          COUNTESS's *clothes, and* MARCELINE.

SUZANNE: (*aside*) Yes, Marceline told me Figaro would be here.
MARCELINE: I wouldn't miss a word of this: I'm going to hide in this pavilion.

Sc.5   *She goes into the pavilion, stage left, that* FANCHETTE *has already*
                              entered.

SUZANNE: You're shivering, Madam! Would your Ladyship be cold?
COUNTESS: The evening's damp. I'm going in.
SUZANNE: If Your Ladyship didn't need me, I'd like to take the air for a moment, underneath the trees here.
COUNTESS: Be careful you don't take a chill – the dew is coming down!
SUZANNE: I'm well prepared for it . . .
FIGARO: (*aside*) Oh yes. For the dew!

Sc.6   SUZANNE *disappears into the wings opposite* FIGARO. CHERUBIN
              comes in, in his uniform, singing to himself.

CHERUBIN:
                    La la la la la la . . .

The lady I'm forsaking
I'll love until I die . . .

COUNTESS: *(aside)* The little page!

CHERUBIN: People walking here. I must be quick and get back to my hiding place! Fanchette will be there already! A woman!!

COUNTESS: Oh Merciful Heaven!

CHERUBIN: Could I be deceived? From the plumed head-dress in the twilight at this distance I'd swear it was Suzanne . . .

COUNTESS: *(aside)* What if the Count were to come?

The COUNT *appears upstage.* CHERUBIN *approaches her and takes her hand: she snatches it back.*

CHERUBIN: Yes, it's the charming girl they call Suzanne! Oh, how could I mistake the softness of this hand, the sudden trembling now. . . . Surely not the beating of my heart!

He tries to touch the COUNTESS's *hand against his heart: again she withdraws it.*

COUNTESS: *(whispering)* Figaro will come.

COUNT: *(aside)* Isn't that Suzanne I can see?

CHERUBIN: I'm not at all afraid of Figaro, because that isn't who you're waiting for.

COUNTESS: Who am I waiting for then?

COUNT: *(aside)* She's with a man.

CHERUBIN: His Lordship, you wicked little thing! He asked you to meet him here this morning when I was behind the chair.

COUNT: *(aside)* It's that infernal page again!!

FIGARO: *(aside)* And they say you shouldn't eavesdrop!

SUZANNE: *(aside)* Little tell-tale!!

COUNTESS: You will oblige me by going away?

CHERUBIN: Not before I have my reward for being obedient.

COUNTESS: You dare!!!

CHERUBIN: Oh yes, I dare all right. You take her place with His Lordship, I take His Lordship's place with you, the only one that's caught out is Figaro.

FIGARO: *(aside)* The little fiend!

CHERUBIN *goes to kiss the* COUNTESS: *the* COUNT *slips in between them and intercepts the kiss.*

COUNTESS: Oh heavens!

CHERUBIN *feels the* COUNT's *clothes.*

CHERUBIN: (*aside*) It's His Lordship!

Sc.7   *He runs into the pavilion, stage left, already containing*
MARCELINE *and* FANCHETTE. FIGARO *goes forward towards the*
COUNT *and* COUNTESS.

FIGARO: I am going to . . .

COUNT: Since you will not kiss me again . . . take that!

He hits out at what he thinks is CHERUBIN *and strikes* FIGARO.

FIGARO: Ouch!!!

(FIGARO *goes off rubbing his cheek*)

(*Aside*) Eavesdropping isn't all advantage, either!

SUZANNE: Ha ha ha ha!!!

COUNT: I cannot understand that child? He gets a slap in the face and goes off roaring with laughter!

FIGARO: (*aside*) I wish he could feel how much it hurt!

COUNT: What? I cannot take a step without . . . (*to the* COUNTESS) let us forget these absurdities – they might well poison the pleasure of finding you here beneath the trees. . . . I did not intercept that kiss in order to deprive you of it!

He kisses her on the forehead.

COUNTESS: Now you're taking liberties!

FIGARO: (*aside*) She is shameless!

SUZANNE: (*aside*) She's charming!

COUNT: But your skin's so soft and smooth. . . . Would that the Countess had as lovely a hand . . .

COUNTESS: (*aside*) Blind prejudice!

COUNT: Are her arms as firm and round? Has she such pretty fingers, so graceful and so mischievous . . .

COUNTESS: Does she love you as much?

COUNT: Love is a romance written by the heart: pleasure is its true history, and that is what brings me here to worship you . . .

COUNTESS: You don't love her any more?

COUNT: I love her very much: but three years together make marriage so respectable . . .

COUNTESS: What was it in her that you wanted?

COUNT: What I find in you, my beauty . . .

COUNTESS: But tell me . . .

COUNT: I don't know: less predictability perhaps, something more provocative in her manner . . . some little thing that fascinates us: sometimes to be refused: . . . who knows?

COUNTESS: (*aside*) Oh, what a lot there is to learn!!

COUNT: The truth is, Suzanne, I have thought a thousand times that if we look elsewhere for pleasure that eludes us in their company, it is because they won't exert themselves sufficiently in learning the art of keeping our appetite alive.

COUNTESS: So they must do everything?

COUNT: And husbands nothing? Would you have us change the course of nature: our task was always to obtain a woman . . . theirs . . .

COUNTESS: And what is theirs?

COUNT: To keep a man. It's too often forgotten.

COUNTESS: Not by me.

COUNT: Nor me.

FIGARO: (*aside*) Nor me.

SUZANNE: (*aside*) Nor me.

The COUNT *takes the* COUNTESS*'s hand.*

COUNT: There is an echo here. We must speak more softly. You've no need ever to think of it: you were made for love, so full of life, and so exquisite. . . . With a hint more wilfulness you'll be the most provocative mistress in the world . . .

(He kisses her on the forehead)

My love, in Castile our word is our bond. Here is all the money that I promised you for the redemption of the rights that are no longer mine, to the delicious moment that you are permitting me. . . . But as the favour that you deign to grant me is beyond all price, I'd like you to accept in addition this diamond ring. Wear it as a symbol of our love . . .

COUNTESS: Suzanne is very grateful, Sir, I'm sure.

FIGARO: (*aside*) Nobody could be more shameless than that!

SUZANNE: (*aside*) We're making a fortune!

COUNT: (*aside*) She's after my money – that is all to the good!

COUNTESS: I can see torches!

COUNT: They are making preparations for the wedding. Let's slip into one of these pavilions for a moment . . . and let them pass . . .

COUNTESS: But there's no light in there . . .

COUNT: What do we need a light for? We haven't anything to read . . .

FIGARO: She's going in, God damn it, I knew she would!

FIGARO *runs forward: the* COUNT, *drawing the* COUNTESS *into the pavilion, turns and sees him.*

COUNT: Who's that going by there?
FIGARO: I'm not going by, I'm coming here on purpose!
COUNT: It's Figaro!!

The COUNT *runs off.*

COUNTESS: I'll follow you!!

Sc.8   *She goes into the pavilion, stage right, the* COUNT *disappearing into the wood upstage.*

FIGARO: I can't hear them any more. They've gone in. Fortunately I don't care: her being unfaithful has no effect upon me whatsoever. So, I've caught them at last!

SUZANNE *comes slowly forward in the dark.*

SUZANNE: (*aside*) I'll teach you to start suspecting me! (*Imitating the* COUNTESS) Who's this?
FIGARO: Who's this? Someone who wishes to God he'd died at birth of some unspeakable disease!
SUZANNE: Oh! It's Figaro!
FIGARO: Your Ladyship!
SUZANNE: Not so loud!
FIGARO: Oh Madam! Thank God you've come just now! Where do you think His Lordship is?
SUZANNE: What should I care about a brute like that? Tell me, is . . .
FIGARO: And Suzanne, my bride, where do you think she is?
SUZANNE: Not so loud!
FIGARO: Suzanne, that everybody thought was such a little innocent and pretended to be so prim. . . . They're in there together with the door locked. . . . I'm going to call for help!

SUZANNE *claps her hand over his mouth, forgetting to disguise her voice.*

SUZANNE: Don't!
FIGARO: (*aside*) It's Suzanne! God damn!
SUZANNE: (*imitating the* COUNTESS) You seem anxious . . . ?
FIGARO: (*aside*) Little trickster! . . . Trying to catch me!
SUZANNE: We must have our revenge, Figaro . . .
FIGARO: You feel a very powerful desire for it . . .

SUZANNE: (aside) Oh God, I could hit him!

FIGARO: (aside) That would be comical, though, just before the wedding!

SUZANNE: But what is revenge without a little love to give it spice . . . ?

FIGARO: Where you see no sign of it, believe me, love is lurking in concealment . . .

SUZANNE: The sentiments may be sincere, but the expression is somewhat lacking in elegance . . .

FIGARO *throws himself on his knees in a comic passion.*

FIGARO: Oh Madam! I worship you! Consider the time, the place, the circumstances, and may grim spite supply the eloquence my protestations lack!! Madam! Your hand!

SUZANNE *hits him, and speaks in her normal voice.*

SUZANNE: You can have it!

FIGARO: Oh! *Demonio!* What a slap!

SUZANNE *hits him again.*

SUZANNE: What a slap! And this one!

FIGARO: *Che es esto?* Damnation! It must be boxing day . . .

She slaps him again and again.

SUZANNE: I'll give you, *che es esto*! It's me, Suzanne! Take that for thinking your suspicious thoughts! And that for your revenges and your infidelities and your excuses and your insults and all your little schemes! Is that love? Go on, tell me, like this morning!

FIGARO *gets up laughing.*

FIGARO: Yes! Santa Barbara! Yes, that's love! Oh, what happiness! Oh, the ecstasy! I can't tell you how happy I am! Hit me, my dearest love, don't stop: but when you've embossed me all over black and blue with bruises, be gentle with me, Suzette. I'm the most fortunate man was ever, ever beaten by a woman!

SUZANNE: Most fortunate. . . . You crafty ragamuffin! That didn't stop you trying to seduce Her Ladyship!

FIGARO *kneels and then prostrates himself in front of her.*

FIGARO: That's what I deserve. On my knees, grovelling, prostrate, flat on my face.

SUZANNE: Ha ha! Oh, the poor Count, think of all the trouble he's gone to . . .

FIGARO: To seduce his own wife!!!

Sc.9   FIGARO *gets up: the* COUNT *appears, going straight to the pavilion, stage right.*

COUNT: (*to himself*) I cannot find her anywhere in the wood: perhaps she went in here . . .

SUZANNE: (*aside to* FIGARO) It's him!

The COUNT *opens the door of the pavilion*

COUNT: Suzanne? Are you in there?

SUZANNE: (*aside to* FIGARO) He didn't recognise her.

FIGARO: Now we'll finish him. Ready?

He kisses her hand: the COUNT *turns and sees them.*

COUNT: A man on his knees before the Countess! Why am I not armed?

He goes forward: FIGARO *gets up, speaking in a disguised voice.*

FIGARO: Forgive me, Madam, I had not dreamed that our familiar trysting place was destined for the celebration of the wedding . . .

COUNT: It's the man in the closet this morning!

The COUNT *strikes his forehead.*

FIGARO: Yes, but it shall not be said that such a footling obstacle could be any hindrance to our mutual raptures . . .

COUNT: (*aside*) I'll slaughter him! Death and Damnation!

FIGARO *leads her towards the pavilion, stage left.*

FIGARO: (*aside*) He's swearing! (*Aloud*) Let us make haste, Madam, and make amends for the ill-usage that we suffered earlier, when I leapt down from the window . . .

COUNT: So! All is revealed at last!

SUZANNE: (*imitating the* COUNTESS) Before we go in, look and see that no one's followed us.

FIGARO *kisses her forehead.*

COUNT: Revenge!!!

Sc.10   SUZANNE *goes inside the pavilion, stage left, already containing*

FANCHETTE, MARCELINE *and* CHERUBIN. FIGARO *is caught by the arm by the* COUNT, *and feigns excessive terror.*

FIGARO: Aaah!! It is the master!!

COUNT: Ah! You scoundrel! So it's you! Halloo!!! Somebody! Somebody!

Enter PEDRILLO, *in riding boots.*   Sc.11

PEDRILLO: Your Lordship! Found you at last!

COUNT: Good! It's Pedrillo! Are you alone?

PEDRILLO: Just arrived from Seville. Disembowelled the horse!

COUNT: Stand here beside me and shout as loudly as you can!

PEDRILLO: (*shouting*) No sign of the page!!! I couldn't find hide nor hair of him! Here is the packet!

The COUNT *pushes him away.*

COUNT: Oh! You animal!

PEDRILLO: Your Lordship said I was to shout.

COUNT: For help! Halloo!! Somebody!! If you can hear me, come over here, all of you!!!

PEDRILLO: There's Figaro and me. That makes two of us. You can't come to much harm with us here.

Enter BRID'OISON, BARTHOLO, BAZILE, ANTONIO, GRIPE-SOLEIL   Sc.12
and the wedding party, all carrying torches.

BARTHOLO: You see, the moment you gave the signal!

The COUNT *points to the door of the pavilion, stage left.*

COUNT: Pedrillo! Guard that door!

PEDRILLO *goes to it.*

BAZILE: (*aside to* FIGARO) Caught him with Suzanne, did you?

COUNT: And all of you, serfs, surround this man for me. You are answerable for him with your lives.

BAZILE: Ha ha ha!

COUNT: Will you be quiet! And now, Lothario, perhaps you will answer my questions . . .

FIGARO: Well, there's no one here that has the power to say I'm not obliged to, Sir. . . . You're in control of everything here, except yourself . . .

COUNT: Except myself!!!

ANTONIO: That's the way to talk to him!

COUNT: (*controlling himself*) You are an innocent bystander, affecting total ignorance. . . . Will you at least be so good as to tell us who the lady is you introduced a moment ago into this pavilion . . .

> FIGARO *points at the pavilion, stage right*

FIGARO: Into this one?

COUNT: Into this one.

FIGARO: That's different. A young person that does me the honour of bestowing her intimate favours upon me.

BAZILE: Ha ha!

COUNT: You heard him, gentlemen?

BARTHOLO: We heard.

COUNT: And this young person: has she any other attachment you're aware of?

FIGARO: There was a noble Lord that took an interest in her for a time: but whether it was because he neglected her, or because she likes me better than someone of a more placid disposition, at present she prefers me.

COUNT: She pref. . . . At least he is frank. So since the dishonour is a public one, it is necessary my revenge should be so too . . .

Sc.13   *He opens the door of the pavilion, stage left, and goes in.*

ANTONIO: That's only right!

BRID'OISON: Has s-s-someone taken s-s-someone else's wife?

FIGARO: I'm afraid that no one's had that pleasure.

Sc.14   *The* COUNT *emerges, dragging an unidentified figure.*

COUNT: There is no use struggling: you are ruined, Madam, and your hour has come! How fortunate it is that so grotesque a union has not borne fruit!

FIGARO: Chérubin!

COUNT: My page!!!

BAZILE: Ha ha!!

COUNT: (*aside*) The diabolical page again!!! (*Aloud*) What were you doing in this tea-house?

CHERUBIN: I was hiding, as you told me to . . .

PEDRILLO: That is what I rode a horse to death for, is it?

COUNT: Go in, Antonio: bring her out to meet her judges: the infamous woman that has dishonoured me.

BRID'OISON: Is it Her La-Ladyship you're looking for?

ANTONIO: By gum, don't say there hain't a righteous Providence above!! The times you done it up and down the countryside!

COUNT: Go inside!!!

(ANTONIO *goes into the pavilion*)   *Sc.15*

You will see, gentlemen, the page was not alone in there!

CHERUBIN: My fate would have been too cruel if some romantic soul had not sweetened the bitterness of it . . .

ANTONIO *comes out, again dragging an unidentified figure.*   *Sc.16*

ANTONIO: Come along, Madam, you don't need asking twice to come on out, when we knows as you went in there . . .

FIGARO: It's my little cousin!

BAZILE: Ha! Ha!

COUNT: Fanchette!!!

ANTONIO: Cor, dang my hide, Your Lordship, that's a caution, that is, making me the one as has to show the company as how my daughter's caused the whole commotion . . .

COUNT: Who knew she was in there???

He is about to storm in himself, but BARTHOLO *steps forward.*

BARTHOLO: Allow me, Your Lordship, I fear there may be complications. . . . I am entirely calm.

He goes in.

BRID'OISON: It is a ve-ve-very complicated c-c-case . . .

BARTHOLO *comes out dragging a third figure.*   *Sc.17*

BARTHOLO: Have no fear, my Lady, no harm will come to you, I will answer for that. . . . Marceline!!!

BAZILE: Ha ha!!

FIGARO: Ha ha, this is madness! You mean my mother's in this too?

ANTONIO: Every one of them worse than t'other!

COUNT: What do I care? The Countess . . .

(SUZANNE *comes out, hiding her face behind a fan*)   *Sc.18*

Ah! Here she comes!

(*He grips her arm*)

Well, gentlemen, what would you say this odious woman deserves . . . ?

(SUZANNE *throws herself on her knees in front of him*)

No, no!

(FIGARO kneels)

No, no!!

(MARCELINE kneels)

No, no!!!

(All except BRID'OISON kneel)

Even if there were a hundred of you!

Sc.19   *The* COUNTESS *comes out of the pavilion, stage right, and kneels with them.*

COUNTESS: At least I'll make one more.

The COUNT *looks from the* COUNTESS *to* SUZANNE

COUNT: What? What is this I see?

BRID'OISON: Good Heavens! It's Her Ladyship!

COUNT: What? Was that you, Countess? I can only ask your generous forgiveness . . .

COUNTESS: You would say 'No, no' if you were in the same position, but for the third time today I do forgive you, unconditionally.

She gets up.

SUZANNE: So do I.

She gets up.

MARCELINE: So do I.

She gets up.

FIGARO: And so do I. There *is* an echo here.

All of them get up.

COUNT: An echo. . . . I thought I was a master of deception and they treat me like a child . . .

COUNTESS: You must have no regrets, my Lord . . .

FIGARO, *dusting his knees with his hat.*

FIGARO: It's days like this that train you for diplomacy.

COUNT: The letter with the pin in it . . . ?

SUZANNE: That was dictated by Her Ladyship.

COUNT: Then she deserves the answer . . .

He kisses the COUNTESS'*s hand.*

COUNTESS: Everyone shall have what's theirs by right.

She gives the purse to FIGARO *and the diamond ring to* SUZANNE.

SUZANNE: Another dowry!

FIGARO: That makes three. This one took some pulling off though . . .

SUZANNE: Like our marriage . . .

GRIPE-SOLEIL: What about the bride's garter, who's having that then?

The COUNTESS *takes the ribbon from her bodice and throws it on the ground.*

COUNTESS: Her garter? It was with her clothes.

The other pages try to pick it up, but CHERUBIN *is quicker and picks it up first.*

CHERUBIN: Anyone that wants it has to fight me for it!

COUNT: For such a ticklish young gentleman, what did you find so funny about being struck just now?

CHERUBIN *draws back, half drawing his sword.*

CHERUBIN: Me, Colonel?

FIGARO: He took it here, on my cheek! That is how men in power deal out justice!

COUNT: I hit you? Ha ha ha!!! What do you say to that, my dear?

The COUNTESS, *day-dreaming, doesn't hear at first, then answers:*

COUNTESS: I. . . . Yes, my Lord, always, I promise, faithfully for ever.

The COUNT *slaps* BRID'OISON *on the back.*

COUNT: Well, Brid'oison, what's your opinion now?

BRID'OISON: Of what I've seen tonight, Your Lordship? Well, for my p-p-part, I don't know what to say . . . that's to my way of thinking.

ALL: What a wonderful judgement!

FIGARO: I was poor and everyone despised me: I showed I had some brains and everybody hated me: now, with a pretty wife and money . . .

BARTHOLO: There'll be a rush to love you again . . .

FIGARO: Will there?

BARTHOLO: I know them.

FIGARO: Setting my wife and my money aside . . . you would make me most proud and happy if you did . . .

The vaudeville is played. They sing:

BAZILE:

>Beauteous wife, endowed thrice over
>Say, what husband could complain?
>On a Lord or infant lover
>Squander jealousy in vain
>With the proverb we discover
>Fortune smiles on industry . . .

FIGARO interrupts.

FIGARO: I know . . . 'Let the well-born man rejoice!' (*Singing*) *Gaudeant bene nati* . . .

BAZILE: No, 'Let the well-endowed rejoice' (*Singing*) You'll be entertained by me . . .

SUZANNE:

>Let a husband turn deceiver
>'Tis his pride, a charming game
>Let his wife once lapse he'll leave her
>See her punish'd for her shame:
>Should such fierce injustice grieve her
>Need she wonder at the cause
>'Tis the strong that make the laws
>'Tis the strong that make the laws.

FIGARO:

>John Weejohn, insanely jealous
>Yearned to keep his wife and wits
>Bought a dog, a hound of hell as
>Fierce as sin, and prone to fits
>Night by night wild screams would tell us
>All were bit save her amour
>Rover's owner last but four
>Rover's owner last but four

COUNTESS:

>One is proud and self-sustaining
>Though she loves her spouse no more
>T'other at her bonds is straining
>Swears he's all that she'll adore
>Least to blame is who unfeigning
>Watches how she loves and cares

To swear oaths she never dares
To swear oaths she never dares.

COUNT:

Country wives, though fine and buxom
Cumbered round with petty care
O, alas, I never plucks 'em
Give me women with an air
Like the coin bringing luck some
Prince displays but never spends
Love their husband, please his friends
Love their husband, please his friends.

MARCELINE:

Who can e'er forget the mother
At whose breast he saw the light
Myst'ry deep as any other
'Tis love's secret, love's delight . . .

FIGARO:

. . . For that myst'ry, here's another
How an ugly, mean old scold
Has a child as good as gold
Has a child as good as gold

'Tis the chance of birth decided
Who's a shepherd, who's a king
Cruel fate their lives divided
Wit alone a change may bring
Kings in life with pomp provided
Death will throw their altars down
Voltaire wears the immortal's crown
Voltaire wears the immortal's crown.

SUZANNE:

If amidst this mad cavorting
Any truth may shyly hide.
'Neath the teases of our courting
'Tis let reason be your guide
So wise Nature us supporting
Our desires directs and tends
Bends our pleasure to her ends
Bends our pleasure to her ends.

BRID'OISON:

> G-gentles all, our p-play is ended
> To your judgement we shall bow
> F-faults apart, it was intended
> To show life, both then and now:
> How your freedom is defended
> 'Gainst the pow'rs would do you wrong,
> Then as now the same old song,
> Then as now the same old song.

THE NEW TARTUFFE

OR

A MOTHER'S GUILT

A Drama In Five Acts In Prose
BY BEAUMARCHAIS

First Performed At The Théâtre Du Marais
On 26 June 1792
And Played Again In A Revised Version
On The 16th Floréal of Year V (5 May 1797)
By The Former Company Of The
Théâtre français

*There's gratitude enough in any family
when you get rid of a troublemaker.*
(Last line of the play)

DRAMATIS PERSONAE

COUNT ALMAVIVA a Spanish Grandee, aristocratic and proud, but without the least arrogance.

COUNTESS ALMAVIVA very unhappy, a woman of angelic piety.

LEON their son, a young man, like all passionate spirits of the modern age, with an ardent love of liberty.

FLORESTINE ward and godchild of Count Almaviva: a young woman of great sensibility.

BEGEARSS an Irishman, a major in the Spanish infantry, formerly diplomatic secretary to the Count: a very deep man, a great hatcher of plots, stirring up trouble with dexterity.

FIGARO the valet, personal physician and confidant of the Count: a man who has learned his lessons from his experience and events.

SUZANNE the Countess's first lady's maid: Figaro's wife, an excellent woman, devoted to her mistress, and beyond the illusions of youth.

MONSIEUR FAL the Count's notary: a precise and very honest man.

WILHELM Monsieur Bégearss's German servant: too simple a man for such a master.

The action is set in Paris, in the house occupied by the Count's family, at the end of 1790.

ACT I

A heavily ornate drawing-room: SUZANNE *alone, making a*   Sc.1
bouquet of dark red and black flowers.

SUZANNE: I wish her Ladyship would wake up and ring the bell: so sad
what I'm doing, but it's finished now. (*She sits down, unhappily*) Not
nine o'clock yet, and I'm exhausted. . . . It was the last thing she told
me to do as I was putting her to bed, and I couldn't sleep all night for
thinking of it. 'In the morning, Suzanne, as soon as it's light, tell them
to get all the flowers they can, and put them in my rooms.' And she
told the porter: 'I don't want to see anyone all day.' 'Make me a little
bouquet of black and dark red, with one white carnation in the
middle. . . .' There I've made it. Poor mistress! She was crying so. . . .
Who can it all be for . . . ? Oh!! If we were in Spain, today would be
her son Léon's saint's day.* (*Darkly*) And someone else's too! But
he's no more. (*She looks at the flowers*) Red for blood and black for
mourning! (*She sighs*) She was so badly hurt, I don't think she'll ever
recover! I'll put black ribbon round them; that was what she wanted,
poor sad lady . . .

(*She ties the ribbon.* FIGARO *comes in, looking inquisitive*)   Sc.2

Do come in, Figaro! You look like a lover creeping into your wife's
bedroom by mistake!
FIGARO: Is it safe to talk?
SUZANNE: Yes, if you leave the door open.
FIGARO: What would be the point of doing that?
SUZANNE: The person in question could come in any minute.
FIGARO: (*stressing his words*) The Honourable Mr Hypocrite Bégearss?
SUZANNE: I said he could come: and you shouldn't call him names all
the time: it could get back to him and then you'd be in trouble.
FIGARO: He is the Honourable.
SUZANNE: Not Mr Hypocrite though . . .
FIGARO: God help us!

SUZANNE: Now you're in a sulk.

FIGARO: I am in a stamping rage! (*She gets up*) Whose side are you on? Do you seriously think you are helping me, Suzanne? I am trying to stop a disaster happening. You can't still be taken in by him. He is a very dangerous man!

SUZANNE: No. But I don't think he trusts me any more: he never tells me anything now. I am afraid, the truth is, he thinks we've made up our quarrel.

FIGARO: Well, we must make him think we still hate each other.

SUZANNE: But why are you in such a terrible temper? Have you found out something else?

FIGARO: Let me just remind you how this all began! Since we have been in Paris, and Mr Almaviva . . . I have to call him that now, since he won't allow himself to be called His Lordship any longer . . .

SUZANNE: (*warmly*) But that's good! Her Ladyship goes out alone, without any fuss. We look just like anybody else!

FIGARO: Since, as I was saying, his rake of an eldest son was killed in an argument over a game of cards, you know how his attitude to us has altered; how the Count's got more and more gloomy and desperate!

SUZANNE: You've been surly enough yourself.

FIGARO: How he seems to have taken against his other son; almost as though he hated him.

SUZANNE: All too clear, that is.

FIGARO: How unhappy Her Ladyship has been.

SUZANNE: It's a crime the way he treats her.

FIGARO: How much fonder he's got of his ward Florestine? Most of all, how he's been trying to sell off his property.

SUZANNE: My poor old Figaro! Do you know, I think you must be going senile! If I know all this, what's the use of telling me?*

FIGARO: All the same, I must be clear, so I can be certain we both understand. Now, we know for sure this shifty Irishman, the bane of this family's existence, had charge of the Count's diplomatic codes when he was working as his secretary, and somehow found all their secret papers. That this crafty operator managed to drag them all the way from sleepy, easy-going Spain to this country, where everything's in turmoil from top to bottom, hoping that here he'll be able to make better use of the differences between them to separate husband and wife, marry their adopted daughter, and rob the family of every penny they possess when they are already half bankrupt as it is.

SUZANNE: And where do I come in? What can I do about all that?

FIGARO: Never let him out of your sight: keep me posted about everything he does . . .

SUZANNE: But I tell you everything he says.

FIGARO: Ah! What he says . . . is not necessarily what he means: but when you are talking, notice what words he uses, any little movement, any impulsive gesture: that's the way to read a man! There's evil brewing, I know it! He must feel very confident: I've noticed he seems more false, more treacherous, more conceited: like some of the fools here in France, who think they've won before the battle's half over! You must be even more two-faced than he is, mustn't you? Lead him on, encourage him; whatever he wants, don't refuse him . . .

SUZANNE: That's a lot!

FIGARO: Everything will be all right, everything will go according to plan as long as I'm told about it straightaway . . .

SUZANNE: Can't I tell my mistress too?

FIGARO: It isn't time for that yet; they're all too much under his influence. You wouldn't be believed: you'd sink *us* without saving *them*. Follow him everywhere, like his own shadow. . . . I'll watch what he does whenever he leaves the house . . .

SUZANNE: My dear, I've told you he doesn't trust me: and if he caught us together. . . . There! He's coming downstairs. . . . Be quiet. . . . Pretend we're quarrelling! (*She puts the flowers on the table.*)

FIGARO: (*raising his voice*) And I'm not having it! If I catch you once more . . . !

SUZANNE: (*raising her voice*) Well, you will! I'm not afraid of you!

FIGARO: (*pretending to slap her face*) Oh, aren't you? Well you take that you insolent slut!

SUZANNE: (*pretending to have been struck*) Hitting me! And in Madam's room too!!

MAJOR BEGEARSS *comes in, in uniform, with a black armband.*   Sc.3

BEGEARSS: Why do you have to make such a noise? The household in mourning for that poor unfortunate child! An hour now you've been at each other's throats! I can hear you from my room up there!

FIGARO: (*aside*) An hour!

BEGEARSS: I come down and now the woman's in tears!

SUZANNE: (*pretending to weep*) He hit me, the brute!

BEGEARSS: How outrageous! Mr Figaro! No real gentleman ever strikes a member of the opposite sex!

FIGARO: (*rudely*) God help us! Please leave this to me, Sir! I am not a real gentleman; and this woman is not a 'member of the opposite sex': she's my wife, and what is more, she is an insolent slut, always up to mischief of some kind, and convinced she can thumb her nose at me because there are some people here always take her side. There's only one language she understands . . .

BEGEARSS: How could anyone be so utterly uncivilised?

FIGARO: Sir, if I choose anyone to act as arbitrator in my relations with her, you would be the last person I would ever come to: and you know perfectly well why!

BEGEARSS: You have too low an opinion of me, Sir: I shall report you to your employer.

FIGARO: (mockingly) Too low an opinion of you? Impossible!

[He goes]

Sc.4

BEGEARSS: My poor child, I'm amazed. What can have made him so angry?

SUZANNE: He came here to pick a quarrel: he said all kinds of wicked things about you. He told me I was never to see you or ever dare to speak to you. I defended you; we started shouting at each other; in the end he hit me. He's never done that, ever; but I've had enough, I want a separation . . . you saw what he was like . . .

BEGEARSS: Never mind about that. I felt a faint shadow of doubt about whether I should trust you: but this quarrel has dispelled it.

SUZANNE: That's not very comforting to me! Is that all you can say?

BEGEARSS: Have no fear, I'll see he suffers for it. It's time I settled accounts with you, my poor Suzanne! For a start I'll tell you a big secret. But are we sure that door is shut? I'll make sure.

(SUZANNE goes to the door)

(Aside) Ah! If I can have just three minutes with the jewel-case with the secret compartment I had made for the Countess! The letters I need are in there . . .

SUZANNE: (coming back) Well, what's the great secret?

BEGEARSS: Help your old friend: you'll do yourself no end of good. I am going to marry Florestine: it's all settled: her father's absolutely in favour of it.

SUZANNE: What father?

BEGEARSS: Were you born yesterday? If there's one thing you can be sure of, my little one, when an orphan girl turns up in a household, either as an adopted child or else as a goddaughter, the husband is always her father.* (Firmly) The point is I have permission to marry her . . . if you can make her amenable.

SUZANNE: Oh, but Léon's so much in love with her.

BEGEARSS: Their son? (Coldly) I'll break that attachment soon enough!

SUZANNE: (*amazed*) Ah! . . . And she . . . she's very fond . . .

BEGEARSS: Of him?

SUZANNE: Yes.

BEGEARSS: (*coldly*) I'll cure her of that, you'll see.

SUZANNE: (*still more taken aback*) Ah! Ah! . . . But Her Ladyship knows all about it, and she wants them to get married . . .

BEGEARSS: We'll make her change her mind.

SUZANNE: (*dumbfounded*) Her too? . . . But there's Figaro; from what I can see, Léon really trusts him . . .

BEGEARSS: He is the least of my anxieties. Wouldn't you be quite relieved to be rid of him?

SUZANNE: As long as he came to no harm . . .

BEGEARSS: Oh, shame on you! The very thought is deeply upsetting to anyone of any moral sensitivity. When they are made to see more clearly what is in their own best interests, they themselves will change their minds of their own accord.

SUZANNE: (*incredulously*) If you can do that, Sir . . .

BEGEARSS: (*with emphasis*) I will do it. You must realise that love doesn't play any part in this whole business. (*With sudden charm*) I've never really loved anyone but you.

SUZANNE: Oh, if Her Ladyship had said yes . . .

BEGEARSS: I would of course have consoled her, but she very arrogantly rejected my advances. According to the Count's present scheme of things, the Countess will be going to a convent.

SUZANNE: (*sharply*) I won't be party to any plot against her.

BEGEARSS: What do you mean, woman? He's only complying with her own wishes. You yourself are always saying she's too good for this world, I've heard you.

SUZANNE: (*angrily*) Yes, but there's no need to persecute her.

BEGEARSS: (*laughing*) No: but at least we'll be taking her a little further away from this world she's always been too good for. . . . And since, under these new and glorious laws, divorce is now permitted . . .*

SUZANNE: (*sharply*) The Count wants to be separated from her?

BEGEARSS: If he can.

SUZANNE: (*angrily*) Oh, men are so evil! They ought to be hanged, every one of them!

BEGEARSS: (*laughing*) I like to think you'd make an exception in my case.

SUZANNE: Oh do you? Well I wouldn't be so sure.

BEGEARSS: (*laughing*) I love you when you're in a real rage: it only shows what a good heart you have! As to our passionate young knight of Malta,* Léon, the Count has plans for him to travel . . . for a very long time. Figaro, being a man of wide experience, will go with him as companion and guide. (*He takes her hand*) And what matters to us: the Count, Florestine and I will all be living in the same house: and our dear Suzanne, who knows all our secrets, will be in charge of us all, run the whole household, have the last word in everything. No husband to beat you, no brute to stand in your way. A future sewn with silk and gold, the happiest life you've ever dreamed of . . .

SUZANNE: All this sweet talk meaning you want me to put in a good word for you with Florestine I presume . . .

BEGEARSS: (*lovingly*) I'll tell you the truth: I had assumed you'd do what you could. You always were the best woman there ever was! I'll see to all the rest: that I leave to you. (*Impetuously*) Damn it, there is one vital thing you can do!

SUZANNE looks at him closely.

SUZANNE: And what's that?

BEGEARSS recovers himself.

BEGEARSS: I say one vital thing – because he seems to think it's important. (*Coldly*) But in fact it's a mere detail. . . . The Count, it seems is thinking, as a wedding present, of giving his daughter a set of diamonds exactly the same as the Countess has. He wouldn't want anyone to know about it.

SUZANNE: (*surprised*) Oh! Oh!

BEGEARSS: It's not such a bad idea. Beautiful diamonds have a way of clinching things. It could be that he'll ask you to bring him his wife's jewel-case, just to compare the originals with what his jeweller has made.

SUZANNE: Why like Her Ladyship's? It seems a strange idea to me!

BEGEARSS: He wants to be sure they're as beautiful. As far as I'm concerned, you realise, it's of no importance whatsoever! Now quick, do you see? Here he comes.

Sc.5   The COUNT comes in.

COUNT: Major Bégearss, I was looking for you.

BEGEARSS: I was on my way to your apartments, Sir, I came to warn Suzanne you were intending to ask her for that jewel-case . . .

SUZANNE: Unless Your Lordship thinks . . .

COUNT: Oh! Leave off that: Your Lordship this, Your Lordship that! Did I or did I not give orders that when we crossed the French frontier . . .

SUZANNE: Well in my opinion, Your Lordship, not saying 'Your Lordship' makes us feel inferior.

COUNT: That is because you are more concerned with appearances than real pride. When you are living in a foreign country you should never offend local prejudices . . .

SUZANNE: All right, *Sir*, but at least you'll give me your word of honour . . .

COUNT: (*proudly*) Just who do you think you're talking to?

SUZANNE: I'll go and fetch it. (*Aside*) After all Figaro did tell me to give them whatever they asked for!

[SUZANNE *goes off*]   *Sc.6*

COUNT: That's her problem solved.

BEGEARSS: There is one other, Sir, that worries me far more: you seem so unhappy . . .

COUNT: You're an old friend, I'll tell you. When my son died, it seemed the worst thing that could ever happen. But now there's something else is tormenting me even more: it keeps the wound open, it is making life unbearable.

BEGEARSS: If you hadn't criticised me already for arguing, I'd have said your second son . . .

COUNT: (*sharply*) My second son! I haven't a second son!

BEGEARSS: Now don't upset yourself, Sir. Let us be reasonable. The loss of a much-loved child may be causing you to misjudge the other one, your wife, even yourself. Facts like that can't be determined on the strength of mere suspicions . . .

COUNT: Suspicions! Oh, I am all too sure of it! What makes me so despairing is to have no proof. While my poor son was alive, it didn't seem to matter. He would inherit my name, my responsibilities, everything I had. . . . What did this other creature matter to me? My contempt, a meaningless title, the Cross of Malta, and an allowance would have been adequate punishment for his mother and for him. But can you imagine my despair, losing a son I adored, at the prospect of an outsider, not my flesh and blood, inheriting the title, everything that was mine, and, to turn the knife in the wound, coming in every morning and calling me, of all the hideous names, 'his father?

BEGEARSS: Sir, I am afraid of making you more bitter when I am only trying to comfort you: but your wife's pious way of life . . .

COUNT: (*angrily*) That is another outrage on top of all the rest. Playing the perfect wife to cover up a filthy scandal! Twenty years of

irreproachable behaviour and relentless piety, universally admired
and respected for it. Her giving everyone an utterly false impression,
to make it seem that *I'm* responsible for everything that goes wrong
as a result of what is described as my strange behaviour. It only
makes me hate them even more!

BEGEARSS: But what would you have had her do, even supposing she
was in the wrong? There can't be any crime known to humanity that
twenty years' repentance can't finally atone for! Were you yourself
entirely innocent? This young Florestine you call your ward, you are
so deeply attached to . . .

COUNT: All the more reason she should ensure I am revenged! I am
going to sell up everything I possess, leave it all to her. There is
already three million in gold arrived from Vera Cruz.* That will be
her dowry when she marries: so you will be the one that has it. The
only help I need from you is in keeping that gift entirely secret. When
you receive the money and propose to her, pretend you've come into
some inheritance, a legacy from some distant relative . . .

BEGEARSS: (*showing the crêpe band on his arm*) You see this crêpe
band on my arm? Your wish is my command. I am already in
mourning.

COUNT: As soon as I have the King's assent to the forfeiture of all my
estates in Spain against investments here in Paris I'll find some way of
making sure you hold them jointly.

BEGEARSS: (*with feeling*) I am sorry, Sir, I could not accept that. You
cannot seriously think, on the basis of mere supposition – ill-founded
for all we know as yet – that I would make myself a party to the utter
ruination of a man that is your legal heir? Of a young man of very
great abilities? You must admit he has great gifts . . .

COUNT: (*losing his temper*) Greater than my son, I suppose you mean?
You think that, and so does everybody else: that makes me even
angrier with him!

BEGEARSS: If your ward accepts my hand, and if, from the main body
of your investments, you set aside for her marriage settlement this
three million in gold from Mexico; I could never bear the thought of
ever possessing such a sum, and I refuse to accept it unless the
contract contains a clause stating that I have made it over to her.
That is my duty if I love her . . .

COUNT: (*embracing him*) You are very frank and you're a good friend!
What a husband I've found for my daughter!

Sc.7   SUZANNE *comes in*

SUZANNE: Sir, there is the jewel-case: don't keep it too long: I ought to put it back where it was, before I draw the curtains in Her Ladyship's room.

COUNT: Suzanne, as you're going out, tell them no one is to come in unless I ring.

SUZANNE: (*aside*) I must tell Figaro about all this.

[*She goes off*]   *Sc.8*

BEGEARSS: Why did you want to see the case?

The COUNT *takes from his pocket a bracelet set with diamonds.*

COUNT: You see this bracelet set with diamonds? I have no desire to conceal the facts of my wife's infidelity from you any longer. Listen. There was a man called Léon d'Astorga; he used to be my page, they nicknamed him Chérubin.

BEGEARSS: I knew him well. We served in the same regiment. It was you commissioned me a major. But he must have died twenty years ago . . .

COUNT: That is precisely why I am suspicious. He had the temerity to fall in love with her. I thought she was infatuated with him: I got him away from Andalusia by giving him a commission in the brigade. A year after the birth of the son, I have now lost in that detestable duel . . . (*he puts his hand to his eyes*) when I went abroad as Viceroy of Mexico: instead of staying in Madrid, or in my palace at Seville, or living at Aguas Frescas, which is a glorious place to be, where do you think, my dear man, that my wife decided to go to? To a contemptible little house at Astorga, an old manor on a barren tract of land I had bought from the page's family. That is where she preferred to spend the three years I was away: where she gave birth – after nine or ten months, I don't know exactly – to this wretched child, with his despicable father's eyes and nose and mouth! Some years earlier when my portrait was being painted for the bracelet I gave the Countess, the painter thought the page was very pretty and asked if he could draw him: it is one of the best pictures in my study.

BEGEARSS: Yes . . . (*He averts his eyes*) So much so, your wife . . .

COUNT: (*quickly*) . . . Will never look at it? Well, from that portrait I have had this one made, inlaid in this bracelet, like hers in every way, made by the same jeweller that set all her diamonds: I am going to substitute his portrait here for mine. If she is too terrified to mention it, you will appreciate, I'll have my proof. If she says anything about it, I shall question her, and the whole shameful matter will be out in the open.

BEGEARSS: If you want my opinion, I do not approve of the plan.

COUNT: Why not?

BEGEARSS: Surely it offends your pride to have to stoop to devices of that kind? If, by some happy or unhappy chance, you found yourself in possession of possible proof, I would forgive you for going into it more thoroughly. But setting traps! Trying to trick her into a confession! Oh, surely no man of any decency would do anything so underhand, even to his sworn enemy?

COUNT: It is too late to stop now: the bracelet is made, the portrait of the page . . .

BEGEARSS: (*taking hold of the case*) Sir, for the sake of your own honour . . .

The COUNT *takes the bracelet out of the jewel-case.*

COUNT: Ah, I've always loved that portrait of me! Now I have it back! I shall at least have the satisfaction of seeing it adorn my daughter's wrist; she is a hundred times more worthy to wear it. I will put the other bracelet in the jewel-case. In its place . . .

He substitutes the other bracelet. BEGEARSS *pretends to want to stop him. They each pull at the case from either side:* BEGEARSS *skilfully opens the false bottom.*

BEGEARSS: No! No! I cannot allow it!!

COUNT: Let go of it!!

BEGEARSS: (*angrily*) Oh! Now we've broken the box.

COUNT: (*looking into it*) No. It's a secret drawer that came open as we were pulling at it. A compartment underneath with papers in.

BEGEARSS: (*trying to stop him*) I trust, Sir, you will not take advantage . . .

COUNT: (*impatiently*) You yourself said a moment ago 'If by some happy chance, you found yourself in possession of possible proof, I would forgive you for going into it more thoroughly.' Well, by chance I have, and I am going to do just what you advised. (*He tears out the papers*).

BEGEARSS: (*passionately*) As I hope to live, I will not be party to this outrage! Put those papers back, Sir, or forgive me if I have nothing to do with it. (*Aside*) So, he's seen enough . . .

He moves away. The COUNT *holds the papers, reading them:* BEGEARSS *watches him out of the corner of his eye, secretly very pleased with himself.*

COUNT: (*wildly*) I don't want to read any more: put the rest away; I'll keep this one.

BEGEARSS: No, whatever it is, you wouldn't sink to . . .

COUNT: (*proudly*) Sink to what? Go on! Say it! There's no need to spare me!

BEGEARSS: (*bowing*) Forgive me, Sir, you have been very generous to me. If I hadn't been so distressed I'd never have said such a thing . . .

COUNT: I don't think any the worse of you. On the contrary, it makes me respect you all the more. (*He throws himself into an armchair*) Rosine! She was unfaithful . . . . I may have been foolish, but she is the only woman I ever felt . . . with the others it was conquest! Oh, I can tell from my own rage now, how much that despicable passion. . . . I hate myself for loving her!

BERGEASS: In the name of God, Sir, put that dreadful piece of paper back.

Enter FIGARO. *The* COUNT *gets up.*   Sc.9

FIGARO: You rang, Sir?

COUNT: What do you mean, blundering in here? What do you want?

FIGARO: I came because the bell rang.

COUNT: (*angrily*) Well I didn't ring it! You are a servant, and you'll keep your nose out of matters that don't concern you!

FIGARO: Ask the jeweller: he heard it too.

COUNT: The jeweller? What does he want?

FIGARO: He says he's got an appointment; about a bracelet he made.

BEGEARSS, *aware* FIGARO *is trying to see the jewel-case on the table, tries to stand in his way.*

COUNT: Oh! . . . Tell him to come back another day.

FIGARO: (*maliciously*) But seeing as you have Her Ladyship's jewel-case open, Sir, it might be quite convenient . . .

COUNT: (*angrily*) You are very inquisitive! Now, you get out, and if you say one word about this . . .

FIGARO: *One* word? Oh, I wouldn't be able to say it in *one* word, Sir. I never do anything by halves.

He looks at the jewel-case, the paper the COUNT *is holding, glares*   Sc.10
defiantly at BEGEARSS, *and goes off.*

COUNT: We must shut this wretched case. I have the proof I was looking for. I have it and it makes me utterly miserable. Why did I have to find it? Oh God, read it, read it, Bégearss!

BEGEARSS: (*refusing to look at the paper*) God forbid I should ever be accused of prying into other peoples' secrets!

COUNT: It's a poor kind of friend who won't share a man's troubles! I suppose it's true: the only person we ever feel sorry for is ourselves . . .

BEGEARSS: What! Because I wouldn't look at that piece of paper? (*Quickly*) Put it away, here comes Suzanne.

Sc.11   *He quickly closes the secret drawer. The* COUNT *puts the letter in his inside pocket, close to his heart, grief-stricken.*

SUZANNE: (*running in*) The jewel-case, the jewel-case! Her Ladyship's ringing her bell!!!

BEGEARSS: (*giving it to her*) There, Suzanne; everything in order, as you see.

SUZANNE: What is the matter, Sir? You're upset.

BEGEARSS: Only mildly irritated by your clumsy lout of a husband, bursting in when he had been expressly forbidden to do so.

SUZANNE: (*archly*) Well, I told him, and from my tone of voice, I'd have thought he'd have understood.

Sc.12   *She goes off. The* COUNT *is about to go, but sees* LEON *coming in.*

COUNT: Now here's the other one.

LEON *tries shyly to kiss the* COUNT.

LEON: Father, good morning: did you sleep well?

COUNT: (*coldly, pushing him away*) And where were you last night, Sir?

LEON: Father, I was taken to a wonderful meeting . . .

COUNT: Where you read a paper?

LEON: I was asked to read them an essay I had written about the evils of celibacy in religious orders and the individuals' right to be released from their vows . . .

COUNT: (*bitterly*) And that would include your own vows in the Order of Malta?

BEGEARSS: I am told it was very well received.

LEON: I think they were being kind on account of my age, Sir.

COUNT: So, instead of making preparations for your military service to earn election to the order, you are making trouble? You go in for writing, for public speaking, anything as long as it's fashionable?

Soon we shan't be able to tell the difference between a gentleman and an intellectual!

LEON: (*shyly*) Perhaps then father, it will be easier to tell the difference between ignoramuses and men of education, and between free men and slaves.

COUNT: That is dangerous talk! Easy enough to see what you want!

The COUNT *makes as if to go.*

LEON: Father . . . !

COUNT: (*contemptuously*) You will be good enough to leave that vulgar style of speaking to the working men in their slums. People of our class express themselves more elegantly. Whoever heard of anyone saying 'Father' at Court? *Sir*! Call me Sir! You stink of the common herd! His father indeed!

He goes off: LEON *follows him, looking at* BEGEARSS, *who gives a shrug of sympathy.*

COUNT: Come along, Bégearss, come along!

ACT II

The COUNT'*s library.*

Sc.1   COUNT: Now I am alone at last, I must read this amazing document
that fate has somehow allowed to fall into my hands.
(He takes the letter from the jewel-case out of his breast pocket,
and reads it, giving weight to every word)
'Desperate, unhappy man! What we most feared has happened. Your
daring to come to me at night without warning, in a house where you
grew up, where you knew every corner, every turn of the wall: the
violent struggle that followed: the crime you committed, and I
committed too' . . .
(He stops)
. . . 'and I committed too, has now been suitably punished. Today,
the feast of San Léon – patron saint of this place and after whom you
were named – I have given birth to a son, my shame, my despair.
I have taken trouble, with a heavy heart, to spare my husband's
self-respect. But mine has gone for ever: I am condemned from this
day on to weep and never be comforted, knowing all too well that
tears can never wash away a crime . . . whose consequences will be
with me for ever. You are never to see me again. That is my final
decision. In misery, Rosine. . . . After this, I do not dare sign any
other name.'
(He presses the letter against his forehead, pacing up and down)
'After this I do not dare sign any other name'! Oh Rosine! And all
the days . . . ? But she has put herself beyond the pale. . . .
(He moves restlessly)
But that's not what a wicked woman would have written! Damn him
for seducing her. . . . But let me see: there's an answer written on the
letter.
(He reads:)
'Since I am not allowed to see you again; I have come to hate being
alive, and I shall die happily in a frontal attack on a fort I have no

orders to take part in. I am sending back all your hard words, the drawing I did of you, and the lock of hair I stole. The friend who will give you this, when I am no more, is a man you can trust. He has witnessed all my misery. If the death of anyone so worthless is capable of stirring any last remains of pity in you, whatever the names you give the child ... of another man, more fortunate than me ... I hope the name Léon will sometimes remind you of the wretched creature ... who dies adoring you, and signs, for the last time,

'Chérubin, Léon d'Astorga'.

Then there's blood:
'I have been mortally wounded, I have opened this letter again and write with my life's blood, in agony, farewell for ever. Remember ...'
The rest is smudged with tears. ...

(*He moves restlessly*)
And that's not what a wicked man would have written either! It was a terrible accident. ...

(*He sits down, still brooding*)
I feel so torn!

BEGEARSS *comes in, stops, looks at him and bites his finger,*   Sc.2
uncertain what to do.

BEGEARSS: Sir?
COUNT: Ah, my dear friend, come in! ... I am, as you see, utterly broken.
BEGEARSS: I was alarmed for you, Sir. I didn't dare to move a muscle.
COUNT: I have just read the letter. No. They had no desire to hurt me. They did nothing unnatural: they were half mad with unhappiness, as they say themselves ...
BEGEARSS: I had imagined it as you did ...

The COUNT *gets up and paces to and fro.*

COUNT: Poor women, they let themselves be seduced; they have no idea of the misery they're letting us all in for! ... They go on, they go on. ... from one humiliation to the next ... and society, being frivolous and unfair, blames a father for remaining silent, for swallowing down his sorrow in secret! ... He is accused of being heartless if he's less affectionate to another man's child, the living proof of adultery! ... However badly we behave as men, they never suffer any real loss: in any case we can never rob them of the certainty they are mothers, all the endless resources of motherhood! And yet one silly little whim of theirs, a fancy, a meaningless affair of no importance whatsoever, can ruin a man's happiness ... the one happiness in his whole life, the security of being a father. Oh, there's good reason for us attaching so much importance to a woman remaining faithful! All the blessings of society, all its curses depend on how they behave: it's heaven or hell in a family, entirely according to the way they make us think of them.

BEGEARSS: Be calm. Here comes your daughter.

Sc.3   FLORESTINE *comes in with flowers pinned at her waist*

FLORESTINE: Sir, they told me you were so busy, I was afraid of wearying you by asking how you were.

COUNT: Busy on your account my darling! My daughter! I like to call you that because I have looked after you since you were a baby. The man your mother was married to was never well; when he died he left nothing behind him. And when she herself lay dying, she entrusted you to my care. I gave her my word; you're my daughter and I shall honour that pledge by finding you a husband with the finest and highest ideals. I speak freely in the presence of this friend who loves us. Look about you: make up your own mind! Is there no one here you see who is worthy of your love?

FLORESTINE: (*kissing his hand*) Only you, Sir, but if you're asking my opinion in the matter, I can tell you that what would make me happiest would be to go on living exactly as we are now. When your son marries – because I'm sure he can't want to go on being a Knight of Malta these days – when your son marries, he may go away and leave his father. But please let me be the one to look after you in your old age! It is my duty, Sir, but I shall be very happy doing it.

COUNT: Now none of that, none of that *Sir* for me. Keep it for those you have no feelings for: no one would think it odd to hear so appreciative a child as you are call me something more affectionate! Call me 'Father'!

BEGEARSS: She deserves all the trust you put in her, and that's the truth! My dear young lady, you've had a good, a loving man to look after you: give him a kiss. You owe him more than you think. His being your guardian is no more than you deserve. He was your mother's friend ... your mother's closest friend ... and to tell you the whole truth ...

Sc.4   FIGARO *comes in, announcing the* COUNTESS *in a loose gown.*

FIGARO: The Countess.

BEGEARSS *glares furiously at* FIGARO.

BEGEARSS: (*aside*) God damn the man!

COUNTESS: (*to the* COUNT) Figaro told me that you were unwell. I was alarmed, I came at once before I had finished dressing, but I see . . .

COUNT: . . . That this interfering fool has lied to you yet again.

FIGARO: Sir, I saw you go by, I thought you looked so drawn and pale . . . well, it's a good thing there's nothing the matter.

BEGEARSS: What?

BEGEARSS *looks at him closely.*

COUNTESS: Good-day, Major Bégearss. . . . There you are Florestine: you look quite radiant. . . . Do you see how well and beautiful she looks? If God had given me a daughter, I would have wanted her to be just like you, looks and character. You'll have to take her place. Will you, Florestine?

FLORESTINE: (*kissing her hand*) Oh My Lady!

COUNTESS: Flowers at this hour of the morning? Who is your admirer?

FLORESTINE: (*happily*) No admirer, My Lady, I picked them myself. Isn't it San Léon's day today?

COUNTESS: Sweet child, you remember everything!

She kisses her forehead. The COUNT's face is contorted. BEGEARSS
restrains him.

COUNT: (*aside*) San Léon . . .

BEGEARSS: (*aside*) Calm yourself, Sir.

COUNTESS: (*to* FIGARO) Figaro, since we are all together now, tell my son we'll take our chocolate here.

FLORESTINE: While they go and get it ready, guardian, do let us see the beautiful bust of Washington they told us about in your rooms.

COUNT: I have no idea who can have sent it me: I didn't order it. I expect it's for Léon. It is fine. I have it there in the study: you can all come.

BEGEARSS, *the last to leave, turns back twice to stare at* FIGARO,   Sc.5
who stares back, each silently threatening the other. FIGARO, *left
alone, arranges the table and the cups for breakfast.*

FIGARO: Viper! Gorgon more like! Eyeing me up and down, looking daggers at me! If looks can kill it'll be mine that do the killing! Where does he collect his post, though? That's what I can't fathom! Never has any letters delivered to the house here with the ordinary mail! He can't be the only demon climbed up out of hell. There must be some other devil writing to him ... but I'm damned if I know where he is ...

Sc.6   SUZANNE *runs in, looks round, and whispers excitedly in* FIGARO's *ear.*

SUZANNE: It's him the girl's marrying! The Count's given him his word. He's going to cure Léon of being in love with her – break Florestine's attachment – make Her Ladyship agree to it – have you thrown out of the house – imprison the mistress in a nunnery till she's divorced – cut young Léon out of his inheritance and make me mistress of everything I survey. That's what he's doing this morning.

Sc.7   [*She runs off*]

FIGARO: No, if it's all the same to you, Major Bégearss, I think I'd rather we discussed it first. I am going to teach you a lesson: only idiots celebrate a victory before they've won. Thanks to Suzanne, who will be playing Ariadne, I have got hold of the thread through the labyrinth, leading to a nasty end, for the Minotaur.... I am going to rip your mask off.... But what can he need so desperately, he makes an elementary mistake like that, telling her everything? Perhaps he thinks he's safe ...? Fools always have a high opinion of themselves! Fancy, a politician, being so open and trusting! Well, that's one game he's thrown away. And now, I think, my service!

Sc.8   *Enter* WILHELM *with a letter.*

WILHELM: Maitchor Betchorras? Aha! I see he ist not hier.

FIGARO: (*arranging the breakfast*) You can wait for him. He'll be back in a minute.

WILHELM: (*shrinking*) Mein Gott! I hem not vaiting hier. Not togezzer viz you! Mein master vould not like zat, I hem tamn sure of it!!

FIGARO: Oh, told you not to talk to me, has he? Well, give me the letter, I'll see that he gets it as soon as he comes back.

WILHELM: (*shrinking back again*) Gif you ze ledders? Oh hell, no! He vould soon kiv me mein marshing orters, I ton't mind delling you.

FIGARO: (*aside*) I am going to have to pump the poor idiot. You-come-from-post-yes?

WILHELM: Oh hell no! I to not come.

FIGARO: I expect it's some packet from the Irish gentleman ... from the relative who just left him everything in his will. You know about that, don't you, Little Wilhelm?

WILHELM: (*with a foolish snigger.*) Ha! Ha! Ha! Ledder from a ted man! Ha! Ha! Vot? No, pliss! I don't sink from him: my Gott, no. It vill be more bropaply from somevun else, I sink. Perhaps it could come from vun of zese who are not . . . not content. Oafer ze porder.

FIGARO: Discontented elements abroad you mean?

WILHELM: Yes. Putt I hem nod inschured.

FIGARO: (aside) It could be: there aren't many pies he hasn't got a finger in. (To WILHELM) We could tell from the stamp, then we'd know for certain . . .

WILHELM: Zat is nod inschured eizzah. Vy? Because ze ledders, iz coming to ze house von Mr O'Connor: ent denn I ton't know vot iss 'damp'.

FIGARO: (quickly) O'Connor! The Irish banker?

WILHELM: My gootness, yes!

FIGARO: (recovering, more calmly) Near here, in the back street, behind the house?

WILHELM: A ferry bretty house I would heff sett, goodness yes. Most jarming indiwiddle, you know him? Dreats me ferry hansome.

He strolls upstage.

FIGARO: (to himself) Oh, what a piece of luck!

WILHELM: (coming back) Nod a vord apout zis penker, nobody in ze verld!! Iss ein secret, you understend? I shouldn't even heff told. . . . Ach, verdammt, der Teufel!!

He stamps his foot.

FIGARO: Oh go on, I don't mind. Don't worry . . .

WILHELM: Mein master, he say to me, you are tamm clever, I hem tamm schtupit. He iss right ja? Putt all ze same I hem a liddle discontent I heff told you zis.

FIGARO: Why?

WILHELM: I don't know. You know, ze dreacherous falet, unt so forss? To be like zat, iss ein most horriple sing, a grime, a wile wile grime, I schpitt on it.

FIGARO: I quite agree. But you didn't say anything . . .

WILHELM: (in tears) Mein Gott! Mein Gott! I ton't know, vot I hem suppose to say, vot I hem nod suppose to say. . . . I vill vait here.

He moves away, sighing deeply, and looks inanely at the books in the library.

FIGARO: (aside) Now we've discovered something! Fate is obviously on my side! (He fetches a notebook) But I still can't understand how a man as devious as that employs this moron. It must be like burglars, keeping well away from anything too bright. He's not bright at all, but at least you can see straight through him. (*He writes in his notebook*) O'Connor, Irish banker. That is where I shall begin my informal inquiries. Not the most constitutional of methods. *Ma per dio!* Ends always justify the means. That's what the police say, anyway! (*He writes*) Four or five gold sovereigns to the boy that collects the post, to have a drink on the way and open any letter with the Honourable Major Begearss's handwriting on it. . . . I'll give him Honourable! Hypocrite! But not for much longer. Someone up there has put me on your trail. (*He puts away his notes*) Fate, the unknown god. In olden times they called him Destiny! Nowadays we call him something else . . .

Sc.9   *The* COUNTESS, *the* COUNT, FLORESTINE, BEGEARSS, *come in:*
BEGEARSS *sees* WILHELM, *and takes the letter crossly.*

BEGEARSS: Why didn't you bring it to my own apartment?
WILHELM: I sought zis vas your own apartment.

[*He goes*]

COUNTESS: (*to the* COUNT) The bust is very good indeed, Sir: has your son seen it?
BEGEARSS: (*who has opened the letter*) Ah, a letter from Madrid! From the Minister's Secretary. There is something here of interest to you. (*He reads*) 'Tell Count Almaviva that the King's assent to the selling up of all his estates is in the post that will leave tomorrow.'

FIGARO *is listening and silently indicates that he has heard.*

COUNTESS: Figaro, don't stand there! Go and tell my son we are having breakfast here.
FIGARO: Madam, I will let him know.

Sc.10   [*He goes out*]

COUNT: (*to* BEGEARSS) Major Bégearss, I wish to inform my purchaser at once. I'll have some tea in my inner study.
FLORESTINE: Dear Papa, I will get it.
COUNT: (*aside to* FLORESTINE) About the man you are to marry. . . . I haven't told you much, but think about it seriously. Sweet girl.

Sc.11   *He kisses her on the forehead and goes off.* LEON *comes in, and looks downcast.*

LEON: Whenever I come into a room, my father goes away. He's been so fierce . . .

COUNTESS: (*severely*) Now, what kind of talk is that? You will insist on seeing injustice in everything! Your father has to write to the man who's buying his estates.

LEON: That's true . . .

FLORESTINE: (*brightly*) You wanted father to stay? So did we. But, as he knows today is your saint's day, he asked me to give you these flowers.

She curtseys and pins the flowers in his buttonhole.

LEON: He could not have asked anyone who would make me more grateful to him.

He kisses her, but she pretends to struggle.

FLORESTINE: You see Madam, whenever I tease him he always takes advantage of it . . .

COUNTESS: (*smiling*) Dear one, on his saint's day I think he might be forgiven.

FLORESTINE: (*averting her eyes*) As a punishment, Madam, make him read his speech they said was so successful at the meeting last night.

LEON: If my mother thinks I did anything wrong, I'll go and fetch my punishment . . .

FLORESTINE: Oh Madam, tell him he must.

COUNTESS: Bring us your speech, my dear: I shall find some needlework to help me listen with more attention.

FLORESTINE: (*brightly*) He is so stubborn! Well done, and I shall hear it now, whatever you say!

LEON: (*tenderly*) Whatever I say? When it was your idea? Oh Florestine, honestly!

COUNTESS: I'll go and find some needlework to help me listen with more attention . . .

LEON: I'll go and fetch my punishment . . .

[*The* COUNTESS *and* LEON *go off separately*] Sc.12

BEGEARSS: (*whispering*) Well, young lady, have you guessed who it is you are to marry?

FLORESTINE: (*joyfully*) Dear Major Bégearss! You are such a dear friend to all of us, that I will risk thinking aloud with you. Now who can I see? My guardian definitely said, 'Look about you, make up your own mind!' He couldn't be kinder than that: it must be Léon. But I'm so poor, surely I shouldn't . . .

BEGEARSS: (*in a terrifying voice*) Who? Léon? His son? Your brother?

FLORESTINE: (*hurt*) Oh! Oh! Sir!

BEGEARSS: Didn't he say to you: 'Call me "father"'? Come to your senses, my dearest child! This is a wicked dream, resist it! It could have terrible consequences . . .

FLORESTINE: Oh. Yes, for both of us.

BEGEARSS: You must realise such a secret must never be revealed to a living soul!

Sc.13   *He goes off, looking at her.* FLORESTINE *is left alone, weeping.*

FLORESTINE: Oh God! He is my brother, and I almost fell into. . . . It's all so horribly clear now . . . . And after a dream like that it's so cruel to be awake.

Sc.14   *She falls into a chair sobbing.* LEON *comes in with a piece of paper.*

LEON: (*happily, aside*) My mother still not back and Major Bégearss gone: too good an opportunity to miss! (*Aloud*) Florestine, you look so beautiful this morning, you always look so perfect: you seem so happy, you spoke so lovingly just then, that I began to hope again that . . .

FLORESTINE: (*in despair*) Oh Léon!

She falls back.

LEON: Oh God! You're crying: you look so upset! Something terrible must have happened.

FLORESTINE: Very terrible. Oh Léon, only for me, now . . .

LEON: Florestine, don't you love me any more? You must know what I feel. . . .

FLORESTINE: (*severely*) Whatever you feel . . . please don't ever tell me. . . .

LEON: What? Nothing but the purest love . . .

FLORESTINE: (*in despair*) Stop this cruel talk or I shall have to go away at once . . .

LEON: But for pity's sake! What happened? Major Bégearss was talking to you. I must know what he said to you.

Sc.15   [*The* COUNTESS *comes in*]

Mother, please help me. I am terribly unhappy. Florestine does not love me any more.

FLORESTINE: (*weeping*) Oh mother, not love him any more! My guardian, you and he are all I've ever lived for.

COUNTESS: My dear, I'm sure that's true. I know how good and loving you are by nature. But why is he so upset?

LEON: Mother, you approve of me loving her as passionately as I do?

FLORESTINE: (*throwing herself into the arms of the* COUNTESS) Do tell him to be quiet. (*Weeping*) I'm so unhappy, I'll die if he goes on . . .

COUNTESS: My dear, I don't understand you. I am as much at a loss as he is. She's shaking! What has he done that you don't like?

FLORESTINE: (*standing back*) Mother, it's not that I don't like him, I love him and respect him as if he was my own brother: but please don't let him ask for more than that.

LEON: You hear her, mother! You heartless girl, tell me what you mean!

FLORESTINE: Leave me alone! Leave me alone, or this will kill me! I swear it will!

FIGARO comes in with the tea things: SUZANNE from the other side with a piece of needlework.

Sc.16

SUZANNE: Your needlework, Madam.

FIGARO: I'll put the chocolate on the table, Madam.

COUNTESS: No, clear everything away again: there is no question of breakfast or reading now. Figaro, take some tea in to your master: he is writing in his study. And you, Florestine, come to my room and tell me what the matter is; I hope I'm still a friend. My dear children, I'm so devoted to both of you. Why must you always make me suffer, one after the other? Have pity on me. I'm sure this is something I must clarify for my own sake.

The COUNTESS and FLORESTINE go out.

Sc.17

SUZANNE: I don't know what the matter is: but I wouldn't mind betting Bégearss was behind it. I want to be sure and see to it my mistress is well prepared . . .

FIGARO: Wait till I've found out more: you and I can work out a joint plan of attack tonight. Oh, there is one thing I've discovered.

SUZANNE: No hopes of your telling me I suppose . . .

[She goes off] Sc.18

LEON: (*in despair*) Oh God!

FIGARO: What is this all about, Sir?

LEON: I wish I knew! I'd never seen Florestine in such high spirits; I knew she'd been talking to my father. I leave her alone for a moment with Monsieur Bégearss: I come back, I find her alone, in floods of tears, telling me she never wants to see me again. What can he possibly have told her?

FIGARO: If you hadn't got such a quick temper, I'd tell you one or two things you really ought to know. But seeing as we need to proceed with extreme caution, one word out of turn from you could ruin ten years' patient work on my part.

LEON: Oh, if it's only a question of discretion. . . . What do you think he told her?

FIGARO: That she is going to have to marry the Honourable Major Bégearss, Léon, and that it's all been arranged by your father and himself.

LEON: By my father and Bégearss! The brute will have to kill me first!!

FIGARO: You carry on like that, Sir, the brute won't kill you, but he'll have the woman you love, and every penny you possess as well.

LEON: Very well. You're a good friend. Forgive me. Tell me what to do.

FIGARO: Find the answer to the riddle of the Sphinx: before he eats you alive. Put it this way: control yourself, let him talk . . . don't let him see what you're thinking.

LEON: (*furiously*) Control myself! I'll control myself all right! But I'm so angry inside! To want to take Florestine from me! Ah! Here he comes: I'll say what I have to say, in a perfectly matter-of-fact way.

FIGARO: If you lose your temper, we're lost!

Sc.19   BEGEARSS *comes in.*

LEON: (*controlling himself with difficulty*) Sir, Sir, I wonder if I could have a word? I would advise you, unless you're looking for trouble, to give me a straight answer. Florestine is desperately unhappy. What did you say to Florestine?

BEGEARSS: (*icily*) And who said I was talking to her? Can't she be upset without my having anything to do with it?

LEON: (*aggressively*) Do not avoid the question, Sir. She was in a sweet mood, very happy: after she had been with you she was in tears. Whatever the cause of her unhappiness, I love her and I share it. You will tell me the cause or give me satisfaction.

BEGEARSS: If you were a little less domineering, I'd tell you whatever you want. I never give in to threats.

LEON: (*furious*) Very well! You filthy liar, it's a fight! Either I kill you or you kill me!

He puts his hand to his sword.

FIGARO: (*stopping them*) Major Bégearss! The son of your best friend? In his own house? When you're living here as a guest?

BEGEARSS: (*controlling himself*) I am perfectly well aware of how to behave. . . . I wish to have this out with him: but I do not want what I have to say to be overheard. Get out. Leave us alone.

LEON: You go, my dear Figaro: you can see he can't wriggle out of this. We mustn't let him have any excuses.

FIGARO: (*aside*) I'll run and tell his father.

He goes. LEON *bars the door.*   Sc.20

LEON: Perhaps it would suit you better to fight than to talk. It is entirely your choice. But I insist on one or the other: nothing else.

BEGEARSS: (*coldly*) Léon! No decent man could butcher the son of his best friend. You could hardly expect me to answer your question in front of a little servant, who prides himself on having worked his way up to a position where he practically dictates to his own master . . .

LEON: (*sitting down*) Come to the point, Sir. I am waiting.

BEGEARSS: Oh, you're going to be very sorry you lost your temper. It was madness!

LEON: We'll see soon enough.

BEGEARSS: (*affecting a cold dignified manner*) Léon. You love Florestine: I saw that long ago. While your brother was alive, I did not think it my duty to encourage a doomed attachment that couldn't possibly have any happy outcome for you. But when that dreadful duel, in which he lost his life, put you in his place, I was arrogant enough to think my influence was sufficient to persuade your father to let you marry the girl you love. I tried everything: every argument met with the same invincible resistance. Very upset at seeing him reject a plan that seemed to me guaranteed to make everybody happy. . . . Forgive me, dear boy: what I have to say will distress you, but I must tell you now, in order to save you endless suffering. Try to take this as philosophically as you can: it will come as a great blow. I forced your father to break his silence and tell me the secret. 'My friend', says the Count at long last 'I know how much he loves her: but how can I let him marry Florestine? Everyone believes she is my ward. . . . She is my natural daughter: his own sister.'

LEON: (*stunned*) Florestine? . . . My sister?

BEGEARSS: That was what it was my unhappy duty. . . . Oh, I am duty-bound to both of you: not to have said anything would have been condemning you both to disaster. Well, Léon? Do you want to fight me?

LEON: You are a good, kind friend! I have been unspeakably ungrateful
. . . inhuman. . . . Please forget . . . that mad tantrum.

BEGEARSS: (*obviously false*) Only on condition this terrible secret never
becomes known. . . . Disclosing anything so discreditable about your
own father would be an abominable thing to do . . .

LEON: (*throwing himself into his arms*) Oh, never!

Sc.21   FIGARO: (*running in*) There they are! There they are!

COUNT: In one another's arms! Are you out of your mind?

FIGARO: (*dumbfounded*) Well, Sir, I'd say anybody would be quite
surprised.

COUNT: (*to* FIGARO) Perhaps you would care to explain the joke?

LEON: (*trembling*) If anyone should explain, it's me, father. Forgive
me! I'm so ashamed I could die! Something very petty . . . I . . . lost
my temper. Behaved very badly. Being very generous by nature,
Major Bégearss has been good enough not only to bring me to my
senses, but to overlook my outburst and forgive me. I was thanking
him when you came in.

COUNT: A hundred times over he has given you cause to be grateful to
him: more than that. We are all in his debt.

FIGARO: (*aside*) His debt!

> FIGARO *silently strikes his forehead.* BEGEARSS *notices, and*
> *smiles.*

BEGEARSS: Mr Figaro?

COUNT: (*to* LEON) Please leave us, Léon. If it weren't for your having
confessed, I'd be a great deal angrier.

BEGEARSS: Oh please, Sir, it's all over and forgotten.

COUNT: (*to* LEON) Léon, go to your room. You should be thoroughly
ashamed of yourself, being impertinent to my closest friend, your
closest friend, one of the best men I've ever met!

FIGARO: (*aside, angrily*) A whole legion of demons all buttoned up in
one suit of clothes!

LEON: (*going off*) God, I'm so miserable!

Sc.22   COUNT: (*to* BEGEARSS, *aside*) And now, my friend, to this business we
have already begun. (*To* FIGARO) And instead of jumping to absurd
conclusions in such an irresponsible manner, you can bring me the
three million in gold you were responsible for collecting from Cadiz.
Sixty bankers' drafts: I told you to make a note of the numbers.

FIGARO: I've done that.

COUNT: Well, bring me the portfolio.

FIGARO: Portfolio, Sir? The three million, you mean?

COUNT: Obviously. Well? What are you waiting for?

FIGARO: (*crestfallen*) Me, Sir? I haven't got them any more.

COUNT: What? You haven't got them?

FIGARO: (*proudly*) No, Sir.

BEGEARSS: (*aggressively*) What have you done with them?

FIGARO: When my master asks me questions, I owe him some explanation of what I have been doing. Not you. I don't owe you anything.

COUNT: (*angrily*) You insolent oaf! What have you done with them?

FIGARO: (*coldly*) I deposited them with Monsieur Fal, your lawyer.

BEGEARSS: And whose idea was that?

FIGARO: Mine. And I still think it's quite a good one.

BEGEARSS: I'll bet he's done no such thing!

FIGARO: Seeing as I am in possession of the signed receipts, that is a bet you are in some danger of losing, Sir.

BEGEARSS: Or if he did agree to take it, the money will have been used for gambling on the stock market. These people go fifty-fifty.

FIGARO: You ought to be more polite about someone who's done you a good turn . . .

BEGEARSS: I owe him nothing whatsoever!

FIGARO: I believe you. If you've just come into forty thousand doubloons . . .

COUNT: (*becoming angry*) No doubt you also have some observation you'd care to make about that?

FIGARO: Who, me, Sir? I'd hardly have any reason to doubt that, Sir, seeing as I was personally acquainted with the relation who left this gentleman everything he had. A rather dissolute young man to be frank, a gambler, squandered his money, always fighting: no idea of self-control, no moral fibre, no character to speak of, nothing he didn't get from other people, not even the bad habits that killed him: then a duel he should never have . . .

COUNT: How dare you!!

The COUNT *stamps his foot.*

BEGEARSS: (*angrily*) For the last time, will you tell us why you put this money on deposit?

FIGARO: Well, Sir, so I wasn't responsible for it. Someone might have stolen it. You never know. You wouldn't believe the thieves get into a house like this.

BEGEARSS: (*fretting*) Be that as it may, your master wants it back!

FIGARO: My master can send someone to get it then.

BEGEARSS: But is the lawyer likely to hand it over without the receipt?

FIGARO: I am just about to give it to my master: and having done my
duty, if anything goes wrong, he can't blame me!

COUNT: Bring it to my study. I'll be waiting.

FIGARO: (*to the* COUNT) I must warn you, Monsieur Fal will only hand
it over to you personally: those were my instructions.

Sc.23   [*He goes off*]

BEGEARSS: (*angrily*) The scum of the earth. You give them what they
want and see what they turn into! The truth is, Sir, I must tell you
this as a friend: you trust that man too much; he has guessed our
secret. He began as your valet, your barber, your medical attendant,
now you've put him in charge of all your finances, all your private
papers, made him a kind of general factotum. Everybody knows that
man twists you round his little finger!

COUNT: As far as loyalty is concerned, I can't criticise him; but I agree
his arrogance is . . .

BEGEARSS: There is a way you could be rid of him and reward his
services at the same time.

COUNT: I often wish I could.

BEGEARSS: (*confidentially*) When you send Léon off to join the Knights
of Malta, I imagine you'll want a man you can trust to look after
him. That man'll be only too flattered to be offered a position of such
trust and respect; he can't fail to agree to go: and there you are, shot
of him for some considerable time.

COUNT: You are quite right, my friend. I'm also told he is getting on
very badly with his wife.

Sc.24   [*He goes off*]

BEGEARSS: (*alone*) Another step nearer my objective! Ah, the high-
minded spy! The perfect clown! The good and faithful servant, trying
to snatch the prize from under my nose, and calling me names, as if I
was a figure in a comedy. Thanks to the tender solicitude of the
Honourable Mr Hypocrite you will be sharing the hardships of a long
patrol at sea, and be obliged to take your nose out of our affairs.

ACT III

SUZANNE: More flowers, Madam . . .

The COUNTESS's *sitting-room; flowers everywhere.* Sc. 1

COUNTESS: Here, in my sitting-room . . . thank you, Suzanne. I couldn't get anything out of the child. She does nothing but sob and weep! She seems to think she has offended me somehow, begged me over and over again to forgive her: says she wants to go into a convent. In the light of her behaviour to my son, I can only think she's blaming herself for having listened to his talk of love, and having encouraged him, when she thinks she isn't good enough a match for him. So like her to be so sensitive! The thought is touching but she really is carrying it too far! Major Bégearss, it seems, made some passing mention of it, and that was what made her feel so sorry for herself. It's just that he's so scrupulous and concerned about moral questions himself, he takes things too seriously and imagines danger and sees horrors where no one else would ever think of it.

SUZANNE: I don't know what has caused the trouble: but there's something strange going on here, I know! It's as if someone had put the Evil Eye on us. The master's gloomy as can be, can't bear anybody near him. You're always crying. The young lady sobbing her heart out: the young master miserable as sin! There's only Major Bégearss: all serene, above it all, never seems to let any of it bother him, watches you all suffering as if he had no feelings at all.

COUNTESS: Dear girl, of course he sympathises in his heart of hearts. I'm afraid without him to comfort us, to heal our differences, be there to guide and advise us, soothe us when we've been too harsh to one another, and calm my husband when he gets angry so easily, our life would be a great deal worse!

SUZANNE: I just hope you're not mistaken, Madam.

COUNTESS: I have known you be more generous about him in the past. (SUZANNE *averts her eyes*) Anyway, he's the only one can stop me being so upset by that child. Please ask him to come down to see me.

SUZANNE: (*aside*) Talk of the Devil! (*Aloud*) Here he comes now; I'll
do your hair later.

Sc.2   [*She goes off*]

BEGEARSS: Dear Countess . . .

COUNTESS: (*mournfully*) Oh my poor Major, what is happening to us?
We seem to be moving towards the disaster I've always dreaded: so
long I've seen it coming! The Count seems to hate my poor son more
and more every day. He must finally have some dreadful glimmering
of the truth.

BEGEARSS: Madam, I'm sure not.

COUNTESS: Ever since my eldest son was taken from me as a punish-
ment, I can see my husband's absolutely changed: instead of doing
everything in his power, with our ambassador in Rome, to have Léon
released from his vows, I've watched him growing more determined
to send him to Malta. I also know, Major Bégearss, that he is selling
up all his property and intends to leave Spain altogether and settle in
this country. The other day at dinner, in front of thirty people, he
was arguing in favour of divorce in a way that terrified me.

BEGEARSS: I was there. I remember it only too well!

COUNTESS: (*in tears*) I'm so sorry, you're the only friend I can trust,
the only person I don't mind seeing me in tears.

BEGEARSS: You must always tell me when you're sad: I pride myself I
am sensitive enough to understand.

COUNTESS: Please . . . was it him, or was it you that made Florestine
so dreadfully upset? I've always wanted her to marry my son. I know
she was born with no advantages, but she's so fine, and beautiful and
good, and she's grown up with us: now my son's come into the
inheritance, surely he has enough for both of them?

BEGEARSS: Too much perhaps: that's the cause of all the trouble!

COUNTESS: I don't know: it's as if I'd been spared punishment all these
years only for it to be more terrible when it came: I've cried enough
about the thoughtless way I behaved: now it seems that everything is
coming together at once, to destroy all the hopes I ever had. My
husband detests my son. Florestine refuses to marry him. Whatever it
is that has made her so bitter, she says she never wants to see him
again. It'll kill the poor child! That's all true, there's no question
about it. (*She clasps her hands*) God is not mocked! I've spent twenty
years weeping and reproaching myself, and now it seems it is His Will
that I am finally to be found out! Oh, I wouldn't mind so much if I
was to be the only one to suffer! Dear God, I have no complaint! But
I pray my son will not be blamed for an offence in which he, of all

people, was entirely innocent! Major Bégearss, there is so much wrong. Is there no answer?

BEGEARSS: I respect you deeply as a woman; I came on purpose to set your mind at rest. When we are afraid of something, it begins to occupy our whole attention, the danger becomes exaggerated in our minds. No matter what we say or do, the anxiety eats its way into everything! In fact, I can explain all these apparent mysteries. You will be happy again.

COUNTESS: How can I be, when I feel so much remorse?

BEGEARSS: Your husband has not been avoiding Léon: as far as the secret of his birth is concerned he suspects nothing!

COUNTESS: Major Bégearss!

BEGEARSS: And all the signs you have interpreted as hatred are only evidence of his own uneasy conscience. I know what I have to say will be of immense comfort to you!

COUNTESS: (*passionately*) Dear Major Bégearss!

BEGEARSS: But what I tell you is of enormous import; and however great your relief may be, it must never go further. You have a secret, which is Léon's true parentage. He has a secret too: the true parentage of Florestine. (*Lowering his voice*) He is her guardian: he is also her natural father . . .

COUNTESS: (*clasping her hands*) Almighty God! Praise be!

BEGEARSS: Imagine his anxiety when he saw the two children in love with one another! Unable either to tell them the truth, or to allow his silence to be seen as encouraging their attachment to one another, he has remained dejected and unpredictable: and if he seems in favour of sending his son abroad, it is with the intention, if possible, by means of this enforced absence and the vows Léon has taken, to put an end to this unfortunate affair he believes he cannot condone.

COUNTESS: (*praying with fervour*) Oh God, Father of all mercies, to allow me in some measure to atone for the sin a reckless, headstrong man once caused me unwillingly to commit! To find me, too, something to forgive my poor husband I've always felt so guilty towards! Oh Count Almaviva! The last twenty years have been hard, they've made me cold and heartless. Now at last I shall be able to love you again. Florestine is your daughter: now I know that, she's as dear to me as if I had carried her in my own womb. We must neither of us ever speak of it, simply forgive and be forgiven. Oh Major Bégearss, what else?

BEGEARSS: My dear, I didn't want to interrupt you. Your response was just what I would have expected, knowing your good, generous heart.

It's misery that does the harm, not relief: for your peace of mind, though, hear the rest of what I have to say.

COUNTESS: Go on: you're a generous friend, I owe you so much. Go on.

BEGEARSS: Your husband, seeking a means of protecting his Florestine from what he believed would be incest, suggested I should marry her: but quite apart from my real and perhaps excessive tenderness towards you, that I have, out of respect for your grief . . .

COUNTESS: (*mournfully*) Oh my dear, you didn't want to hurt me!

BEGEARSS: We will not speak of it again. In trying to introduce the subject, your husband said something ambiguous that made Florestine think he was talking about Léon. She's very young: she was thrilled, and then a servant came in to say you were on your way. I couldn't tell her what it was her father intended: but I tried to say a word about the restraint incumbent on a brother and a sister, and that produced the outburst, this onset of irrational terror that neither your son nor you were able to understand the cause of.

COUNTESS: Léon never suspected anything like that, poor child.

BEGEARSS: Well, now that you at least are acquainted with the facts, ought we to pursue your husband's plans for our marriage? It could make good all the damage that has been done . . .

COUNTESS: (*quickly*) We must, my dear. I know in my mind and I feel instinctively it is right, and it is up to me to see it happens. That way the truth about both of them is safe: no one outside the family will ever know. For the first time in twenty wretched years we shall be happy together again, and it is you the family will have to thank for it. Dear friend!

BEGEARSS: (*raising his voice*) To ensure there's no more trouble, there is one further sacrifice will have to be made, and I believe you are sufficiently courageous to make it.

COUNTESS: Anything! I'll do it willingly.

BEGEARSS: (*solemnly*) The letters, the papers of a man who is now, alas, dead and gone, must be destroyed. You must burn them.

COUNTESS: (*grief-stricken*) Oh, God!

BEGEARSS: When that dear man was dying, and ordered me to give them to you, his last command was to protect your good name and leave no evidence that could damage it.

COUNTESS: God! God!

BEGEARSS: I have begged you in vain for twenty years now to be rid of them: God knows, they've made you unhappy enough. . . . But even setting aside the harm all this is doing you, think of the risk involved!

COUNTESS: But what is there to be afraid of?

BEGEARSS: *(looking to see if they are overheard, then speaking more quietly)* I do not suspect Suzanne: but any maid who knew you kept these papers could make a fortune out of them one day! If a single one of them fell into your husband's hands, and he might well have to pay a high price for it, you would be in the most terrible trouble.

COUNTESS: No, Suzanne has too good a heart . . .

BEGEARSS: *(speaking louder and with great firmness)* My dear, I admire you: you have done everything that love, or grief or anything else could possibly have demanded: and if you approve of the way I have behaved as a friend, this is the only reward I ask. You must burn all those papers, obliterate every memory of an offence you have sufficiently atoned for: but so we never need mention this painful subject ever again, and it's a sacrifice that must be made, I insist you do it now, this instant.

COUNTESS: *(trembling)* It's like listening to the voice of God! As if I was being ordered to forget him: to stop mourning for him, to throw off this despair that has made my life so dismal ever since he died. Oh God! Yes, I will obey the friend Thou has given me. *(She rings the bell)* He asks it in Thy name, my own conscience has long prompted me to do it: but my own weakness prevented me.

SUZANNE *comes in.*　　　　　　　　　　*Sc.3*

SUZANNE: Madam.

COUNTESS: Suzanne! Bring me the jewel-case with my diamonds in it. No, I will fetch it myself, you would have to get the key . . .

　　　　　　　　　　　　　　　[She goes off]　*Sc.4*

SUZANNE: *(a little upset)* Major Bégearss, what's going on? They've all gone raving mad. It's like a lunatic asylum! The mistress in tears, the young lady sobbing her heart out. Master Léon's talking about drowning himself: the master locked himself in his study and won't talk to anybody. And why's everyone so interested in this jewel-case?

BEGEARSS: *(putting a finger to his lips, mysteriously)* Shh! No questions now! You'll know in a moment. . . . Everything's going according to plan: everything's fine. . . . Today has been worth. . . . Shh! Here comes the Countess.

The COUNTESS *comes back with the jewel-case.*　　*Sc.5*

COUNTESS: Suzanne, bring us the little charcoal stove from my dressing-room.

SUZANNE: If it's for burning papers, the night-light is still here in the Greek urn.

She brings it forward.

COUNTESS: Watch the door. Don't let anyone come in.

SUZANNE: (*going off, aside*) I'll have to tell Figaro first!

Sc.6   BEGEARSS: I have so often longed for this moment for your own sake!

COUNTESS: (*sobbing*) Oh my dear! What a day to do it! The day my poor son was born! I have spent this day, every year, with these letters, praying to God for forgiveness, and weeping as I read them again. At least I convinced myself that it was more a tragic mistake on our part than a mortal sin. Oh, must I burn all I have left of him?

BEGEARSS: What, Madam? Will you be destroying the son that constantly reminds you of him? Do you not owe it to him to make a sacrifice that will save him from untold danger! You owe it to yourself! Your whole future security could depend on this one solemn act!

Give me the box.

He opens the secret drawer in the case and takes out the letters.

COUNTESS: (*surprised*) Major Bégearss, you are better at opening it than I am! Let me read them just once more!

BEGEARSS: (*severely*) No, I will not allow it!

COUNTESS: Only the last one, with his final words, written in the blood he shed for my sake, giving me a lesson in courage I am badly in need of now.

BEGEARSS: (*resisting her*) If you read a single word we shan't burn anything. Offer God a sacrifice that is complete, courageous, made of your own free will, and free of any taint of human weakness: or if you don't dare do it, then I must be strong and do it for you. There, they will all burn together.

He throws in the bundle of letters.

COUNTESS: (*quickly*) Major Bégearss! You are a cruel friend! That is my life you are burning! Let me keep a corner of one of them!

She tries to reach the burning letters. BEGEARSS *holds her in his arms.*

BEGEARSS: No, I will not allow it!

COUNTESS: Let me go!!

BEGEARSS: I will scatter the ashes.

SUZANNE *runs in with the* COUNT *and* FIGARO.   *Sc.7*

SUZANNE: The master's coming! He's just behind me! It was Figaro called him, not me.

FIGARO: That's right, get me into trouble!

COUNT: (*surprising* BEGEARSS *with his arms round the* COUNTESS) What is this I see, Madam? What is the cause of all this disorder? Why this fire? This jewel-case? These papers? What is the argument about? Why are you in tears?

BEGEARSS *and the* COUNTESS *stand confused.*

You refuse to answer?

BEGEARSS: (*recovering, then speaking with some embarrassment*) I hope, Sir, you are not asking us to explain ourselves in the presence of your servants. I have no idea what your purpose was in suddenly bursting in on your wife like this! As far as I am concerned, I am determined to defend my good name by telling you nothing but the whole truth.

COUNT: (*to* FIGARO *and* SUZANNE) Get out, both of you!

FIGARO: But Sir, to clear my name, you will at least admit I have handed over the lawyer's receipt there was all the fuss about just now.

COUNT: By all means: my apologies, I misjudged you. (*To* BEGEARSS) You may be sure, Major Bégearss, this is the receipt. (*He puts it back in his pocket.* FIGARO *and* SUZANNE *cross on their way out*).

FIGARO: (*whispering to* SUZANNE *as they go*) See him talk his way out of that . . .

SUZANNE: (*whispering*) He's very clever . . .

FIGARO: (*whispering*) I've done it! He's finished!

[*They go off*] *Sc.8*

COUNT: (*in a grave tone*) Madam, we are alone.

BEGEARSS: (*still affected by emotion*) I will say what has to be said. I will answer any questions you may wish to put. Have you ever known me tell an untruth, Sir, on any occasion?

COUNT: (*drily*) Sir, I am not suggesting that.

BEGEARSS: (*recovering*) Though I by no means approve of this interrogation, that seems to me uncalled for, I am honour-bound to repeat what I said to your wife, when she asked for my advice. 'No one entrusted with secrets should ever keep any papers if they could compromise the friend or loved one, now deceased, who left them in our care. Whatever grief we may feel in parting with them, however advantageous it might be for us to preserve them, we have a sacred duty to the dead, and that must be our first consideration. (*He points to the* COUNT) An unexpected accident, and they could end up in hostile hands . . .

COUNT: Major Bégearss . . .

The COUNT *tugs at his sleeve to stop him.*

BEGEARSS: Would you have spoken any differently in my position, Sir? Anyone seeking a counsel of caution, or shameful half-hearted support should not come to me! Both of you have proof enough of that, and you in particular, Your Lordship, (*the* COUNT *signals to him*) which is why, when this lady asked me, and without making any attempt to discover what the papers might contain, I advised a course of action I could see she hadn't the courage to carry out: I had, and I had no hesitation to use it to overcome what I considered to be ill-advised procrastination on her part. That was what we were arguing about whatever anyone may think, I have no regrets, either as to what I said or as to what I did. (*Raising his arms*) Friendship is a sacred trust: the word means nothing unless we are prepared to meet the harshest demands it can make on us! And now with your permission I will go.

COUNT: (*inspired*) You're the best man there ever was! No, you mustn't leave us. Madam, he will soon be bound to us more closely still: I am giving him my ward Florestine.

COUNTESS: (*eagerly*) Sir, you could not make better use of your authority as her legal guardian. I certainly consent to the choice, if you think it necessary, and the sooner the better.

COUNT: (*hesitating*) Very well! . . . Tonight . . . a quiet service . . . your chaplain will officiate . . .

COUNTESS: (*warmly*) Very well! As I am the only mother she has, I will go and prepare her for the ceremony: but you won't think your friend is the only one that cares for the dear child? I hope you don't.

COUNT: (*embarrassed*) Oh Madam . . . believe me . . .

COUNTESS: (*joyfully*) Oh yes, Sir, I do believe you! Today is my son's saint's day: if we can celebrate both events together, it is a day that will make me very happy indeed.

Sc.9   [*She goes off*]

COUNT: (*watching her go*) I am amazed. I cannot understand it. I expected arguments, endless objections: and I find her fair, kind and generous to my child! You heard her: 'I am the only mother she has.' No, she is not a wicked woman! There is a dignity in everything she does that compels me to ... a way of saying things that forestalls criticism, even when I am furious with her. But friend, I should be ashamed of myself for having looked so surprised when I saw those papers burning ...

BEGEARSS: I was not surprised in the least, seeing it was Figaro you came in with. No doubt the little reptile came hissing in your ear, telling you I was about to betray your secrets? Slander of that sort has no effect on me, I am fortunately above it; safe from such slimy insinuations. But after all, Sir, those papers couldn't have mattered to you. You'd taken everything you wanted to keep, albeit against my will. I only wish to God she'd asked me earlier! You would not have such irrefutable proof against her.

COUNT: (*sadly*) Yes, irrefutable. (*Passionately*) Out! I can't bear it to touch me: it's as if it were burning my skin! (*He takes the letter from his breast pocket and puts it in an outside one*) This letter ...

BEGEARSS: (*continuing gently*) I might have more success in fighting on behalf of the man the law says is your son. After all, he surely can't be held responsible for the unfortunate turn of events that's brought him so close to you.

COUNT: (*becoming angry again*) He'll never be close to me. Never!

BEGEARSS: Nor can he be blamed for loving Florestine: and yet, as long as he's here with her, I can't see how the child and I are to be married. It may be she is infatuated with him: she may only consent in deference to you. Her feelings will be so badly hurt ...

COUNT: Dear man, I understand you. And what you say convinces me he must be sent away at once. Yes, I shall be less miserable too when that terrible spectre is no longer there to cause me pain by his very presence; but how am I to broach the matter with her? Will she ever let herself be separated from him? What if she openly defies me?

BEGEARSS: Defies you? There is such a thing as divorce: this is a dangerously progressive country: it is now legal here: you can always have recourse to that.

COUNT: And trumpet my humiliation from the housetops? A few poor craven individuals have done it! This century has sunk low, but this is its vilest achievement. Public contempt is all they deserve: those who commit the outrage and the miserable creatures who drive them to it!

BEGEARSS: I have acted both towards her, and towards you as decency dictated. I am not in favour of violent means, least of all when it concerns a son ...

COUNT: Don't call him that: he's no flesh and blood of mine! And I intend to spee⌐ nim on his way as soon as possible.

BEGEARSS: You won't forget the insolent valet . . .

COUNT: I am too weary of him to want to keep him. Please, go straight to my lawyer, as quickly as you can. Use this receipt to draw the three million in gold he has on deposit. Then you will be within your rights to make whatever generous settlement you want to in the contract: and that must be rushed through with all possible haste, today. There: it is now yours.

(*He gives him the receipt, takes him by the arm, and they go off*)

And at midnight tonight, with no fuss, in Her Ladyship's private chapel . . .

We do not hear the rest.

ACT IV

The COUNTESS's *sitting-room, as before.* FIGARO *comes
in alone, uneasy, looking to left and right.*

FIGARO: 'Come to the Mistress's sitting-room at six o'clock', she says,
'that's the safest place to talk. . . .' I rush to finish everything I had to
do while I was out, come back in a muck sweat and where is she?
(*He paces up and down, mopping his brow*) I mean, I'm not mad! I
saw them coming out of this room with the Master giving Bégearss
his arm! Ah well, you lose one piece, you don't throw away the game.
You don't see public speakers sneaking out of a debate every time
they have an argument shot from under them. . . . But what a filthy
humbug! (*Quickly*) He persuades Her Ladyship to burn her letters so
she shan't see there's one of them missing: he's asked to explain, and
he slithers out of it! He's the pure embodiment of evil that Milton
writes about in *Paradise Lost.** (*In a mocking tone*) I was right when
I was in a rage just now: The Honourable Major Bégearss is the Devil
in the Bible who says 'My name is Legion'*: if you look close enough
you'll see he's got a cloven hoof. According to my mother, that is the
only part of him the Devil can't cover up! (*He laughs*) Ha ha ha! I
must be feeling better again: well, first because I've left the gold from
Mexico safe with Monsieur Fal, which gives us time. (*He strikes a
letter against the palm of his hand*) And then . . . Doctor of Hypocrisy,
the Demon Major, Molière's original Tartuffe, thanks to chance that
governs everything that happens, thanks to my grasp of tactics,
thanks to various gold coins I have planted, I have here a note
promising me one of your letters, in which, I am informed, you
appear in your true colours in a manner that leaves nothing to be
desired! (*He opens the note and continues*) The fiddler who opened it
wants fifty sovereigns. Well, he can have it, if the letter's worth it: it'll
be a year's wages well spent if I can open the Master's eyes to what's
going on: he's been very good to us over the years. But where's
Suzanne? She ought to be here, laughing. *O, que piacere!** Have to

leave it till tomorrow then! I can't see anything too terrible happening tonight! But why waste time? Whenever I did I always regretted it.... (*With great enthusiasm*) Not a moment to be lost: I'll go and lay the fuse; sleep on it; have a night to think it over: and tomorrow morning we'll see which of us blows the other one to smithereens!

Sc.2   BEGEARSS *comes in.*

BEGEARSS: (*taunting him*) Aha, aha, aha! Master Figaro! How this simple room is transfigured by your presence in it, Sir!

FIGARO: (*imitating his tone*) If only in anticipation of the exquisite pleasure of having me thrown out of it. Again.

BEGEARSS: Oh, fancy! A little thing like that still rankles, does it? How good of you to spend time brooding on it: we all have our little hobbies.

FIGARO: And yours is conducting your own defence *in camera*, I believe, Sir.

BEGEARSS: (*slapping him on the back*) Ah, but a man of your remarkable genius and insight doesn't need to hear the evidence, he can imagine it.

FIGARO: Well, Sir, we try to make use of those few talents heaven has seen fit to bestow on us.

BEGEARSS: And is our great manipulator of men hoping to win immense amounts of money with those he is now displaying?

FIGARO: Well, not having any money on the game, all I have to do to win . . . is to make sure my opponent loses.

BEGEARSS: (*nettled*) I shall observe your masterly tactics with interest.

FIGARO: Oh, nothing flashy; not the kind of thing that makes them gasp up in the gallery. (*He assumes an air of stupidity*) But God helps those who help themselves, as Old King Solomon used to say.

BEGEARSS: (*smiling*) What an original epigram! Didn't he also use to say 'It's a long road that has no turning'?*

FIGARO: (*proudly*) Yes, he did. Just as he was spearing a viper that was about to bite the hand foolish enough to feed it.

Sc.3   [FIGARO *goes off*]

BEGEARSS: (*watching him go*) He makes no secret of his intentions any more. Pleased with himself, is he? That's a good sign: he can't have any idea what I mean to do: he'd be looking very morose if he knew that at midnight.... (*He searches nervously in his pockets*) What? What have I done with the paper? Here it is.

(*He reads:*)
'Received of Monsieur Fal, Solicitor, three million in gold as specified in the attached statement, Paris the. . . . Signed, Almaviva'.

That's good. I have the girl, I have the money! But that is not enough: the man is weak, he'll never make any sensible use of the rest of his fortune. The Countess's influence is very strong. He's afraid of her; he still loves her. . . . She'll never go to a nunnery unless I set them at one another's throats, unless I make him tell her everything . . . as brutally as possible. (*He paces up and down*) Damnation! I can't risk a sordid scene of that kind here tonight! If you try to make events run too fast they can run away with you! There will be time tomorrow, when I have tied the sweet and solemn knot that will shackle them to me!
(*He presses both his hands against his breast*)
Oh, it's so evil, the sense of exhilaration. It's uncontrollable, the way my heart swells within me! It'll kill me, the violence of it, or give me away like a fool, if I don't let it off the leash a little while I'm here alone. So pious, so touching, so gullible! Allowing the bridegroom to walk away with a fortune! And when the pale moon is up, goddess of the night, letting her become my unwilling little wife! (*He rubs his hands with joy*) Bégearss! Well done Bégearss! Why call yourself Bégearss? Are you not well on the way to being His Excellency Count Almaviva? (*With terrifying intensity*) One step more, Bégearss, and I shall be that, in name and in reality! But there's more to do before that . . . Figaro infuriates me: I can't breathe easily with him here. . . . He called him in just then, I know it. Any trouble now and I'd be finished. That valet will be my undoing. . . . You'd say the man had second sight! I must do it now. Now! He must go, and so must his knight errant!

SUZANNE *runs in, crying out in surprise at not seeing* FIGARO *as she expects.*   *Sc.4*

SUZANNE: Oh! (*Aside*) It isn't him!
BEGEARSS: You seem surprised! Who did you expect it to be?
SUZANNE: (*recovering*) Nobody. I thought I was alone . . .
BEGEARSS: Since you're here, a word before the committee assembles.
SUZANNE : What do you mean? What committee? Honestly, in the last two years, all anybody talks about in this country is politics. I don't understand a word of it . . .
BEGEARSS: (*smiling sardonically*) Ha! Ha! (*He gathers a pinch of snuff from his snuff-box, apparently pleased with himself*) This particular

committee, my dear, is a conference between the Countess, her son, our young ward, and myself on the important matter I mentioned to you earlier.

SUZANNE: After that scene when I was there? You can't still be hoping . . .

BEGEARSS: Hoping? No. Only . . . I'm marrying her tonight.

SUZANNE: (*quickly*) Even though she's in love with Léon?

BEGEARSS: Dear simple-minded woman. You remember saying 'If you can do all that, Sir . . .'

SUZANNE: Well, who'd have thought it!

BEGEARSS: (*taking snuff several times*) So, what are they saying? Are they all talking? You're part of the family, highly respected, trusted – do they have a high opinion of me? That is what I want to know.

SUZANNE: What I want to know is what magic spell you use to have them all in your power like that. The Master never mentions you without praising you to the skies, the Mistress worships you; his son thinks you're the only one will ever help him! Florestine says she respects you . . .

BEGEARSS: (*in a very conceited tone, dusting snuff from his jabot*) And you, Suzanne, what do you think?

SUZANNE: Well, Sir, quite frankly, you amaze me! In the middle of all this terrible trouble you've caused here you are the only one who's perfectly calm and composed: I think you're like one of those Eastern mystics who can move everything by willpower.

BEGEARSS: (*very pleased with himself*) My little one, it couldn't be simpler. Firstly, there are only two pivots everything in this world turns on: morals and politics. Morals are really of no consequence whatsoever; being honourable and telling the truth: they produce, or so they'd have us believe, a kind of grinding, run-of-the-mill goodness.

SUZANNE: And politics?

BEGEARSS: (*with warmth*) Ah! Politics is the art of creating facts: the effortless domination of men and events, first for the hell of it: always for personal advantage, always by means of intrigue: never too fond of the truth, a dazzling prism of endless glittering possibilities. As deep as Etna, seething and rumbling long before it finally erupts: but when it does there's nothing can stand in its way: it demands skills of the highest order: the only insuperable disadvantage is having any principles. (*Laughing*) That's what's called negotiation.

SUZANNE: You may not find morals very exciting, but politics gives you a real thrill, doesn't it?

BEGEARSS: (*on his guard, recovering himself*) Oh! It's not politics . . .

it's you. Telling me I can make things happen by willpower! Here's
Léon: leave us.

SUZANNE goes. LEON comes in.

Sc. 5

LEON: Major Bégearss, I am desperate!

BEGEARSS: (*in a protective tone*) What has happened, my dear boy!

LEON: My father has just informed me, very brutally, that I have two
days to make all my preparations for going to Malta: no one is to
come with me but Figaro, and one servant to be sent on in advance.

BEGEARSS: Yes, his behaviour is strange, if we didn't know the truth;
but you and I have seen through him, and we must feel sorry for him.
What's making him send you away is an anxiety it's very easy to
understand. Your joining the Knights of Malta is only an excuse: the
true cause is he's alarmed at who it is you've fallen in love with.

LEON: (*sadly*) But, dear Major Bégearss, why, when you're marrying her?

BEGEARSS: (*confidentially*) If, as her brother, you believe it can serve
any purpose to delay your departure, and I know you don't want to
go . . . I can see only one means possible . . .

LEON: Oh, dear Major Bégearss, tell me!

BEGEARSS: If your mother could overcome the natural timidity that
prevents her from ever telling him what she thinks: her submissiveness
does you more harm than if she was too obstinate. Suppose someone
has unfairly prejudiced him against you: who more than a mother has
the right to force a father to see reason? Ask her to try . . . not this
evening but . . . tomorrow, and tell her to speak her mind.

LEON: Dear Major Bégearss, you are right: I know his real reason is
because he's afraid. I'm sure my mother is the only one who can
make him change his mind. Here she comes now with . . . someone I
must not allow myself to love any more. (*Painfully*) Oh my friend!
Please make her happy!

BEGEARSS: (*fondly*) I will. By talking to her every day about her
brother. . . . Madam! Red and black! It suits you wonderfully!

LEON: Oh yes, Madam, it does . . .

The COUNTESS comes in, her hair dressed, wearing jewellery, a red
and black dress, and holding the flowers of the same colours.

Sc. 6

COUNTESS: Suzanne, bring me my diamonds.

SUZANNE goes to fetch them.

BEGEARSS: (*with a pretence of dignity*) Madam, young lady, I will
leave you with this dear young man: I endorse in advance everything

that he has to say to you. I say this with a heavy heart, but do not take into consideration my happiness at becoming a member of your family: your ultimate peace of mind must be your sole concern. I wish only to fulfil whatever role you may apportion to me: but whether this young lady accepts my proposal or no, you have my solemn word of honour that the entire fortune I have inherited is settled on her at my instructions, by contract or in my will. I am going now to have the deeds drawn up: it is for the young lady to choose. After what I have just said, it would not be fitting that my presence here should make the decision more difficult for her: she must be free to take it alone: but, whatever it may be, dear friends, you must know I shall hold it sacred: I accept it without reserve.

Sc.7   *He bows low and goes off.*

COUNTESS: (*watching him go*) He must have been sent from heaven to put right everything that has gone wrong.

LEON: (*with passionate grief*) Oh Florestine! We'll have to give in: when we were first told we could never live with each other, we were so desperately unhappy we swore we'd never live with anyone. But I will keep that vow for both of us. I shan't be losing you altogether: I hoped to find a wife, and I've found a long-lost sister. We can still love each other.

Sc.8   SUZANNE *brings in the jewel-case: the* COUNTESS *puts on earrings, rings, and her bracelet without looking at them.*

SUZANNE: Your jewel-case, Madam. Earrings, rings ...

COUNTESS: And a bracelet – Florestine! Marry Bégearss: everything he does proves you're right to do so: and since it is what your guardian most wants, you must do it today. Thank you, Suzanne.

SUZANNE: Very good, Madam.

Sc.9   SUZANNE *goes out, taking the jewel-case.*

COUNTESS: (*to* LEON) You and I, my son, must not fret for what we cannot have. You are crying, Florestine.

FLORESTINE: (*weeping*) You must feel some pity for me, Madam. Oh, how am I supposed to stand so many shocks in one single day? I barely find out who I am, and I am told I must give up everything I ever wanted, and be.... I am so miserable and terrified I could die.... I have nothing against Major Bégearss but I feel agony at the thought of him becoming my.... But there it is: I must: I must make this sacrifice for the sake of my dear brother; so that he can be happy, if I can't make him happy myself. You say I'm crying! What I am doing for him is worse than if I was giving up my life for him! Mama, you must feel some pity on us! Bless your children! Life has been very cruel to us!

She throws herself on her knees: LEON *does the same.*

COUNTESS: *(laying her hands on their heads)* Bless you, my children. My Florestine, I am your mother now. If you knew how very dear you are to me! You will be happy, my daughter, happy in a quiet conscience: and that may more than make up for any other kind of happiness.

They get up.

FLORESTINE: But Madam, do you think my doing what he wants will make him fonder of Léon, his own son? Because there's no point in deceiving ourselves: he's so unfair to him, I sometimes think he hates him.

COUNTESS: Dear girl, I hope it will . . .

LEON: That is what Major Bégearss thinks: he told me so: but he also said it would be a miracle and that Mama was the only person who could do it. Will you be strong and stand up to him? For me?

COUNTESS: I have often tried, my son, but not apparently to any effect.

LEON: Oh poor Mother, you are too generous! You were too conciliatory and I suffered as a result. Your being so afraid of contradicting him prevents you from making use of the influence you should have; you're so good, so deeply respected by everyone: if you were really firm with him he couldn't refuse.

COUNTESS: Dear son, do you think so? I will try, when you are here. Your reproaching me upsets me almost as much as his unkindness.
But so you don't undo all the good I try to do when I talk about you, go into my study: you will be able to hear me from there, arguing a perfectly fair case: you won't be able to accuse your mother of lacking courage when it comes to defending her son!

She rings the bell.

Florestine, it wouldn't be proper for you to stay here: go to your room, shut the door and pray I have some success, and that peace may finally be restored to my unhappy family!

[FLORESTINE *goes*]   *Sc.10*

SUZANNE: Did you want something, Madam? You rang.

COUNTESS: Ask the Master, from me, if he'll come here for a moment to my room. Yes, ask him to come now.

SUZANNE: (*alarmed*) Madam! You're frightening me! Oh heavens! What will happen? Eh? He's never once come here without there being . . .

COUNTESS: Do as I say, Suzanne, and don't worry.

SUZANNE: Oh dear!

Sc.11   SUZANNE *goes off, lifting her arms to heaven in terror.*

COUNTESS: You'll see, my son, whether your mother is weak in defending your interests! But give me time to collect myself and say a prayer to prepare me for it. So much depends on how I put your case.

LEON: I'll wait in your study . . .

Sc.12   LEON *goes into his mother's study. The* COUNTESS *kneels at her armchair.*

COUNTESS: This is how I imagine it will be at the Last Judgement. My blood is almost frozen in my veins. . . . Oh God! Give me the strength to touch my husband's heart! (*More softly*) Thou alone knowest the cause of my long silence! Oh, if my son's happiness were not at stake, Thou knowest, oh Lord, I would never presume to say a word. But if it be true that twenty years' repentance is sufficient to obtain Thy generous pardon for my sin, as a wise friend has assured me, oh God, give me the strength to touch my husband's heart!

Sc.13   *The* COUNT *comes in:* LEON *concealed.*

COUNT: (*drily*) Madam, I am told you sent for me.

COUNTESS: (*timidly*) I thought, Sir, we could talk more freely here than in your rooms.

COUNT: Well, here I am. What is it?

COUNTESS: (*trembling*) Sit down, Sir, please, and listen to what I have to say.

COUNT: No, I can hear perfectly well standing up: you know I can't sit still when I'm talking.

COUNTESS: (*sitting down, with a sigh, and speaking in a whisper*) It's about my son, Sir.

COUNT: (*abruptly*) Your son, Madam?

COUNTESS: What other reason could I have, would make me overcome my reluctance to mention a question you've never wanted to talk about? But I have just seen him in a state that would have made anyone take pity on him: confused and terribly hurt at your having

ordered him to leave immediately: and, most of all, at how brutally
you spoke when you sent him into exile. What can he have done to
have fallen out of favour with a f . . . , with a man as fair-minded as
you are? Since that dreadful duel took our son from us . . .

COUNT: (*covering his face with his hands, with an expression of
suffering*) Oh!

COUNTESS: This child, who should never have known a moment's
unhappiness, has been more and more affectionate and thoughtful,
trying to console us in ours!

COUNT: (*pacing quietly up and down*) Ah!

COUNTESS: His brother's hot-headedness, his chaotic way of life, his
extravagance, his drinking and gambling, his wildness, caused us
both a great deal of distress. God's will is harsh but there is wisdom
in what He allows to happen: by depriving us of that child He may
perhaps have spared us even greater suffering later.

COUNT: (*as if in pain*) Oh! Oh!

COUNTESS: But in any case, you must admit the son that we still have
has never disappointed us. We've never had the slightest cause to
criticise him. He's pointed out as an example to all the young men of
his own age: everyone respects him: he is loved, sought after, always
being asked for his advice. The man who is his favourite person in all
the world, my husband, is the only one who seems unable or unwilling
to recognise his quite outstanding qualities: everyone else is delighted
by him . . .

(*The* COUNT *paces more quickly, but says nothing. The*
COUNTESS, *encouraged by his silence, continues with increasing
confidence*)

On any other question, Sir, I would think it a matter of principle that
I should bow to your will, that my feelings and my opinions, for what
little they are worth, should conform to yours, but we are talking
about . . . a son.

(*The* COUNT *becomes more restless in his pacing*)

When he had an older brother, the great weight of a family tradition
dictated that as a younger son he should take a vow of celibacy and
be condemned to belong to the Order of Malta. At the time, tradition
may have blinded us to the unfairness of discriminating in that way
between two sons . . . (*timidly*) . . . with an equal right . . .

COUNT: (*more restless still, half-choking, aside*) . . . with an equal right!

COUNTESS: (*a little louder*) But since that terrible disaster two years
ago . . . has meant that he is sole inheritor . . . do you not think it is
strange you should have done nothing to release him from his vows?

It is common knowledge your only reason for leaving Spain was to sell your estates, either to raise capital or to make investments here in France. If it was purely in order to prevent him having them, Sir, surely that is excessive, even if you hated him. Then you order him out of the house, as if he weren't allowed to live with his own f . . . , family. Forgive me for saying so, but, from a rational point of view, your treatment of him is unforgivable. What has he done to deserve it?

COUNT: (*stops, in a terrible voice*) What he has done?

COUNTESS: (*alarmed*) I really didn't mean to offend you, Sir.

COUNT: (*louder*) What he has done, Madam? You, of all people, ask me that?

COUNTESS: (*undone*) Sir! Sir! You are frightening me!

COUNT: (*furiously*) Since you have provoked an explosion of resentment that only human decency has held in check until this moment, I'll tell you what I have against him, and against you!

COUNTESS: (*more distressed*) Oh Sir, oh Sir!

COUNT: You asked me what he has done?

COUNTESS: (*raising her arms*) No, Sir, don't say any more!

COUNT: (*beside himself*) Just think, you unfaithful woman, what you did yourself! You took an adulterous lover in your arms, you brought a child into the house that is nothing to do with me, and you dare to call him my son!

COUNTESS: (*in despair, trying to get up*) Let me go, please!

COUNT: (*holding her down in her chair*) No! You are not going! You won't escape until you've been tried and convicted! (*Showing her the letter*) Do you recognise this handwriting? It is your, your handwriting and you are guilty! And the answer scrawled in blood . . .

COUNTESS: (*barely able to speak*) You're killing me! You're killing me!

COUNT: (*ferociously*) No, no. You are going to listen to the sentences I have underlined.

(*He reads like a madman:*)

'Desperate, unhappy man! What we most feared has happened. Your daring to come to me at night without warning, in a house where you grew up, where you knew every corner, every turn of the wall: the violent struggle that followed: the crime you committed, and I committed too, has now been suitably punished. Today, the feast of San Léon – patron saint of this place and after whom you were named – I have just given birth to a son, my shame, my despair' . . .

(*He stops reading*)
And that child was born on San Léon's Day, more than ten months after I had left for Vera Cruz!

He goes on reading very loudly, and we hear the COUNTESS, *at the same time, muttering disjointed phrases, delirious.*

COUNTESS: (*praying, with her hands clasped*) Great God! So Thou dost not allow even the most secret sin should remain unpunished!

COUNT: And then in the fornicator's writing: 'The friend who will give you this, when I am no more, is a man that you can trust!'

COUNTESS: I deserve it all, oh Lord, I must be punished.

COUNT: (*reading*) 'If the death of anyone so worthless is capable of stirring any last remains of pity in you, whatever the names you give the child . . . of another man, more fortunate than me . . .'

COUNTESS: (*praying*) Accept this torture in expiation of my sin!

COUNT: (*reading*) '. . . I hope the name Léon . . .' (*He stops reading*) And the son is called Léon!

COUNTESS: (*delirious, her eyes closed*) Oh God, my crime must have been very terrible if it was equal to this punishment. Thy will be done on earth . . .

COUNT: (*louder*) And branded with this infamy, you dare to call me to account for being insufficiently affectionate to him?

COUNTESS: (*still praying*) Let me not resist thy chastisement, oh Lord, for Thy hand is heavy upon me!

COUNT: When you plead for the child of this wicked man, with my portrait on your wrist!

COUNTESS: (*taking it off, looking at it*) Sir, Sir, I will give you back your bracelet then! I know I have no right to wear it. (*In the greatest amazement*) God! What is happening? Oh, I'm going mad! It must be my guilt! I'm seeing ghosts! Come to reproach me! I always knew it would – I can see it and know it isn't there. . . . It is not you; it's him, beckoning me to follow, to be with him in the grave . . .

COUNT: (*upset*) What? No, no, that's only . . .

COUNTESS: (*delirious*) So terrible, haunting me! Leave me alone!!

COUNT: (*crying out in pain*) It is not what you think it is!

COUNTESS: (*throwing the bracelet to the ground*) Wait! Yes, I will obey you . . . !

COUNT: (*more distressed*) Madam, listen to me!

COUNTESS: I will go . . . I will obey you . . . I will die . . . (*She faints*).

COUNT: (*in terror, picking up the bracelet*) I went too far. . . . She is ill. . . . Oh God, I must get help!

Sc.14   *He runs off. Convulsed with grief, the* COUNTESS *slips to the floor.*
                                    LEON *runs in.*

LEON: (*crying out*) Oh mother! Mother! This is my fault! I've killed
    you! (*He lifts her up and puts her back in the armchair, unconscious*)
    Why didn't I go, without asking anyone for anything? I could have
    prevented all this horror ever happening!

Sc.15   *The* COUNT *comes back with* SUZANNE.

COUNT: (*crying out*) And her son!
LEON: (*confused*) She is dead! (*Putting his arms round her and crying
    out*) I will not live without her!
COUNT: (*in terror*) Smelling salts! Smelling salts! Suzanne, any money
    if you can save her!
LEON: Oh, my poor mother!
SUZANNE: Madam, inhale from the bottle! Hold her head, Sir: I'll try
    and loosen her clothes . . .
COUNT: (*like a madman*) Cut anything, tear anything! Oh, I should
    have spared her this!
LEON: (*shouting deliriously*) She's dead, she's dead!

Sc.16   FIGARO *runs in.*

FIGARO: Who's dead? Madam? Not so much of the shouting! You're
    making enough noise to kill her. (*He takes her pulse*) No, she's not
    dead: it's only a seizure: a violent rush of blood. We mustn't waste
    any time though, she needs a sedative to calm her nerves. I'll go and
    get it.
COUNT: (*beside himself*) As fast as you can, Figaro! You can have
    every penny I possess!
FIGARO: (*sharply*) Look! I hardly need persuading! Her Ladyship's life
    is in danger!
Sc.17   [*He runs off*]
LEON: (*holding the bottle under her nose*) If only we could make her
    inhale! Oh God, bring my poor mother back to life for me! She's
    coming round . . .
SUZANNE: (*weeping*) Madam! There, Madam!
COUNTESS: (*coming to her senses*) Oh, it's so hard to die!
LEON: (*desperate*) No, Mama, you are not going to die!
COUNTESS: (*desperate*) Oh God! The judgement! My husband and my
    son! They know everything. . . . I have destroyed both your lives. . . .
    (*She throws herself face down on the floor*) Punish me for what I've

done, both of you! I know you can't forgive me now! (*Horrified*) A mother's guilt! Not a proper wife! One single moment and everything ruined! I have brought horror into the family! I've let loose civil war between a father and his children! Righteous God! It was inevitable this crime should be found out! I hope my death will make amends.

COUNT: (*in despair*) No, be reasonable! It has hurt me terribly to see you suffering like this! In this chair. Léon. Come on son! (LEON *reacts violently*) Suzanne, in this chair.

FIGARO: (*running in*) Has she come round?   *Sc.18*

SUZANNE: Oh God, I'm going now! (*She unlaces her own bodice*).

COUNT: (*crying out*) Figaro, help us!

FIGARO: (*out of breath*) Wait a minute, everyone stay calm! She's not in danger any more. I was out, for God's sake! I only just got back in time! She frightened me, I tell you! There, there, Madam, be brave now . . .

COUNTESS: (*praying, her head thrown back*) Oh God, in Thy loving kindness, help me to die!

LEON: (*settling her more comfortable*) No, Mama, you are not going to die, and we'll see to it that all is well. Sir – I shall never anger you again by calling you anything else – keep your titles, everything that belongs to you: I had no right to them. I didn't know. But be generous: don't destroy this poor woman by publicly humiliating her: after all, she was your. . . . In all justice, a mistake paid for by twenty years of remorse is not a crime. My mother and I will leave your house at once.

COUNT: (*passionately*) No! You must never go, ever!

LEON: She will go to a convent: and I shall take my own name, Léon, join the army as a private soldier, and defend the freedom of our adopted country. No one will know who I am, and I shall either die for France, or serve as a patriotic citizen.

> SUZANNE *is weeping in one corner:* FIGARO *is lost in his own thoughts in the other.*

COUNTESS: (*pitifully*) Léon, my dear child! Your courage gives me strength! I can bear to live if my son is generous and doesn't despise his mother. If you can suffer with dignity you could have inherited nothing better. I did not marry him for money; we shall not ask anything of him now. For what little time is left to me, I shall keep myself by working: you will be serving your country.

COUNT: (*in despair*) No, Rosine! No! I am the one who is guilty. A sad old age I'd have had without all that goodness.

COUNTESS: You'll be surrounded by it: you still have Florestine and Bégearss. Florestine, your own daughter, your favourite child.

COUNT: (*amazed*) What? How do you know that? Who told you?

COUNTESS: Sir, give her everything you have, my son and I will do nothing to prevent it: it will be a comfort to us to know she is happy. But before we separate, could I ask one question as a favour? Tell me how you came into possession of that awful letter I thought was burned with all the rest? Was it someone who had given me his word . . . ?

FIGARO: (*shouting*) Yes, it was! That filthy liar Bégearss! I caught him red-handed giving it to the Master.

COUNT: (*speaking quickly*) No, no, it was an accident. This morning he and I were looking at your jewel-case for a different reason entirely, without suspecting for a moment it had a secret compartment. There was an argument, we both were holding it, and the secret drawer suddenly came open: he was amazed. He thought he'd broken the box.

FIGARO: (*shouting louder*) Amazed there was a secret drawer? That man is a monster! He was the one who had it made!

COUNT: Is that possible?

COUNTESS: I'm afraid it is all too true!

COUNT: We caught sight of some papers: he had no idea they were there, and when I tried to read them to him, he refused to look at them.

SUZANNE: (*shouting*) He's read them hundreds of times with the Mistress!

COUNT: Is it true? He knew what was in them?

COUNTESS: It was he who gave them to me. He brought them when he left the army, after that poor man was killed.

COUNT: The friend he said you could trust, that knew everything?

FIGARO:
COUNTESS: } (*together, shouting*) Bégearss!!!
SUZANNE:

COUNT: What an evil trick! When I think how clever he was, leading me on! I see it all now!

FIGARO: You think so?

COUNT: Well, I can see what the wretched man is after. But to be absolutely sure, let me try to uncover the whole mystery. From whom did you find out about my Florestine?

COUNTESS: (*quickly*) He was the only one who knew: he told me in confidence.

LEON: (*quickly*) He made me swear to keep it a secret.

SUZANNE: (*quickly*) He told me too.

COUNT: (*horrified*) He is a monster! And I was going to let him marry my daughter! Give him every penny I possess!

FIGARO: (*energetically*) He'd have more than a third of it already if I hadn't taken your three million in gold, without telling you, and left it on deposit with Monsieur Fal. You were going to let him do whatever he wanted with it: fortunately I didn't trust him. I gave you the receipt.

COUNT: (*quickly*) The cunning devil just came and collected it so he could draw out the entire sum.

FIGARO: (*in despair*) Oh, take me out and shoot me! If he's got the money, all the work I've done is wasted! I'll run all the way to Monsieur Fal's. Pray God it's not too late!

COUNT: (*to* FIGARO) He can't be there yet, the lying traitor!

FIGARO: If he's dawdled on the way, we've got him! I'll run!

He is about to go.

COUNT: (*energetically, stopping him*) But Figaro! The terrible secret you've just been told must never go any further.

FIGARO: (*very emotionally*) My dear Master! Twenty years now I haven't breathed a word about it, and ten years I've been trying to stop a very evil man from using it against you. But please, do nothing whatsoever until I get back.

COUNT: (*quickly*) You mean he'd try to deny it?

FIGARO: He'll try everything. (*He takes a letter from his pocket*) But this is the antidote. Read what it says in this letter: it is diabolical: like looking in through the gates of hell. You'll be grateful I went to all the trouble to get that. (*He gives him the letter*) Suzanne! Give your mistress her drops. You know the way I make them. (*He gives her a bottle*) Make her lie down on her day-bed, and no noise. Only don't start again, Sir; we'd lose her, no doubt about it!

COUNT: (*passionately*) Start again? I'd never forgive myself!

FIGARO: (*to the* COUNTESS) You heard what he said, Madam? He's himself again. That's my Master talking. You know what I've always said about him? A quick temper in a good man, means he can't wait to forgive you.

He runs off. The COUNT *and* LEON *support the* COUNTESS, *on either side: they all go off together.*

ACT V

The great drawing-room as in Act I. The COUNTESS *without make-up, her clothing still in disarray.*

LEON: (*supporting his mother*) You are better here in the drawing-room. It is too warm in the inner rooms, mother. Suzanne, bring up an armchair.

They help her to it. The COUNT, *very much softened, arranges the cushions.*

COUNT: There, are you comfortable? What's this? Still crying?

COUNTESS: (*lifelessly*) Oh let me weep a little, with relief! The terrible things I've had to hear have left me quite broken! Especially that dreadful letter.

COUNT: (*raging*) A wife in Ireland, and trying to marry my daughter! Everything I possess in a bank in London, supporting a gang of thieves till all of us were dead. And, Great God, who knows how he intended . . .

COUNTESS: Poor man! Please don't upset yourself! But it is time to ask Florestine to come down. She was so wretched at the thought of what she had to face! Go and fetch her, Suzanne, but you're not to say a word of what has happened.

COUNT: (*with dignity*) What I said to Figaro, Suzanne, applies to you as much as to him.

SUZANNE: Sir, anyone who has seen the Mistress weeping and praying for the last twenty years would be too upset by the suffering she's been through to want to do anything that would make it worse.

[*She goes off*]

COUNT: (*with sudden feeling*) Oh! Rosine! Don't cry any more: and damn anyone who ever hurts you again! My dear . . .

COUNTESS: Kneel, my son and thank your father for being so generous in looking after you: thank him for your mother's sake.

LEON *is about to kneel, but the* COUNT *raises him up.*

LEON: Sir, I . . .

COUNT: Let's forget the past, Léon. Don't let's ever speak of it for fear we might distress your mother. Figaro says she must have absolute peace. But, above all we must remember Florestine is still young: we must see to it she never knows the reason all this happened.

FLORESTINE *runs in.* Sc.3

FLORESTINE: Goodness, mother, whatever's the matter?

COUNTESS: Nothing that won't make you very happy when you hear it. Your guardian will tell you all about it.

COUNT: I am sorry to say, dear Florestine, that I tremble when I think of the moral danger I was about to expose you to. You're so innocent. Thank God, from whom no secrets are hid, you will not be marrying Bégearss! No, you will not be the wife of that treacherous and ungrateful man!

FLORESTINE: Oh God! Léon . . .

LEON: Dear sister. He convinced all of us!

FLORESTINE: (*to the* COUNT) His sister!

COUNT: He deceived us. He made use of each of us to deceive the others: and you were the one he was out to capture by his repulsive, two-faced scheming. I am going to throw him out of the house.

COUNTESS: Florestine, you were always afraid of him: your instinct was more use to you than all our experience. Dear child! Thank God you've been saved from danger!

LEON: Dear Sister.

FLORESTINE: (*to the* COUNT) Sir, he keeps calling me his sister!

COUNTESS: (*exultant*) Yes, Florestine, you are a true member of the family now. That is the best secret of all. That is your father, that is your brother, and I shall always be your mother. Never forget, will you? (*She stretches out her hand to the* COUNT) Almaviva! True. She's my daughter, isn't she?

COUNT: (*exulting*) And he is my son: these are our two children.

All four hug one another. FIGARO *runs in with Monsieur Fal, the* Sc.4 *solicitor, throwing off his coat.*

FIGARO: Damn the man! Bégearss has got the money! I saw the crafty beggar taking it away just as I got to this gentleman's office.

COUNT: So, Monsieur Fal. You didn't waste any time!

MONSIEUR FAL: (*energetically*) No, Sir, quite the contrary. Bégearss stayed with me for more than an hour: made me complete the contract, add a clause about the settlement he intends to make. Then he gave me the receipt, with yours attached to it, and said the money was his, he'd inherited it, and had given it to you in confidence to look after . . .

COUNT: The blackguard: there's nothing he hasn't thought of.

FIGARO: Except what's coming to him!

MONSIEUR FAL: In the light of what he said, I could hardly refuse to surrender the portfolio. Three million, payable to the bearer: if you prevent the marriage from taking place and he wishes to keep the money, I can see very little hope of averting disaster.

COUNT: (*vehemently*) I would happily lose all the money in the world as long as I was shot of him!

FIGARO: (*throwing his hat on to an armchair*) I'll be hanged if he keeps a farthing of it. (*To* SUZANNE) Watch the front door Suzanne.

[She goes off]

MONSIEUR FAL: Have you any means of making him confess in front of witnesses that he was given this immense amount of money by your Master? Without that I fail to see how anyone can make him part with it.

FIGARO: If his German servant tells him what's happened here, he won't come back.

COUNT: All the better! There's nothing I'd like more! Oh, let him keep it!

FIGARO: (*quickly*) Let him keep your children's inheritance just because you despise him? That's no way to behave: that is being weak.

LEON: (*angrily*) Figaro!

FIGARO: (*more strongly*) I said weak and I meant it. (*To the* COUNT) What are you going to give people you can trust if you pay that amount of money to people who betray you?

COUNT: (*becoming angry*) But if we try to get it back and fail we're only offering him another chance of breaking us!

Sc.5   SUZANNE: (*at the door, shouting*) Major Bégearss is coming back!

Sc.6   *She goes off. A general stir.*

COUNT: (*beside himself*) Oh, the treacherous devil!

FIGARO: (*very quickly*) There's no time to make any proper plan: but, listen to what I say, and support me, make him feel he's absolutely safe, and I am prepared to bet my life on it we'll win!

MONSIEUR FAL: Will you mention the portfolio or the contract?

FIGARO: (*very quickly*) No: he knows too much to mention it as suddenly as that! We must lead him round to it gradually till he gives himself away of his own accord. (*To the* COUNT) Pretend you're going to sack me.

COUNT: (*confused*) But, but, what for?

SUZANNE: (*running in*) Major Bégearss!!

She finds a place near the COUNTESS *and* BEGEARSS *comes in*   Sc.7
apparently much surprised by what he sees.

BEGEARSS: Well!!

FIGARO: (*crying out as he sees him*) Major Bégearss! (*Humbly*) Ah well, what's one more humiliation now? Your Lordship, you insist on me making a full confession before you consider forgiving me.... (*To* BEGEARSS) Major Bégearss, I hope you will be equally generous.

BEGEARSS: (*amazed*) But what is going on? Why is everyone here together?

COUNT: (*brusquely*) To get rid of a criminal!

BEGEARSS: (*still more surprised, seeing the lawyer*) And Monsieur Fal?

MONSIEUR FAL: (*showing him the contract*) Wasting no time to see your wishes are carried out. All very much to your advantage.

BEGEARSS: (*surprised*) Ha! Ha!

COUNT: (*impatiently, to* FIGARO) Be quick: I find this very exhausting.

During this scene, BEGEARSS *looks narrowly at each of them in turn.*

BEGEARSS: (*aside*) Are they in league against me?

FIGARO: (*addressing the* COUNT *as if asking forgiveness*) Since there's no sense in lying, I will cut the whole unfortunate story short. Yes, as I say, I wanted to make trouble for Major Bégearss, and I am ashamed to say I started spying on him, following him about and making things difficult for him whenever I could. (*To the* COUNT) For instance, you didn't ring this morning, Sir, but I came in to your study because I wanted to know what you were both doing with the Mistress's jewel-case, and it was lying there, wide open.

SUZANNE: Shame on him!

BEGEARSS: It was! Open, very much to my regret!

COUNT: (*with a sign of irritation*) How dare you?

FIGARO: (*bowing, tugs at the* COUNT's *coat to warn him*) Ahem, Master . . .

MONSIEUR FAL: (*terrified*) Sir!

BEGEARSS: (*to the* COUNT, *aside*) Control yourself, Sir, or we shall never know the truth.

The COUNT *stamps his foot:* BEGEARSS *looks at him.*

FIGARO: (*with a sigh, to the* COUNT) And when I knew the Mistress was with him, with the door shut, burning certain papers I knew were important, that was why I rushed in and asked you to come.

BEGEARSS: (*to the* COUNT) Didn't I tell you?

The COUNT *bites his handkerchief in rage.*

SUZANNE: (*whispering to* FIGARO *behind their backs*) Go on, get on with it!

FIGARO: Well, seeing you were all in it together, as you might say, I confess I did everything I could to provoke a violent argument between the Mistress and yourself . . . which did not turn out quite as I'd anticipated . . .

COUNT: (*to* FIGARO, *angrily*) Is this speech ever going to end?

FIGARO: (*very humbly*) I'm afraid so, Sir. I have nothing more to say; the conversation that followed led to Monsieur Fal coming here to complete the contract. This gentleman must have been born lucky: whatever I've done he's always won! Sir, I've been working for you for . . . thirty years . . .

COUNT: (*angrily*) It is not for me to judge. (*He paces quickly up and down*).

FIGARO: Major Bégearss?

BEGEARSS: (*who has regained his self-assurance, ironically*) Who? I? Dear friend, I had no idea I was so beholden to you. (*Raising his voice*) When I see my dearest wishes speeded to fulfilment by these squalid manoeuvres intended to frustrate them! (*To* LEON *and* FLORESTINE) My dear young people! What a lesson! Let us set our feet upon a path of honesty. You see how the criminal sooner or later brings about his own destruction.

FIGARO: (*with excessive humility*) How true!

BEGEARSS: (*to the* COUNT) Sir, this time surely he must be dismissed!

COUNT: (*to* BEGEARSS, *harshly*) If that is your decision: very well, I agree.

FIGARO: (*passionately*) Major Bégearss, the way I have behaved to you, I deserve it. But I see Monsieur Fal wants to get on and complete the contract. . .

COUNT: (*irritably*) I am familiar with all its clauses . . .

MONSIEUR FAL: Except this one, Sir. I will read out the settlement this gentleman is making. . . . (*looking for the place*) The Honourable . . . Honourable . . . Honourable Major Jacques Bégearss . . . here we are:

(he reads:)

' . . . and to give his wife to be, in lasting proof of his affection, the said honourable gentleman, her future husband, entirely makes over to her his whole fortune consisting at the time . . . *(reading with particular emphasis)* . . . as declared and set forth in the presence of the notaries hereinafter named, three million in gold, hereto attached, in bonds payable to the bearer . . .'

He puts his hand out for them as he reads.

BEGEARSS: Here they are, in this portfolio.
    (He gives the portfolio to MONSIEUR FAL)
Less two thousand sovereigns I drew out to cover the expenses of the wedding.

FIGARO: *(quickly, indicating the* COUNT) But the Master's decided to pay for all that: I have the banker's order here.

BEGEARSS: *(taking papers out of his pocket and handing them to the notary)* In that case, count them in: have the settlement in full!

> FIGARO *turns his back, putting his hand over his mouth to stop himself from laughing.* MONSIEUR FAL *opens the portfolio and puts in the papers.*

MONSIEUR FAL: *(pointing to* FIGARO) Perhaps, Mr Figaro, you would be kind enough to confirm the figures, while we complete.

> *He gives the portfolio open to* FIGARO, *so that he can see the contents.*

FIGARO: *(ecstatically)* I suddenly understand the benefit of repentance. What do they say? Virtue is its own reward.

BEGEARSS: And what reward is that?

FIGARO: I was just touched to see both of you being so generous! God bless you, two perfect friends. We don't need this in writing. *(To the* COUNT) Those are your bonds! Yes, you recognise them. Between Major Bégearss and you, Sir, it's always a contest who can be more generous. One of you gives all his worldly wealth to the bridegroom: the other gives it all back to the bride! *(To* LEON *and* FLORESTINE) Miss Florestine! You have such a good man to look after you: I know you'll love him! But I shouldn't be saying all this. . . . It's just that I am very moved: I hope I haven't said anything out of place . . .

No one speaks. BEGEARSS, *a little taken aback, recovers and makes up his mind to speak.*

BEGEARSS: You've said nothing out of place, if my friend here has no objection to confessing: if he will ease my conscience by letting me admit it was indeed he who gave me these bonds. A good heart never wearies of gratitude: and I would not have rested happy if I had not acknowledged it. (*Pointing to the* COUNT) It is to him I owe my happiness and everything I have: and when I share it with his dear, deserving daughter, I am doing no more than restoring to her what is hers by right. Give me the portfolio: I only ask the honour of presenting it to her myself, in all humility, as we sign this blessed contract.

He moves to take it.

FIGARO: (*jumping for joy*) Gentlemen, you heard him! You can all testify if necessary! There is your money, Master! Give it to the man it belongs to; if you still feel he deserves it!

He gives him the portfolio.

COUNT: (*getting up, to* BEGEARSS) Great God! Give them to you! You vile blackguard, get out of my house! You are more devious than any devil in hell! Thanks to this faithful old servant of mine, I've been spared the consequences of my stupidity. Get out of my house this moment!

BEGEARSS: My dear friend! You have been deceived yet again!

COUNT: (*beside himself, strikes him across the face with his own letter*) And this letter, you monster! Is that lying to me too?

BEGEARSS *sees it: furious, he tears the letter out of the* COUNT's *hands and shows himself in his true colours.*

BEGEARSS: So! You've found me out! But I'll have my revenge!

LEON: You have put this family to every kind of horror! Leave us in peace!!

BEGEARSS: (*furious*) You reckless little fool! You can pay for the rest of them! Fight me! I challenge you!!

LEON: (*quickly*) I can't wait!

COUNT: (*quickly*) Léon!

COUNTESS: (*quickly*) Son!

FLORESTINE: (*quickly*) Brother!

COUNT: Léon, I forbid it. (*To* BEGEARSS) Defend your honour! You have no honour. That's not how men of your kind end their lives!

BEGEARSS: Aaah!!

> BEGEARSS *makes a terrible gesture, but does not answer.*

FIGARO: (*stopping* LEON *quickly*) No, young man! Don't do it! Your father's right. Everyone's against duelling now:* it was a craze, insanity. The only fighting we'll be doing here from now on is against the enemies of France! Let him rage! And if he ever dares attack you, defend yourself as you would against a murderer. There's no crime in killing a mad animal. But he won't dare! Any man who can sink to the depth he has sunk to is not just a coward: he is contemptible.

BEGEARSS: (*beside himself*) Damn you!

COUNT: (*stamping his foot*) Will you get out? I feel sick at the very sight of you!

> The COUNTESS *sits distressed in her chair:* FLORESTINE *and*
> SUZANNE *are comforting her.* LEON *goes to join them.*

BEGEARSS: (*through clenched teeth*) Yes, by God, I'll go! But I possess proof that you are a traitor! Your only motive in asking His Majesty's permission to sell your estates in Spain was so you could stir up trouble with impunity from this side of the Pyrenees!

COUNT: You monster! What are you saying?

BEGEARSS: That I am going to denounce you in Madrid. That bust of Washington in your study is evidence enough. I can have every one of your estates confiscated!

FIGARO: (*shouting*) That's right! Denounce a man who gave you a third of everything he has!

BEGEARSS: But just in case you try selling everything, I am going straight to our Ambassador to see he stops His Majesty's Warrant of assent that will be arriving by this post.

> FIGARO *pulls an envelope out of his pocket.*

FIGARO: (*shouting*) The King's warrant? There! I thought you might try that! I have just collected this packet from the secretary at the Embassy, on your behalf: the post from Spain had just arrived.

> The COUNT *quickly takes the packet.* BEGEARSS, *furious, strikes*
> *his forehead, takes two steps to go, and turns back.*

BEGEARSS: You'll not see me again! Depraved family: no morals and no sense of honour! Go on in your infamy, celebrate this abomination of a marriage, make a brother couple with his own sister: but there's not a soul on earth won't know the obscene truth!

[*He goes*]

FIGARO: (*like a madman*) Let him slander you: it's all cowards can do! He's no danger to you any more: we've uncovered him for what he is, he's finished, he hasn't a penny in the world. Oh, Monsieur Fal, I'd have cut my own throat if he'd kept the two thousand sovereigns he'd taken out of that portfolio! (*He is serious again*) Besides, he knows better than anyone these two aren't related either by blood or by law: they've nothing whatsoever to do with each other!

COUNT: (*embracing him and crying out*) Oh Figaro! Madam, he is right.

LEON: (*very quickly*) Oh God! Mama! You mean there's hope?

FLORESTINE: (*to the* COUNT) What, Sir? You're not . . . ?

COUNT: (*drunk with happiness*) Children, we'll look into it: and we will consult enlightened lawyers using assumed names: men of intelligence and honour. Oh children! There is an age coming when noble minds will forgive one another the sins and weaknesses they were guilty of in the past! We'll see a gentler love take the place of the stormy passions that once divided them. Rosine – as your husband I shall call you that again – come and rest: today has tired us both. Monsieur Fal, Sir! Don't go. Come, my two children! Suzanne, kiss your husband! And may the cause of all our quarrels be buried for ever! (*To* FIGARO) The two thousand sovereigns he drew out are yours until I can reward you properly as you deserve.

FIGARO: (*quickly*) Me, Sir? If it's all the same to you, I'd rather not. Why spoil a good turn I've been able to do you by taking money for it? My reward will be to end my days with you. When I was young I often made mistakes: let's hope what I've done today makes up for it! When I'm an old man I hope I'll be able to forgive myself for what I did when I was younger: I'll be proud if I can. One day has changed our lives!* No shameless hypocrite! No one to exploit us! Everybody's done their duty: don't let's complain if there have been times of trouble! There's gratitude enough in any family when you get rid of a troublemaker.

A RESTRAINED LETTER ON THE FAILURE OF *THE BARBER OF SEVILLE* AND ITS CRITICS

The Author is discovered, modestly costumed and in
a bending posture, presenting his play to the reader

Sir,

It is my privilege to present you with another little novelty of my own workmanship. I hope I find you at one of those happy moments when you are free of all anxiety, satisfied with your health, your business, your mistress, your dinner and your digestion, and can afford to grant yourself a moment's luxury to read my *Barber of Seville*: for all that is necessary if you are going to be someone capable of being amused and a sympathetic reader.

But if by some unhappy chance your health should be upset, your position threatened, if the lady has proved unfaithful to those vows that once she made, if dinner was bad or you are suffering from indigestion – ah, put my *Barber* down: now is not the time for it: go through your accounts, study your opponent's case against you, read through once more that letter written to another man you caught Rose with red-handed, or leaf through Tissot's* masterpiece on Temperance: muse on politics, economics, dietary principles, philosophy or morals.

Or, if your position is so appalling you can't bear to think about it, settle yourself down deep in a comfortable armchair, open the *Journal established in Bouillon with Encyclopaedia, by Royal Licence and Assent,** and enjoy an hour or two of untroubled slumber.

What charm could you hope to find in so trivial a piece, labouring as you are through the black fogs of despair? And what possible interest could it be to you whether or not Figaro the Barber made a buffoon of Bartholo the Doctor by helping a rival to make off with his mistress? We find it hard to laugh at other men's merriment when we ourselves are out of humour on our own account.

Again, what does it matter to you if this Spanish Barber, on reaching

Paris, encountered a certain amount of opposition, or if his being prevented from performing made my particular pipe-dreams seem of more importance than they really were? We are scarcely going to pay much heed to other people's affairs unless we are free from any qualms about our own.

But anyway, you're all right? Eating like a horse, good cook, mistress telling the truth and a good night's sleep? Then let's have a chat, by all means, and give my *Barber* a hearing.

I am all too well aware, Sir, that the days are gone when I could sit on my manuscript like a flirtatious girl, saying nobody could have it, when I was longing passionately all the time to surrender it: when I used, very grudgingly, to grant a private reading to a few favoured individuals, who thought they were under some obligation to repay my generosity by lauding it to the skies in a very pompous manner.

Ah, happy days! The place, the time, the audience worshipping me, and the bewitching charm of a clever reading assuring my success, I would skim over any weaknesses and take my time when I was on firmer ground: then, assessing the favourable verdict out of the corner of my eye with a great affectation of modesty, I would enjoy a triumph that was all the sweeter for some crafty actor not filching three-quarters of it on his own account.

But, ah me, what is there left now of all that glorious haul? At a time when it would take a miracle to hold you enthralled, when Moses' Rod* would barely be enough, I haven't even Jacob's walking stick* to lean on: no more sleight of hand, no tricks, no fluttering of the eyelashes, inflections of the voice, theatrical illusion, nothing. You are about to see such capacities as I possess stripped entirely naked: and you must form your judgement accordingly.

So do not think it strange, Sir, if I suit my style to my position, and don't aspire, as some writers do, to call you casually *Reader, Friend and Reader, Dear Reader, Benign,* or even *Blessèd Reader,* or some other condescending, I would even say offensive, form of address, by which these unwise writers try to put themselves on an equal footing with their judge, and which often does no more than make him hate them. It has always been my experience that affectation cuts no ice with anyone, and that a note of modesty in an author's tone of voice is all that can ever inspire any sympathy on the part of his proud reader.

And – dear me – what writer ever needed your indulgence more than I do? It would be useless for me to try to deny it. I made the mistake in the past, Sir, of presenting you, at different times, with two poor miserable *Dramas,** unnatural, monstrous productions as we all know, for between Tragedy and Comedy,* it has now been established, there is nothing, only a vacuum: that is the official view, the master says so, and it's all round the school. I myself am so convinced of it, that if I were now to present on stage a mother in tears, a wife whose husband is unfaithful, a sister in distress or a son cut out of his inheritance, so as to bring them before the public with any *decency*, I would never dream of doing so until I had imagined a glorious kingdom for them to reign over to the best of their ability, away in some archipelago or other distant corner of the earth: knowing for certain, after that, that the implausibility of the story, the enormity of the events described, the exaggerated nature of the characters, the grotesque ideas expressed, and the inflated grandeur of the language, far from being held against me, would rather be a guarantee of my success.

Show men belonging to the middle class, overwhelmed by events and in despair, shame on you! Men of that kind must never be seen as anything but objects of derision. Absurd citizens and nobly unhappy kings – that is all the theatre recognises to exist or will ever exist, and that's the end of it: it's all over and done with, and I have no desire to argue.

And so I made the mistake in the past, Sir, of writing *Dramas*, which were not *in the proper form*, and I bitterly regret it.

Since then, under the pressure of events, I ventured to print my wretched legal *Memorials*,* which my enemies did not find *in the proper style*, and I am still assailed by pangs of the most cruel remorse.

Today I am sliding under your nose a very light-hearted *Comedy*, that certain authorities on taste do not consider *proper* at all, and I am utterly disconsolate.

It may be that one of these days I shall risk afflicting your ears with an *Opera*: then I shall no doubt be told by young people in the future that the music is not *in proper French*, and I am already thoroughly ashamed of myself in advance.

In this way I shall spend my life making mistakes and then begging to be forgiven, committing sins and inventing excuses: deserving your sympathy and tolerance for the naïve good faith with which I acknowledge the one and overwhelm you with the other.

As to *The Barber of Seville*, I am not adopting this respectful tone of voice in order to corrupt your judgement: but I have often been told that once an author had emerged, albeit battered, victorious in the theatre, it only remained for him to be accepted by yourself – a Reader, Sir – and be torn to shreds in various papers, and he would be certain, in literary circles, of the laurel crown. My glory is therefore guaranteed

if you deign very graciously to accept my little work, persuaded as I am
that there are several gentlemen of the press who will not refuse me the
honour of their abuse. One of them, *established in Bouillon with Royal
Licence and Assent*, has already paid me the *encyclopaedic* compliment
of telling his subscribers that my piece was conceived without a plot, is
lacking in unity, has no real characters, is bereft of any intrigue and is
devoid of humour.

Another,* still more naïve, and, to tell the truth, without *Royal
Licence*, lacking in *Assent*, and even devoid of an *Encyclopaedia*, after
a candid exposé of my drama, adds to the crowning laurel of his
criticism some flattering observations of a more personal nature. 'The
reputation of Monsieur *de* Beaumarchais has taken a serious blow, and
decent people have now finally come to see that once his peacock
plumes are plucked, there will be nothing left but an evil black crow, all
brazen gaping beak and hideous greed.'

Since I have indeed been *brazen* enough to write this comedy, *The
Barber of Seville*, so that the prophecy may be fulfilled in its entirety, I
will be so *greedy* as to entreat you, Sir, to judge me for yourself, and
not be influenced by critics, past, present or future: for you know that
by their very position journalists are often hostile to men of letters: I
will even be *greedier* still, and warn you that having taken me up, you
must absolutely be my judge, whether you will or no, by virtue of your
being my Reader.

And you must realise, Sir, that if, to spare yourself the chore, or prove
my argument fallacious, you should stubbornly stop reading and refuse
to go on, you would be begging the question in a manner unworthy of
your intelligence: not being my Reader, you would no longer be the
person I am talking to.

Also, that if, out of spite at appearing to have been put in such a
position of responsibility, you suddenly decided to throw this book
away this very minute, as you are reading it, it would be the same, Sir,
as if in the middle of any other trial you happened to be plucked
unceremoniously from the Court by sudden death, or by whatever other
accident it might be had wrested you from the Bench. The only way you
can escape passing judgement on me is by becoming null and void,
negative, annihilated: by ceasing to exist, at least in your capacity as my
Reader.

And what harm can I do you, treating you as my superior? After the
satisfaction, Sir, of commanding men in battle, what greater honour can
there be than to judge them?

So that's settled. From now on I shall recognise no other judge but you, excluding even the highly-esteemed members of my audience, whose judgement is subject to appeal, and are used to seeing their sentence quashed by your tribunal.

The matter was first argued before them in the theatre, and since those gentlemen laughed a great deal, I might have thought I'd won my case at the hearing. Not so: the journalist *established in Bouillon* claims that they were laughing *at* me. But that, I put it to you Sir, as they say in the Law Courts, is simply a miserable quibble on the Prosecution's part: my aim having been to amuse the audience, whether they were laughing at my play or me, if they laughed loud enough, the intention was equally well achieved: which I call having won my case at the hearing.

The same journalist maintains again, or at least allows it to be understood, that I wanted to win over certain members of the said audience by giving them private readings, as a personal favour, in order to buy their votes in advance. But that again, I put it to you Sir, is no more than the kind of objection you would expect from a Flemish pamphleteer. It is obvious I never meant to do any more than brief them: the readings were a form of legal consultation on the matter in hand. If those I chose to consult, having given their opinion, proceeded to mingle with the judges, you must see that I was powerless to prevent it, and that it was for them to declare their interest, out of delicacy, if they felt they might be biased in favour of my Barber from Andalusia.

Oh if only they had remained biased in his favour, the young stranger and I might have found it easier to bear our brief hour of anguish! But that is how men are: if you are a success they welcome you, support you, hug you and think it an honour to know you: but beware of ever weakening! The first sign of a setback, and oh friends, remember there'll be no more friends. That was precisely our experience, the morning after that dreadful night. The Barber's fair-weather friends were to be observed skulking away, hiding their faces or scattering in panic: the women, always so brave in praising their favourites, shrank back into their hoods, or as far as their plumes allowed, looked embarrassed, avoided our eyes: men rushed to call on one another to make abject apologies for having said anything in favour of the play, and blamed my damned clever way of reading things for any specious charm they might have imagined it possessed: I was totally deserted, absolutely abandoned.

Some looked shiftily away to the left when they saw me coming on the right, and no longer appeared to recognise me: God Almighty! Others, more courageous, but making certain first that nobody was

looking, drew me into a corner and said 'Eh? How did you manage to
make us believe in a thing like that? Because I must confess, friend, your
play is the dullest thing in the world.'

'Alas, Gentlemen, I read you my dull thing as honestly as I could, in
just the same dull way I wrote it: but after your kindness in still speaking
to me after a play of mine has failed, and for the sake of your present
opinion, don't let the piece be performed again on stage: because if, by
some misfortune, they happened to play it as I read it, there you'd be
again, believing in it, and I'd be blamed, because you'd no longer know
which day you were right and which day you were wrong: and heaven
knows, we don't want that to happen!'

No one believed me, they allowed the piece to be performed a second
time, and suddenly I was a genius. Poor Figaro, who had had his bottom
soundly thrashed to the monotonous chanting of the cabal, and almost
been buried on the Friday, did not behave like Candide*: he kept his
head, and rose again on Sunday with an energy that the rigours of a
long Lent and the strain of seventeen performances have still not
sapped. But who knows how long it can last? My guess would be that
in five or six hundred years' time it'll be forgotten altogether, the French
being as frivolous and fickle as they are.

Works for the theatre, Sir, are like children are for women: conceived
with a thrill of intense pleasure, rounded out with some exhaustion,
delivered in agony, and rarely surviving long enough to repay the
parents for their trouble: more of a grief than a pleasure. Follow them
in their career: they hardly see the light of day than they are accused of
being trouble-makers, and censors are applied: as a result, any further
development is often stunted. Instead of gently watching them play, the
cruel denizens of the pit handle them roughly, and often drop them:
sometimes the actor employed to make them presentable lets them fall
so flat they never walk again. Let them out of your sight for a moment,
and you find them, sad to say, playing anywhere, but in rags, unrecog-
nisable, hideously cut about and crawling with critics. If they escape all
those calamities, and shine for a moment in the world, they fall victims
to the greatest of them all, and die a lingering death from being
forgotten: their life is over, they are allowed to sink back into oblivion,
lost for ever in the vast immensity of books.

I asked someone why there should be these battles, this relentless
warfare between audience and author, at a play's first performance,
even when it is destined later to be a success. 'Didn't you know', he
said, 'that Sophocles and the ancient Dionysius died of joy at winning
the prize for dramatic poetry?* We are too fond of our playwrights to

let them be killed off by a sudden wild excess of joy, and lose the pleasure of their company: we want to keep them, so we take great care to see to it their triumphs are never so complete that they drop dead with sheer happiness.'

Whatever the cause of their severity, this child of my idle hours, this young, this innocent *Barber*, so spat upon at the outset, far from taking undue advantage of his victory a few days later, or showing any resentment against his critics, only tried all the harder to disarm them with his natural charm.

A rare and striking example, Sir, in a century of *ergotism*,* when everything, even laughter, is calculated, when even the slightest difference of opinion spawns undying hatred, when what begins as a game always turns into open war, when insult answers insult, and is repaid in turn with yet another insult, until another, wiping out the one that's gone before, fathers a fresh one, engendering several more, prolonging the rancour interminably, so that though we may laugh to begin with, in the end even the most embittered Reader has had enough, and is disgusted, even angered by it.

As for me, Sir, if it is true, as they have said, that all mankind are brothers, and it is a charming idea, I only wish we could persuade our brothers the men of letters to leave the mean and spiteful tone in their arguments to our brothers that deal in libel, and are so proficient at it: and that they would leave personal abuse to our brothers the barristers who aren't unskilled in the department either. I wish most of all we could persuade our brothers the journalists to abandon the didactic, authoritarian tone with which they thrash artists, the children of Apollo, and make fools laugh at the expense of men of wit.

Open a newspaper, and you might think you were in the presence of a grim-faced martinet, cane or rod upraised over naughty children: treating them like slaves if they make the slightest error in their school-work. How could you, brothers? This isn't work! Literature is a way out of our weariness, a gentle recreation after work is over!

As far as I'm concerned, at least, there is no hope of your ever making my imagination, in the inventive games it plays, a slave to any set of rules: it is incorrigible, and the moment school-work is over for the day, it's out, liaising and up to every kind of nonsense, so I can only let it play. Like a shuttlecock bouncing on the racquet, it flies up, drops, so I wonder at it as I watch, soaring up through the air again, turns over and comes spiralling back to earth. If someone is good at the game and wants to join me, knock some light idea of mine about between us, he couldn't be more welcome: if he taps it back with grace and skill, I am delighted, and tl ̣ ̣ ̲game begins. Then you'd see some strokes: forehand, backhand, the shuttlecock merely fielded or returned, or, when we're fighting back, hammered in fast and furious, or rescued at the last second with a grace and skill that would delight those watching as much as it would stimulate those taking part.

That, at least, Sir, is what criticism should be, and that has always been my idea of controversy among cultivated minds engaged in literature.

Let us see, I ask you, whether the criticism written by this *Bouillon* journalist has any of the generosity and, most of all, the honesty I have been urging.

The piece, he says, is a Farce.

We'll overlook the flattery. The vile names a foreign cook may call our good French stews do no harm to their flavour. It is when he gets his fingers in them that they become so hard to recognise.

Let's analyse this *Farce à la mode de Bouillon*.

The play, he said, has no plot.

Could it be because it was too simple, that it eluded the mighty intellectual grasp of our adolescent critic?

An old man in love means to marry his ward the following day: a young lover, cleverer than he is, prevents him from doing so, and that same day makes her his wife, under her guardian's nose and in his house. That is the basic material, from which it would have been possible to construct, with just as much success, a tragedy, a comedy, a drama, an opera, etcetera. What else is Molière's *Miser*? What else is the great *Mithridates*? The form of a theatrical work, like that of any other event, depends less on the substance of things that happen in it than on the characters that bring them into play.

I myself only intended to make use of this plot as the basis of a play that would make people laugh and not bore them, a kind of *imbroglio*. I was perfectly happy if the protagonist, instead of being a villain, was an odd kind of man, who didn't care, and who laughed as much when his schemes succeeded as when they came to nothing: so that the work, far from turning into a serious drama, was a light-hearted comedy: and simply and solely because Bartholo was slightly less of a buffoon than the general run of those who are made fools of on the stage, what resulted was a great deal of action in the play, and most of all the need to give those conspiring against him more energy and invention.

If, instead of staying within the simple world of comedy, I had wanted to complicate, extend and elaborate my plot into a tragedy or a drama, do you seriously think I would have been short of material? I have, after all, shown only the least astonishing episodes of the story on the stage!

Indeed, there can be no one today who doesn't know that at the historic moment when I portrayed the tale as ending happily, the quarrel – behind the scenes, as you might say – between the Doctor and Figaro about the hundred crowns really began to become heated. Mutual abuse gave way to blows. The Doctor, who was being punched and kicked by Figaro, happened, in the struggle, to pull off the *redecilla** or Spanish hair-net the Barber had on his head, at which those present espied, not without some surprise, the outline of a hot spoon, or Doctor's spatula, branded on his shaven scalp.* I trust, Sir, I am making myself clear.

At the sight of this, battered black and blue though he is, the Doctor shouts out ecstatically 'My son! Heavens, my son! My dear son! . . .' But Figaro does not hear him: already he is raining down an even more violent hail of blows on the head of his belovèd father. For he, indeed, it is.

Figaro, who until that moment has had no family in the world other than his mother, is Bartholo's natural son. The physician, in his youth, has had the child by a lady in service, who, as a result of her misdemeanour, has been hounded out of her employment and left entirely destitute. However, before he abandoned them, Bartholo, in floods of tears, and then still only a student, heated his spatula until it glowed red hot, and used it to stamp his son upon the occiput, so that he would recognise him again if one day fate should ever reunite them. Mother and child have spent six years in respectable penury, begging, when a gypsy chief, descended from Bishop Gaurico,* travelling through Andalusia with his troupe, and consulted by the mother as to her son's future destiny, furtively stole the child away, leaving in his place this horoscope:

> After he once his mother's blood hath shed
> Thy son shall smite his cursèd father's head
> Then, turning on himself the fatal blade
> See him legitimate and happy made.

Unwittingly, the poor young man has changed his status in society: unwillingly, he has changed his name: he has grown up as Figaro, and as such he has lived. His mother is Marceline, grown an old woman and become governess in the Doctor's house, her son's dreadful horoscope her only consolation in her loss. But today all is to be fulfilled.

In bleeding Marceline's foot, as is seen, or rather as is not seen, in my play, Figaro fulfils the first line of the prophecy:

> After he once his mother's blood hath shed . . .

When he innocently punches and kicks the Doctor after the curtain has come down, he accomplishes the second line of the prophecy:

> Thy son shall smite his cursèd father's head . . .*

At that moment the most touching reconciliation occurs between the Doctor, the old woman and Figaro: 'It's you, it's him, it's you, it's me . . .' What a moment in the theatre! But the son, in despair at what his own innocent enthusiasm has driven him to, bursts into tears, and taking out his razor, has a very close shave indeed, in the sense of the third verse:

> Then, turning on himself the fatal blade . . .

What a tableau! In not revealing whether he uses the razor to cut his throat or simply the stubble on his chin, it may be observed that I could, had I so chosen, have ended my play on the most elevated note of pathos. But the Doctor marries the old woman, and Figaro, in accordance with the last part of our text, is seen

> Legitimate and happy made.

What a curtain! All I would have needed was a new Act VI! And what an Act VI! There can't have been a tragedy at the Théâtre Français . . .. But that's enough of that. To come back to my play in the state in which it was actually performed and criticised: when I am being bitterly attacked for what I have written, it is probably not the time to praise what I might have written.

The action of the play is implausible, we are told, again by the journalist *established in Bouillon, with Royal Licence and Assent.* Implausible! Let us, if you will, examine that.

His Excellency Count Almaviva, whose close friend it has been my privilege to be for many years now, is, or I should say was, a young aristocrat: for age and great employments have since made him a man of high seriousness, as I am myself. His Excellency was, then, a young Spanish aristocrat, violent and passionate, as all lovers are in Spain, a nation thought to be cold and unresponsive but in fact only hopelessly lethargic.

He has set off secretly in pursuit of a beautiful young woman he has caught sight of in Madrid, and whose guardian has shortly afterwards brought her back to her birthplace. One morning, as he is strolling beneath her windows in Seville, where he has spent a week trying to attract her attention, fate brings to the self-same spot the barber Figaro. 'Ha! Ha! Fate!' my critic will say, 'and if fate had not chosen that particular moment to bring Figaro to that self-same spot, what would have become of the play?' – 'It would have begun, brother, at some other time' – 'It couldn't have, because the guardian, as you told us yourself, is going to marry her the following day.' – 'Then there wouldn't have been a play, brother, or if there had been, it would have been different.' Is a thing implausible because it could have happened otherwise?

Really you are a bad-tempered individual. When Cardinal de Retz* tells us quite simply:

> One day I required a man: to say truth I wanted only a phantom. I desired he might be the grandson of Henry the Great*: that he might have long fair hair: that he be handsome, of goodly stature and a rebel: that he love and speak the language of the markets of Paris: and, lo and behold, fate ordained that I should meet in the city Monsieur de Beaufort, escaped from the King's Prison: he was just the man I had to have.

Are we to say to the Great Suffragan 'Ha! Ha! Fate? What if you hadn't met Monsieur de Beaufort? What about this? What about that? . . .'

Fate, then, brings to the self-same spot the barber Figaro, a great talker and a bad poet, a bold musician, a great prancer with the guitar, and sometime manservant to the Count: set up in Seville, successfully untangling beards, love affairs and marriages, a bleeding-knife in one hand and a clyster-pump in the other: the terror of husbands, the darling of the wives, and just the man we had to have. And as, in every quest, what is known as passion is no more than desire inflamed by being denied, the young lover, who perhaps would have taken no more than a passing fancy to this lady if he had met her in society, falls in love with her because she is locked in and impossible to marry.

But to provide you at this point with a complete résumé of the piece, Sir, would be to call in question your intelligence and your ability to grasp the author's intentions, to pursue the twists and turns of the intrigue as you are reading it. Less prejudiced than the *Bouillon Journal*, which is wrong, *with Royal Licence and Assent*, on every point about the action of the play, you will see that 'all the lover has to do is' not 'simply to deliver a letter', which is no more than a subsidiary and unimportant element in the plot, but to capture a stronghold in the face of vigilance and suspicion, and above all outwit a man who senses constantly where the next move is coming from and forces his opponent into some very swift manœuvring if he is not instantly to come to grief.

And when you see that the whole virtue of the climax lies in the fact that Bartholo, having locked his own front door as he goes out and given the master-key to Bazile, so that only the lawyer can come in to solemnise his nuptials, you will be amazed to learn that our critic, entirely unbiased as he is, either betrays the trust placed in him by the reader, or else genuinely fails to understand! He writes – in the *Bouillon Journal* of all places – 'The Count has taken the trouble to put a ladder up to the balcony and climb in with Figaro, *in spite of the fact that the door below is unlocked.*'

Then, at the end, when you see the unhappy Bartholo made to look a fool by the very measures he has taken to prevent such a thing occurring, finally forced to sign the Count's marriage contract and approve what he has been powerless to prevent, you will leave it to the critic to decide whether Bartholo was an 'imbecile' not to see through an intrigue that was kept entirely concealed from him! Indeed, the critic, from whom nothing was concealed, clearly had no more notion of what was going on than the Doctor himself.

After all, if he *had* understood it, how could he have failed to praise all the finer points of the work?

For having entirely failed to notice the way in which the first act introduces each character in turn and provides such a witty exposition, he may be forgiven.

That he remained unaware of any hint of comedy in the great scene in Act II, where, despite the distrust and rage of her jealous guardian, Rosine succeeds in throwing him off the scent entirely about a letter given her while he was present in the room, and makes him go down on his knees to beg forgiveness for having harboured any such suspicions, I can easily understand.

That he did not even mention the moment of Bazile being so nonplussed in Act III, which seemed so very original on stage and so delighted the audience, I am not surprised at all.

We will overlook the fact that he didn't understand the difficulties the author voluntarily created for himself in the last act, by having Rosine confess to her guardian that the Count has taken the key to the lattice: and the way the author extricates himself in two words and is away, playing on the new anxiety he has planted in the audience's mind, is indeed no great achievement.

I hope it never entered his head that the play, one of the happiest productions to be seen on any stage, contains nothing in the least suggestive, and not a thought or a word that could alarm the purest minds, even in the private boxes: no small claim, Sir, in a century when hypocrisy in matters of decency has become as widespread as the decline in morals. Indeed I sincerely hope it didn't. Nothing of that kind, I am sure, would be worthy of the attention of so major a critic.

But how could he fail to admire what no decent man was able to see without being moved to tears of happiness and pure emotion? I mean the filial piety of the goodhearted Figaro, who can never forget his mother!

'So you know this guardian?' the Count asks him in Act I. 'As well as I know my own mother', answers Figaro. A miser would have said 'As well as I know the inside of my own pockets'. A dandy 'As well as I know my own reflection in the glass'. An ambitious man 'As well as I know the road to Versailles'. The journalist from Bouillon 'As well as I know my publisher', the similes of each drawn always from whatever they love most in all the world. 'As well as I know my own mother', says the affectionate and respectful son.

Again, somewhere else, Bartholo says to him 'Ah, you are charming!' 'So my mother used to tell me, Sir.' And the *Bouillon Journal* never once draws our attention to such poignant moments. It takes a very dessicated brain not to be aware of them, and a hard heart indeed not to find them deeply moving.

Not to mention a thousand other artistic subtleties, bounteously strewn throughout the work. For example, everybody knows that actors have created more and more categories of employment for themselves. Categories like First Lover, Second Lover and Supporting Lover; like First, Second and Supporting Maid; like Clown, Magnifico, Bumpkin, Rustic, Lawyer, Magistrate or Mourner. But no one hitherto had ever been employed as Yawner. And what contribution did the author make to training an actor with very little previous experience of opening his mouth as wide as possible in public? He took the trouble of gathering together for him in one sentence all the yawning syllables in the language – 'No *more* than *hear* him *aaasking* me how I was' – enough to make a corpse yawn, or even prise open the jaws of a certain journalist, even when he's got his teeth into a thing.

In that admirable passage, where, hard-pressed by Bartholo roaring reproachfully 'What do you say to that wretched man, yawning, asleep on his feet? And to the other one who's spent the last three hours sneezing fit to blow his skull off and spatter his brains about? What do you say to them?' the innocent Barber makes reply 'Why, I'd say "God bless you!" to the one that's sneezing, and tell the one that's yawning he ought to go to bed.' An answer so apt, so full of Christian charity, and so admirable, that one of those proud critics who had been granted a seat among the Gods could not stop himself from shouting out in praise of the author: 'Lord 'elp us! Must 'ave taken 'im a week to think o' that one!'

And the *Bouillon Journal*, instead of praising these innumerable beauties, squanders ink and paper, *Royal Licence and Assent*, on dismissing such a work as being beneath criticism! They could cut my throat, Sir, but I would still complain!

Did he not go so far as to say, this cruel fiend, that 'in order to save the *Barber* from dying on stage, they have had to mutilate it, alter it, reshape it, cut it down, reduce it to four acts, and purge it of a great amount of slapstick, puns and play on words – in a word, low comedy'?

Seeing him flailing about in the dark so, it is very evident he didn't understand a word of the work he is dismembering. But I am happy to assure this journalist, together with the young man who has the job of cutting his quill-pens and his pieces, that far from having 'purged' the play of any 'puns', 'play on words', etc. which are supposed to have marred it at its first performance, I restored to those acts that we retained everything I could use from the act that was not performed, in the same way as a careful carpenter rakes through the shavings on his workshop floor for anything he can use to plug and fill in any little hole in what he has made.

Let us pass over in silence his shrill abuse of the young lady as having 'all the faults of a badly brought-up daughter'. It is true that to escape the consequences of making such an allegation, he tries to blame it on someone else, as if he hadn't written it, by resorting to the tedious expression 'One finds the young lady, etc . . .' One finds!

So what would he have her do? Eh? Instead of giving in to the wishes of a young lover of great charm, who is, as it happens, a man of noble birth, he would like our sweet child to marry the gouty old Doctor? A fine match he's making for her there! And just because 'one' does not see eye-to-eye with our high and mighty friend, 'one' has 'all the faults of a badly brought-up daughter'.

Certainly, if the *Bouillon Journal* has made any friends in France with the justice and candour of its criticism, I would think it must have made fewer beyond the Pyrenees, and that it is, in particular, a little hard on Spanish ladies.

But who knows? It may be Her Excellency the Countess Almaviva, a model to wives in those circles in which she moves, and living like an angel with her husband, though she no longer loves him, will one day resent the liberties 'one' allows 'oneself' at Bouillon in writing about her in such a way *with Royal Licence and Assent.*

Could it be that the unthinking journalist has never even paused to consider that Her Excellency, possessing, by reason of her husband's rank, considerable credit at the Ministry, could have obtained him some employment on the *Spanish Gazette*, or on the *Gazette* itself, and that in the career he has chosen to embrace, it is necessary to be more circumspect where ladies in society are concerned? Not that it's any business of mine: it will be appreciated I mention it only for his sake.

It is time to leave this adversary, even though he is the worst offender among several who maintain that 'I was unable to sustain five acts, and therefore divided myself into four to bring back audiences.' Well, what if I did? When we are hard pressed, isn't it better to sacrifice a fifth of all we have rather than see the whole lot carried off by brigands?

But do not, Dear Reader ... I mean Sir, do not, I beg you, make a mistake that many have made and which would do no credit to your judgement.

My play, which appears now to be in four acts only, is, in reality and in fact, composed in five: Act I, Act II, Act III, Act IV and Act V, in the ordinary way.

It is true that on the day of the battle, seeing the enemy relentless, the pit beginning to rise, rough and roaring aloud like the waves of a great sea, and all too well aware that those dull rumblings, heralding a storm, had brought about the wreck of more than one proud enterprise, I came to think that many plays in five acts (like my own), though excellently made in every way (like my own), would not have gone down with all hands (like my own), if the author had taken a firm decision (like my own).

'The God of the cabals is angry' I told the actors with some fervour:

Children! This day demands we make some sacrifice!

Then, giving the devil his due and tearing up my manuscript, 'God of the hissers, sneerers, spitters and disturbers of the peace!' I shouted, 'must you have blood? Then drink my Act IV, and may your fury be appeased!'

That very second you could sense the infernal din that was making the actors blanch and falter beginning to grow fainter, draw off and die away to nothing: applause following in its stead, and from the lower depths of the pit, a general murmur of 'Bravo!' arise, passed round from mouth to mouth, up to the highest benches in the Gods.

From this account, Sir, it follows that my play remained in five acts, which are Act I, Act II and Act III on stage, Act IV in the everlasting bonfire, and Act V with the other three. There is one writer will even try to tell you that this Act IV, that is never seen, is the one most cherished by the audience, simply by virtue of its never being seen.

Let the world say what it will: for me it is enough to have proved my point: it is enough for me, by making my play in five acts, to have paid my respects to Aristotle, Horace, Aubignac* and the Moderns,* and so seen to it the honour of the rule was saved.

By the rearrangement hell claimed its share. My chariot goes as well on four wheels as it ever did on five, audiences are happy, and so am I. But not the *Bouillon Journal*. Why not? Shall I tell you? Because it is very hard to please people who, by reason of their profession, are never allowed to find amusing things serious enough, or serious things sufficiently amusing.

I like to think, Sir, that I am arguing from what are called philosophic principles, and that you enjoyed that little syllogism.

It remains for me to answer certain other observations some people have been flattering enough to make about the least important drama risked upon the boards this century.

I shall ignore the letters written to the actors, and myself, that were unsigned, generally known as anonymous: judging from the clumsiness of their style those who write them have little experience of criticism, and don't seem fully to have understood that a bad play is not a bad deed, and that abusive language of that kind, though wholly suitable when applied to a bad man, is always misplaced in the case of a bad writer. Let us go on to the others.

Connoisseurs have observed that I suffered from the drawback of having to use a wit from Seville, in Seville, to criticise French customs, whereas plausibility demanded he should base his observations on the state of society in Spain. They are quite right. I gave it a great deal of thought, and, in order to make it more completely plausible, I did at first decide to write the play in Spanish and have it played in the same language: a man of taste then pointed out that some of the finer points might perhaps be lost on audiences in Paris, and that was what persuaded me to write in French: so, as you can see, I have sacrificed a great deal for the sake of the jokes: without, however, managing to raise a smile at the *Bouillon Journal*.

Another expert, seizing a moment when there were a great many people in the foyer, took me to task in the most ponderous tone, saying my play was similar to *They Can't Think of Everything*.* 'Similar to it, Sir? I promise you, this is *They Can't Think of Everything*.' 'How is that?' 'Well, they couldn't think of my play!' The expert had no answer to this, and was laughed at all the more for mentioning *They Can't Think of Everything* when he himself was clearly a man who'd never thought of anything in his life.

Some days later, and this is more serious, at the house of a lady that was indisposed, a gloomy gentleman in black, with his hair brushed up and a cane with a crow's head handle, lightly grasping the lady's wrist, politely put forward certain reservations about the truth of those shafts I had directed against doctors. 'Sir', I said, 'are you a friend of one? I should be very unhappy if some foolish joke . . .' 'Not in the least. I see you don't know who I am. I never take anyone's part: my quarrel is for the body as a whole.' This made me ponder very much as to who this man might be. 'When it comes to jokes', I answered, 'you know, Sir, it's never a question of whether it's true, but whether it's a good story.' 'Aha, and you think your work would fail the second test any less lamentably than it does the first?' 'How clever, Doctor!' said the lady, 'What a monster he is! Do you know he had the temerity to attack us too? You and I must band together and defend ourselves!'

At the word *Doctor* it began to dawn on me that she must be talking to her physician. 'I grant you, Madam, and you, Sir', I went on, very demurely, 'that I allowed myself some liberties, but my conscience was all the clearer for their being of so little consequence. Who, after all, could harm two such powerful bodies, universally obeyed, and between them ruling over the whole world? Whatever the envious may say, beautiful women will always have the upper hand by being able to give pleasure, and doctors by inflicting pain: when we are well we need love as much as we need medicine when we are sick.

'All the same, I don't know whether, in the balance, medicine hasn't some slight advantage over beauty: it's often enough a beauty sends us to the doctor, but oftener still the doctor keeps us, and never gives us back.

'So when we mock either, we should perhaps bear in mind who is likely to resent it more. We should remember beautiful women take their revenge by refusing to have anything to do with us, which after all is only a sin of omission, but doctors take theirs by having a great deal to do with us, and the consequences can be grave indeed.

'When doctors have us in their power, they do what they want with us, while beautiful women, for all their beauty, do with us only what they can.

'Spend enough time with a beauty and our need for her is diminished: but make a habit of visiting the doctor, and it can end in his becoming indispensable.

'Finally, the rule of one would seem to have been established only to ensure the continuance of the other: the more youth and inexperience are given over to love, the more our frail old age seems to be spent at the mercy of medicine.

'And since you decided to band together against me, I was justified, Madam, and entirely in the right, Sir, to offer you my excuses at one and the same time. Believe me, it's my nature to worship beautiful women and live in dread of doctors: if I say a word against women I'm lying, and if I make the feeblest thrust at the medical profession I do so with my teeth chattering in terror.

'I am certainly telling the truth as far as the ladies are concerned, and even my bitterest enemies will have to admit that in a melancholy moment, when my displeasure with one beautiful creature was in danger of being vented rather too freely on all the rest, I stopped short at the twenty-fifth verse, and repented very promptly, to make amends in the twenty-sixth to any lady I have ever angered.

> Oh charming sex, should I discover
> Deep within your heart some fire
> Oft unfaithful to your lover
> Ever true to your desire
> If I tease you, oh my treasures,
> Oh my goddesses, forbear
> If I chide, alas, at pleasures
> That I only long to share

'And as for you, Doctor, it is well known that Molière . . ..'

'I deeply regret', said the Doctor, getting up, 'I cannot benefit further from your most illuminating views, but groaning humanity must not suffer for my selfish pleasure.' You'd left me, I swear to you, with my mouth open and the sentence hanging in the air. 'I don't know', said the beautiful invalid laughing, 'whether I forgive you, but I see our Doctor does not.' 'Ours, Madam? He'll never be mine.' 'And why not?' 'I don't know. I would be afraid he might fall below what I required in a doctor if he couldn't rise above a joke at his expense.

'That doctor is not for me. I need a man so good at what he does he can honestly admit when he doesn't know the answer, witty enough to laugh as I do at those who say he is infallible: a man who'll come and talk to me – call it a consultation if you wish: advise me what to take – call it writing a prescription if you must: and devote himself with dignity and humility to the noblest work an enlightened and sensitive mind can aspire to. If he is more intelligent, he will deduce more from what I tell him, and that is all anyone can do in a science that is as valuable as it is haphazard. He explains, comforts me, guides me, and nature does the rest: far from taking offence at my jokes, he will be the first to use them against a pompous colleague. If his conceited friend says "Eighty cases of pneumonia I have treated this autumn, and only one solitary patient died in my care", he will say with a smile "I have tried to help more than a hundred people this winter. I'm sorry to say I only saved the one." That's my dear doctor.' – 'I know him' – 'Then, with your permission, I won't exchange him for yours. I have no more confidence in a pompous pedant when I'm ill than I have time for a prude when I'm well. But I'm a fool. Instead of reminding you of my apologies to the fairer sex, I should have sung you a verse I composed on prudes: it suits him down to the ground:

> To lend a lightness to my verse
> I bid my wit go wander free
> And taught by Fancy, nature's nurse
> I paint, but never what I see
> The woman of the world, and wit
> Smiles on the author, and is kind
> He is unwise, who's shocked at it
> His sneer betrays his simple mind'

'And talking of songs', said the lady, 'it was very handsome of you to have given your play to the Théâtre Français, when all I have is a little box at the Italian Opera. Why didn't you make a comic opera of it? They say that was your intention originally. The play is of a kind that calls for music.'

'I don't know if it would bear it, or whether I was wrong at the outset in supposing so: but without going into all the reasons that made me change my mind, Madam, this will answer your question.

'Our music in the theatre is too much like our concert music ever to have any real effect, or energy to entertain. We shall only begin to make serious use of music on the stage when people come to understand that you can only sing if you have something to say: when our composers come closer to imitating reality, and above all stop insisting on the absurd custom of always going back to the first part of a tune after they have played the second. Do you have repeats and rondos in a drama? The repetition is agony: it is death to the dramatic interest and only indicates an intolerable absence of ideas.

'I have always loved music: unwaveringly, never once unfaithful: and yet often, listening to pieces I am most fond of, I find myself leaning back in my seat getting cross and muttering under my breath: 'Oh, come along now, music! Why always repeat yourself? You are slow enough as it is! Where is the life? You can't get on with it and tell the story, you always have to elaborate! You don't portray the passion, you insist on clinging to the words! The poet works himself to death compressing the event, and here you are extending it!

'What use is there in his making his style energetic and compact if you pad it out with all this futile warbling? Enough of all this sterile profusion: let's be done with an unbroken diet of songs until such time as you have learned the glorious and unbridled language of the passions.'

Indeed, if our declamatory style of speaking is already a travesty of story-telling on the stage, singing, which is a travesty of the declamatory style, is obviously a double travesty. Add to that the way the phrases are repeated, and you can see what dramatic interest there is left. And the more that particular mistake is made, the more the dramatic interest is lost: the action flags. I feel I'm missing something: my attention wanders. I become bored: and if I try to think what I'd like most in all the world, I very often find it would be for the curtain to come down and the opera to be over.

There is another imitative art, in general far less advanced than music, but which seems on this point to provide a very useful lesson. Simple in its variety, the highest form of dancing already offers a model that singing would do well to imitate.

Think of the glorious dignity of Vestris,* or the arrogance of d'Auberval,* as they come on to dance a role. The dancer won't even yet be dancing, but however far away he may appear, the freedom and relaxation of his stance already make the audience raise their heads. He inspires pride: he promises pleasure. Then he is off: the musician restates the same phrase twenty times over, making every movement monotonous, and all the time the dancer is enriching his, making them different every time, creating an infinite number of variations.

See him, coming towards us, light as can be, advancing in little leaps, or taking long steps backwards, making you forget the pure perfection of his art by the negligent ease of his invention. On one foot now, maintaining the most skilful balance, suspended quite still for several bars, amazing us, shocking us with his calm and immobility . . .. And suddenly, as if he regretted the time he has spent resting, he is off like an arrow, flying away upstage, and coming back, spinning on the spot so fast the eye can scarcely follow him.

The tune may begin again, reprise, repeat and warble on: he never once repeats himself. Displaying the male beauty of a supple, powerful body, he portrays the violent movements that rage within his soul: he hurls a look at you with a passion in his eyes made more intense by the gentle opening of his arms: and as if he were soon weary of giving you pleasure, he draws himself up, haughty once again, escaping from the eyes that follow him, and the most ardent of all passions seems to come upon him, growing out of the gentlest intoxication. Imperious and wild, he expresses a rage so violent and so real he drags me from my seat and makes me frown in sympathy. But then he suddenly resumes the movements and demeanour of voluptuous quietness, wandering non-chalantly with a grace, an indolence and such delicacy that he draws applause from as many hands as there are eyes held spellbound by the enchantment of his dancing.

Musicians, compose as he dances, and instead of operas, we shall have melodramas!* But I hear my everlasting critic – I don't know whether he's from somewhere else or still from Bouillon – asking me 'What is the point of an image like that? What I see is a dancer of exceptional merit, not dancing in general. If you take an art you must take it at its most ordinary in making any comparison, not at its most sublime. After all, we have . . .'

Then it's my turn to cut him short. What? If I want to paint a race-horse, and form a true idea of that noble animal, am I to go and look for a poor gelded, vicious old nag suffering between the shafts of a cab, or clattering along under a fat plasterer, whistling on his way home from work? I would take one from the stud-farm, a proud stallion, powerful, unbridled and with a flashing eye, pounding the earth and breathing fire from his nostrils, bucking with desire and impatience, rending and electrifying the air with his fierce whinnying, rejoicing the hearts of men and setting every mare in the countryside a-tremble. Of such stuff is my dancer.

And when I talk about an art, I intend to choose my models from its greatest practitioners, works of genius . . . but I am straying too far from my subject: let us go back to the *Barber of Seville* . . . or rather, Sir, let's not. We have said quite enough about something that is really of no importance whatsoever. Without realising it I should be making the mistake of which we French are all too justly accused: of being frivolous about big issues, and ponderous and boring about little ones.

I am, with the greatest respect,

Sir,

Your very humble and most obedient servant

THE AUTHOR

PREFACE TO
THE MARRIAGE OF FIGARO

In writing this preface it is not my purpose to indulge in idle speculation on whether I have brought upon the stage a good play or a bad – for me it is now too late: but scrupulously to consider, as I always must, whether I have created a work deserving of rebuke.

No man being obliged to write a comedy that is like other comedies, if I have strayed from too well-worn a highway, for reasons that appear to me convincing, am I to be judged, as certain gentlemen have judged me, by laws that are not mine? Am I peevishly to be informed in print that I have 'carried dramatic art back to its infancy', simply for taking it upon myself to clear a new path in that art, whose first and, as it may be, only rule is to amuse and to instruct? But that is not what here concerns me.

The ill we *speak* of a work is often very far from any ill we *think* of it: the moment, it may be, that haunts us, some phrase that, if we will or no, stays buried in our hearts, even as our tongues are taking their revenge in damning all the rest. So we may accept it as established in the theatre, but with regard to those reproaches we make the author, that which has moved us most is that of which we speak the least.

It will perhaps be of some purpose to uncover to the general gaze this double countenance of comedy, and I shall have made good use of mine if, by subjecting it to this scrutiny, I may succeed in fixing public opinion as to what, in the theatre, we are to understand by 'Public Decency'.

By dint of giving evidence at all times of our squeamishness, proof that we are exquisite connoisseurs, and affecting, as I have said elsewhere, a hypocritical regard for decency in the face of moral standards in decline, we are becoming hollow, empty creatures, incapable of being amused or of judging what best may suit us: must I say it? – jaded prudes no longer knowing what it is we want, what we should like, or should reject. Already those worn-out words *good taste* and *good society* – adjusted as they always are to the level of each insipid coterie, and whose application is so wide that none knows where they may begin or end – have destroyed that honest truthful laughter that once distinguished our comic sense from all the rest.

Add to that the finger-wagging abuse of those other great words *decency* and *public morals* – that confer so imposing and high-falutin' a tone, our judges of comedy would be disconsolate were they not allowed to mouth them over every play that appears – and you will have some idea of what it is that throttles talent, intimidates all our writers, and drains the life-blood out of any plot: and without a plot all that remains is coffee-table wit and comedies that close within the week.

Last, but not least in this sorry state of things, every level of society comes to see itself as being above criticism from the stage: we could not play Racine's *The Attorneys*,* but there would be an outcry from all the George Dandins* and the Brid'oisons, and even more enlightened persons, that we were become a people lacking alike in morals and any veneration for the magistrates.

We could not have *Turcaret** performed but we should bring upon our heads Tax Inspectors, Under-Tax Inspectors, Commissioners of Trade and Excise, Duty men, the gatherers of Tolls and Supplementary Tolls, Excess Consumption, Food and Wine, the whole taxing tribe of Royal Revenue Collectors. It is true that nowadays we have no *Turcaret*s. But soften as we might a feature here, a feature there, the obstacles would remain.

We could not play the bores, the Marquesses and parasites of Molière, but we should shock our whole nobility, both the great and lesser aristocracy, modern and antique. His *Female Virtuosos* would enrage our feminine Academies of Wit: but who can begin to calculate the length of lever and the force which needs must be applied, in our own day, to raise on any stage his sublime *Tartuffe*, the Hypocrite! So it is that the author that enters into commerce with his audience *to amuse and to instruct them*, instead of devising his work entirely to his own fancy, is obliged to twist and turn amidst impossible events, to have recourse to ridicule and malice where there should be honest laughter, and to take his models from beyond society for fear he will make himself a thousand enemies he never knew when he sat down to write his turgid drama.

It therefore seemed to me upon reflection that if some man of courage did not undertake to shake the dust off, the tedium of our French plays would drive the nation to the frivolity of Comic Opera, or even further, to the Boulevards, to that pestilential scaffolding of wormy trestles, monuments to our shame, where decent freedom, banished from our French Theatre, becomes unbridled licence, and where youth consorts to suck up licentious trash and lose, together with its moral sense, any taste for decency and the masterpieces of our greatest playwrights. I have tried to be that man and if I have not invested my works with any superior talent, at least my intentions have been manifest in them all.

It was always my opinion, and still is, that neither elevated feelings nor profound morality, nor excellence and truth of comedy are to be had upon the stage without strong situations, which always have their origin in some social incongruity, in the matter selected by the writer. The author of tragedy, bolder in his strokes, dares to make use of monstrous crimes: conspiracies, thrones usurped, murder, poisoning, incest in *Oedipus* and *Phaedra*, fratricide in *Vendôme*,* parricide in *Mahomet*,* regicide in *Macbeth*, etc. etc. Comedy, being less audacious, goes no further than social incongruity, because its images are drawn from our familiar lives, its subjects from our own society. But how are we to castigate avarice, if we do not represent upon the stage a wretched miser? Unmask hypocrisy without showing, as Orgon is shown in *Tartuffe*, an abominable hypocrite *marrying the daughter and lusting after the mother*? A reckless adventurer, without having him dally with a full circle of enchantresses? A desperate gambler without surrounding him with rogues if he is not yet sunk so far himself?

Such persons are all very far from being virtuous: the author does not give them out to be so: he is not the master of any one of them: he is the painter of their vices. And because the lion is fierce, the wolf voracious and a glutton, the fox sly and cunning, can the Fables be said to be without a moral? When the author intends to castigate a fool made even more a fool by praise, he causes the cheese to fall from the crow's beak into the fox's jaws, and his moral point is made: if he were to turn it against low flatterers, he would end his parable as follows: 'The fox's jaws snap shut: he swallows it. But the cheese was poisoned.' The fable is no more than a light comedy, and every comedy no more than an extended parable. Their difference is that in the fable animals may speak like men, while in our comedies men more often than not behave like animals, and foolish wicked animals at that.

So when Molière, who was so tormented by the foolish, gives the Miser a spendthrift and wicked son who steals his casket and insults him to his face, is it from virtue that he draws his moral or from vice? What do his phantoms signify to him? It is you he is at pains to improve. It is true the literary scribblers and scavengers of the time were not slow in instructing the public how they should find it all entirely repugnant. It is also recorded that envious men of great prominence, or prominent men of great envy, also threw themselves into the attack. Observe grave Boileau in his epistle to the great Racine,* avenge his friend, now dead, remembering the facts:

> See Ignorance and Error at the cradle wait
> In purple dress'd and in the Robes of State
> Deigning to curse each Opus at its birth
> And shake their heads at lines of noble worth
> Lord A laments a scene so ill-express'd
> Lord B, enraged, won't stay to see the rest
> C, zealous in the cause of piety so spurn'd
> Demands the author and his works be burn'd
> Declares, Fire-breathing Earl, a War on Wit
> T'avenge the Court so slaughtered in the Pit.

There even survives, in a Memorial addressed by Molière to Louis XIV,* so valiant in his protection of the Arts, and without whose enlightened taste our theatre would have been deprived of every masterpiece that Molière ever wrote, a passage in which we see this philosophic author complaining most bitterly to the king that since he had unmasked the hypocrites, they were everywhere accusing him in print of being '*a libertine, iconoclast, an atheist, a demon clad in human flesh*': and that was printed with the 'Approbation and Privilege' of the king who was his protector: things have become no worse.

But because those impersonated in a play are shown as vicious are they to be banished from the stage? Who are we then to make our quarry in the theatre? Little faults and foibles, mere absurdities? Do such things justify our writing? They are as our fashions are: we are never cured of them, we do but exchange them for others.

Vice and oppression: these are what do not change but reappear in a thousand different guises under the masks they wear in our prevailing way of life: to tear these masks off and to show them as they are – that is the honourable task of any man that consecrates himself to the stage. It may be he will moralise with a smile, it may be he will season his sadness with a moral. Heraclitus or Democritus,* it is his duty, he can do no other: and woe befall him should he shrink from it. Mankind will not mend its ways unless it is made to see itself as it is. True comedy that serves its purpose can never be a lying hymn of praise or some empty address to an Academy.

But let us be wary of confusing this general criticism of humanity, one of the noblest ends of art, with scurrilous and vindictive satire directed against an individual: the advantage of the first is to administer correction without inflicting wounds. Make a just man say upon the stage, embittered by some act of kindness scandalously abused, *'There is no gratitude!'*; though every man be near to thinking as he does, none will take offence. Ingratitude not being possible if there did not exist benevolence and acts of kindness, the reproach itself implies an equal balance of good souls and of bad: we sense its meaning and are comforted. A wag may say *'Ah, but for every act of generosity there are a hundred of ingratitude'* but it may be answered with justice that *'there is perhaps no person guilty of ingratitude as has not many times performed an act of generosity'*. And that again is a consoling thought. And thus it is that by making itself of general application, the bitterest denunciation bears fruit without us being wounded by it: while personal satire, as barren as it is malign, always wounds and never is productive. This latter I everywhere abominate, and believe it an evil so deserving of punishment that I have several times officially invoked the vigilance of the magistrates to prevent the theatre being made an arena for gladiators, where those in power believe themselves justified in having their revenges executed by those prostitute and, unhappily all too numerous pens that sell their venom to the highest bidder.

Have these great men not sufficient as it is, in the thousand and one scribblers, manufacturers of pamphlets and scrawlers on walls, to make a selection of the worst of them, choose one especially distinguished for his cowardice, and let him denigrate whoever it may be that has displeased them? We tolerate such petty irritations because they are of no consequence and the short-lived vermin irritates only for a moment and then perishes: but the theatre is a giant, inflicting mortal wounds on all that fall beneath its blows. We must reserve its deadly power for great abuses of the public ills. It is, therefore, neither the depiction of vice nor of the events it brings in train that constitute an offence against decency in the theatre, but the lack of any moral or didactic purpose. If the author whether out of feebleness or fear of the consequences, does not dare to draw a moral from his material then that it is which makes his play ambiguous or likely to corrupt. When I first had *Eugénie* performed in the theatre – and I am obliged to quote myself since it is always myself that they attack – when I first had *Eugénie* performed in the theatre, all our Inquisition clamouring for *decency*, raised a great rumpus at my having dared portray a licentious aristocrat that dressed his valets as priests and made a pretence of marrying a young woman, who appeared on stage great with child without having been married.

Despite their clamour the play has been adjudged, if not the best, at least the most uplifting drama in our repertory constantly performed on every stage and rendered into every language upon earth. More charitable spirits have seen that its moral, and its dramatic interest, derive entirely from the evil use made by a powerful and corrupt man of his name and of his credit to torment a virtuous, helpless girl he has deceived and abandoned. So everything of worth and value in the work stems from the author's courage in daring to treat the social incongruity with the greatest imaginable freedom.

More recently I wrote *The Two Friends*, a play in which a father confesses to a young woman he claims is his niece that she is his natural daughter: this drama is also highly moral because through the sacrifices made in the name of purest friendship, the author is at pains to set forth the duties imposed on us by nature towards the offspring of a former love that the harsh rigour of social convention, or rather its abuse, so often leaves without support.

Among other criticisms of the piece, I overheard in the box beside mine a young *person of consequence* at Court say gaily to the ladies: 'No doubt the author is some wardrobe man that never sees a soul above a tax clerk or a draper: the back of the shop is where he's gone to find his noble Friends and then he transports them on to the French stage!' 'Alas, Your Lordship', I said, leaning forward, 'at least I was obliged to find them where it is not unthinkable they should exist. You would mock the author more, I fancy, if he had found two faithful friends at Versailles, in the *Œuil de Boeuf** or the *Carrosses*? We must make some effort to be true to life, even in portraying acts of virtue.'

Giving rein to my own optimistic nature I tried since in *The Barber of Seville* to restore to our stage the honest laughter of the past, by mixing it with the lighter tone of humour as it is today: but since even that was a kind of innovation, the play was fiercely attacked: it seemed I had shaken the state to its foundations. The extreme nature of the measures taken to suppress it and the outcry raised against my person bore witness above all to the dread of certain corrupt men at that time at seeing themselves unmasked. The piece was five times banned, cancelled on the hoardings three times upon the very instant it was to be played, even denounced in the Parliament of the day: and though overwhelmed by all this tumult, I persisted in demanding that the public should remain the judge of what I had intended for the public's entertainment. My demand was granted three years later. After the outcry, praise: and everyone said to me under their breath: 'Write more plays in this vein. After all, you're the only one left that dares to laugh outright.'

A writer in despair from being booed and bawled at, but who sees his play will run, takes courage once again, and so did I. The late Prince de Conti, of patriotic memory – speak his name and the very air re-echoes with the old word 'fatherland' – the late Prince de Conti* then challenged me publicly to put upon the stage my Preface to the *Barber*, that made him laugh, he told me, even more than did the play itself, and to portray there Figaro's whole family at whose existence I had hinted in that same Preface. 'Your Royal Highness', I answered him, 'if I were to recall that character to appear a second time, since I must needs portray him older, and therefore more knowing in the ways of the world, there would be another uproar, and who knows if it would ever see the light of day!' Nevertheless, out of respect for His Royal Highness, I accepted the challenge: I composed this *One Mad Day*, which now is the cause of so much hubbub. He graciously agreed to be the first to see it. He was a man endowed with greatness of character, an august Prince, of a proud and noble spirit: dare I say it? He was satisfied.

But God help me, what a trap I was to fall in! I yielded to the judgement of our critics in calling my comedy by the meaningless name of *One Mad Day*! It was actually my intention to unburden it of any ponderous significance, but I was ignorant to what extent an alteration in the playbill can bewilder the mind. If I had left it its true title, the bills would have announced *The Deceitful Husband*. It would have led them off on another scent: they would have hunted me, but in a different manner. But this calling it *One Mad Day* put a hundred leagues between us: they no longer saw anything in the work save what it will never contain: and my none too charitable observation on how easy it was to throw them off the scent is of more general application than might be believed. If Molière, instead of using the name *George Dandin*, had called his drama *The Folly of Alliances*, it would have borne far greater fruit: if Regnard had called his play *The Heir*, *A Batchelor Punish'd*, it would have made us tremble. A thing however he never thought to do: I did it of a purpose. But what a fine chapter might be written on human judgement and theatrical morality entitled *The Influence of the Playbill*.

Be that as it may, *One Mad Day* remained five years in a drawer: the actors knew I had it and at length succeeded in wresting it from me. Whether they were wise to do so or not has only since become apparent. It may be that the difficulty of playing it excited their rivalry, it may be they sensed together with their audience, that to succeed in comedy new efforts were necessary. But there was never a play so difficult performed with such spirit by a company of actors: and if the author – as is said – has suffered by it, there is not one single player whose reputation the work has not established, enhanced or made more solid. But to return to its first reading and its acceptance by the actors.

Upon the exaggerated praise which they bestowed on it, every level of society wished to know what it was about, and from that time forward I was obliged either to enter into every kind of argument or yield to universal demand: from that time forward also the great enemies of the author were assiduous in bruiting it abroad at Court that in this work – which was moreover '*a parcel of inanities*' – he abused religion, the government, all levels of society, public morals and that virtue at the end was trampled under foot and vice triumphant – '*as one*' they added '*might expect*'. If the grave gentlemen that spoke those words so often do me the honour of reading this preface they will see at least that they have been accurately quoted, and the bourgeois integrity I bring to my quotations will only serve to underline the better the noble falsity of theirs.

So, in *The Barber of Seville* I had done no more than shake the state to its foundations: in this new attempt, more infamous and more seditious still, I was overthrowing it from top to bottom. Nothing was sacred any longer if this work were allowed. The authorities were misled with insidious reports; powerful corporations lobbied; ladies of timorous disposition were alarmed out of their wits; enemies made for me in chapel pews and in confessionals; and I, depending on the company I kept where I was, fought off this contemptible campaign by my excessive patience, by my unyielding deference, my obstinate docility, and my appeals – when anyone would listen – to justice and to reason.

This battle lasted for four years. Add the five years in the drawer, and what remains of topical allusions so arduously uncovered in the work? It's sad to say, but when it was written all that today is in full bloom had barely begun to germinate. It was another universe. Through all those four long years of argument I asked for only one censor: they graciously allowed me five or six.* What can they have seen in such a piece of work that so unleashed their fury? The plot could scarcely be more trivial: a Spanish Grandee, in love with a girl he wishes to seduce; the struggles of this girl, already betrothed, and of the man she is to marry, and of the Grandee's own wife, to frustrate in his designs an absolute tyrant whose rank, fortune and prodigality render him entirely capable of encompassing. That is all: nothing more. The play is there revealed in its entirety.

Whence therefore come these piercing shrieks? From the fact that instead of pursuing a single villain – the gambler, the man of unbridled ambition, the miser or the hypocrite, that would have brought down on the author's back only one species of enemy – he had taken advantage of a loose construction, or rather so arranged his plot to be able to introduce criticism of a whole host of evils that affect society. But since that could never be held by the enlightened censor to mar a work, they all, by giving it their approval, restored it to the theatre. It was therefore necessary to endure it: and the very princes of society were scandalised to see, performed upon the stage:

> A brazen servant, in unseemly Strife
> Vie with his Master which shall have his Wife.*

Oh how I now regret I did not take this uplifting subject and make of it a truly gory tragedy! Put a dagger in the hand of the outraged husband – and I would not have called him Figaro – have him in his jealous rage nobly stab the high-born villain: and how he would have avenged his honour in great roaring couplets, line after line like level snores: and my jealous hero, commander of an army at the very least, would have had a rival, some thoroughly atrocious tyrant, reigning at the very worst over a whole nation in despair.* All that, far removed from our daily life, would not, I swear, have given the least offence: they would have yelled 'Bravo!' and 'What a moral work!' We have been saved, both I and my Indian Figaro.

But only seeking to entertain our native French and not to unleash cascades of tears to gush down their poor wives' cheeks, I made of my guilty lover a young landowner of the present day, impetuous, flirtatious to a fault, even something of a roué: something akin to other young landowners of our own era. But what could I have dared to say in the theatre about a landowner without offending all the rest, unless it were to reproach him with his being excessively gallant? Is it not the failing that they themselves would least deny? I can see many of them now, from here, modestly blushing – and it is a noble effort – to admit that I am right.

Wishing therefore to make mine a villain, I had sufficient generous respect for my betters not to give him any of the vices of the common people. Will you say that I could not, without ceasing to be true to life? Then cast your vote in favour of my play, because, after all is said and done, I did not.

Indeed, the failing I accuse him of would have produced no momentum towards comedy at all, had I not had the wit to match him with the most nimble-minded man in all the world, *the real Figaro*, who, while defending Suzanne, his property, makes a mockery of his master's schemes, and waxes humorously indignant that the latter should dare to pit his wiles against him, pastmaster as he is in this variety of duel.

So from a relatively energetic struggle between the abuse of power, the abandonment of principle, reckless extravagance, boundless opportunity, all that is most beguiling in seduction and Figaro's passionate invention, all the resources that the underdog provoked can muster in his own defence, there springs to life in my work an entertaining game of plot and counterplot. In this the *Deceitful Husband*, thwarted, weary, harassed, always blocked in his designs, is obliged three times in the same day to kneel at his wife's feet,* while she, benevolent, forbearing and tender, always in the end forgives – as they always do. And, as to morality, what is so reprehensible in that, gentlemen?

Perhaps you find the grave tone I adopt a little ironic: then you should welcome the other tone that so offends you when you read the work, although you did not look to find it there: that a landlord, corrupt enough to want to prostitute to his whim everyone that is subordinate to him, so that he may debauch every peasant girl in his domains, should come as this one does, to be the laughing stock of all the men that serve him. And that is what the author has roundly expressed when in a fury, in Act V, Almaviva, believing he is about to discomfit a faithless wife, shows his gardener a locked door and says, 'Go in Antonio, bring her out to meet her judges: the infamous woman that has dishonoured me.' And the latter replies 'By gum, don't say there hain't a virtuous Providence above! The times you done it up and down the countryside!'*

The underlying moral is to be perceived throughout the entire work: and if I was minded to show my adversaries that throughout my trenchant parable I have paid more heed to the villain's dignity than one had any reason to expect from the sharpness of my character drawing, I would have them observe that crossed in all his projects, Count Almaviva is constantly humiliated but never degraded.

Indeed, if the Countess used guile to blind his jealousy on purpose to deceive him, she could not have brought her husband to his knees before her without his being degraded in our eyes. If it had been a wife's unchaste design to break her sacred vows, I should have been reproached, and rightly so, with having depicted immorality: for in our moral judgement we always look to women: men we do not hold in high enough regard to ask so much of them upon so delicate a point. But far though she may be from any immoral purpose, what is most clearly established in this work is that no one has any desire to deceive the Count save in preventing him from doing as much to others. It is this purity of motive that puts the means employed above criticism, and because the Countess wants no more than to regain the affections of her husband, all the confusions he encounters are morally improving in their intent and not debasing.

That you may be all the more forcibly convinced of the truth of this, he also sets against this boorish husband a wife that is by inclination and conviction the most virtuous of women. Neglected by a husband she has loved too well, when is she first revealed for your contemplation? In the moment of crisis, when her benevolence for a charming child, her godson, threatens to become a dangerous attachment, if she permits the emotions that inspire it to gain dominion over her. It is the better to underline her love of duty that the author allows her for a moment to contend with a growing affection that wars against it, but oh, the weight that has been laid upon this fragile dramatic mechanism in order to accuse us of indecency! It is allowed in tragedy that every queen, every princess should be possessed of violent passions, to struggle against with more or less conviction and yet in comedy they will not suffer an ordinary woman should contend with even the faintest of temptations! Ah, the great Influence of the Playbills! The dramatic form is altered, so we condemn in the one what we applauded in the other! And yet in both cases the principle remains the same: no virtue but entails a sacrifice.

I would make so bold as to appeal to you, unhappy young women that your misfortune has shackled to Almaviva! Would you always make so nice a distinction between your virtue and your unhappiness at such ill usage if some urgent prompting of affection that bade fair to put them both to flight were not at last to warn you it was time to fight for them? The grief at losing a husband is not what touches us in this instance: such personal suffering is far from being a virtue! What we love and admire in the Countess is her honest struggle against a growing affection she condemns and her justified resentment. Her efforts to regain the affections of her unfaithful husband show her in the kindest light as she stifles both her affection and her anger: we applaud her triumph without giving them a thought: she is a model of virtue, a paragon of her own sex and loved by her own.

If this mystical sense of the honesty of the scenes, if this acknowledged principle of what is 'decent' in the theatre did not strike our judges during the performance, there is no purpose in my unfolding here its development and consequences: a criminal tribunal does not listen to a defence of the accused it has been ordered to condemn, and my Countess has not appealed to any National Parliament: she is to be judged by a secret Commmission.

There is a brief sketch of her delightful character in that charming little play *A Stroke of Luck.**

The growing affection a young woman feels for her little cousin the officer did not seem in that instance to arouse criticism from any quarter, although the constitution of the scenes might have led one to think that the evening could end differently if the husband by 'A Stroke of Luck' had not come home in time. Also by 'A Stroke of Luck' no one was bent on slandering the author: everyone addressed their attention in good faith to the delectable emotions aroused by a virtuous and susceptible young woman attempting to repress the first promptings of love. And note that in that same play the husband appears as no more than a fool, in mine he is unfaithful: my Countess is the more deserving of the two.

Also, in the work I am concerned to defend, our true sympathy is with the Countess! And all the rest exhales the same pure spirit.

Why is Suzanne, the lady's maid, clever, capable and radiant, also entitled to our sympathy? Because, under attack by a tyrannical seducer with more than enough advantages to turn the head of a girl in her position in society, she does not hesitate to bring word of the Count's intentions to the two persons most concerned with watching over her wellbeing – her mistress and the man to whom she is betrothed – because in her entire role, almost the longest in the play, there is not one sentence, not a word, that does not breathe innocence and devotion to her duties. The sole deception she allows herself is for the sake of her mistress, to whom her loyalty is unwavering and whose purposes are wholly honest.

Why, in the liberties he takes with his master, is it that Figaro arouses my amusement, never my indignation? Because, contrary to the general run of valets, he is not – and you know it – dishonest and the villain of the piece: seeing him obliged by his condition in society to repulse ill-usage by his wits alone, we forgive him everything the moment we know he only gulls his master for the purpose of preserving what he loves and rescuing his property.

So it is that, with the exception of Almaviva and his minions, every personage in the play acts according to the dictates of his duty. If you believe them to be dishonest in speaking ill of one another, the rule will hardly hold. Consider the honest men of our age: they spend their lives in doing little else! It will even become so accepted a thing to tear a man to pieces without pity when his back is turned but I, who always defend

them, often hear them mutter 'What a fiend the man is, and so
provoking! Not a creature on earth he hasn't a kind word for!'

So is it after all my little page that so outrages you and the immorality
you condemn as lying at the core of the work only to be found at its
periphery? Oh simpering critics! Unwearying wits! Moral Inquisitors,
that damn in the twinkling of an eye five years of mental labour: for
once be just, we will not take it as a precedent. Is a child of thirteen, at
the first stirrings of love, curious about everything and understanding
nothing, predisposed to worship as one is at that happy age, what is to
him a heavenly body that Fate has made his godmother, a subject of
scandal and concern? Adored by all the household, quick, mischievous
and impassioned like any other clever child: in his impetuous high
spirits and without once intending it, he upsets ten times over all the
Count's nefarious schemes. A child of nature both in years and by
instinct, everything he sees is capable of throwing him in a frenzy:
perhaps in truth he is no longer a child, but he is not yet a man, and
that is the moment I chose to show him, arousing our affectionate
sympathy without anyone being obliged to blush. That which in his
innocence he feels himself, he inspires everywhere in others. Are we to
say he is in love with love? Stern critics – that is not the word that we
should use: you are too enlightened all of you not to know that love,
even the purest love contains some measure of self-interest: it is not yet
love but we know that one day soon it will be. And that is what the
author has playfully put into the mouth of Suzanne when she says to
the child 'Oh, in two or three years I swear you will be the biggest little
rip . . . .'*

In order to establish him more clearly as a child, we purposefully
have Figaro address him in familiar terms. Suppose that he was two
years older, would any valet in the house dare take such liberties? Look
at him just before he leaves the stage: no sooner is he in his officer's
tunic than his hand flies to his sword hilt at the Count's first twitting
him as to whose face has been slapped in the darkness. The little rascal
will one day be a proud Spaniard: now he is a child and no more. Have
I not watched our ladies, in their boxes, grow distracted for love of my
page? What do they want? Alas, nothing: they feel sympathy with him
too, but like the Countess, a pure and innocent sympathy . . . they are
touched and yet not touched.

But is it the figure of our page or his master's conscience that so
torments the latter, every time the Author condemns them to encounter
one another on the stage? Remember this perception, because it may set
you on the right road: or, rather, take it as an indication that the child

was introduced for the sole purpose of enforcing the moral of the work, by showing you that the man who is entirely master in his own house, the moment he enters upon a criminal undertaking, may be thrown into despair by a person of the least importance, who dreads meeting him.

When my page is eighteen, with the eager and passionate nature with which I have endowed him, I shall commit a crime myself if I allow him on the stage. But at thirteen what does he inspire? Some tender, gentle sensation that is not friendship and that is not love and yet possesses something of the two. I should be hard put to it to be believed as to the innocence of these impressions, were we living in a century less chaste, in one of those hard-bargaining ages when, desiring everything before it had by nature come to ripen, like the hothouse fruit, the great married their children off at twelve and bent nature, modesty and inclination to their most sordid customs, eager before all else to wrest from these half-reared creatures beings still less rearable, whose happiness was of concern to none and who were but a pretext for a kind of barter in advantages that bore no relation to themselves but only to their names. Happily, those days are now distant, and the character of my page, in itself of no significance, acquires it in relation to the Count – a point the moralist will grasp at once but which has not yet struck the general run of our judges.

In this work then every important role has some moral purpose. The sole exception seems to be the role of Marceline. Guilty of an indiscretion long before, of which her Figaro was the issue, she should, we are informed, at least be seen to be punished by her guilt and shame at the moment she recognises her son. The Author could have drawn a profounder moral lesson: in the society he wishes to improve, the crime in the seduction of a young girl is committed by men and not herself. Why then did he not do so?

Reasonable critics, he did! Study the following scene that formed the core of the third act, and which the players beg me to suppress for fear so severe a passage would cast a pall over the general gaiety of the action.

When Molière has thoroughly humiliated the trull or trollop in *The Misanthrope** by the public reading of her letters to all her lovers, he leaves her degraded by the blows he has struck her: he is right: what was he to do? Wicked by inclination and by choice, a battle-scarred widow, a woman of the Court, with no excuse for the ill she has committed, making an honest man's life a torment to him, he abandons her to our scorn and so bears home his moral. As for myself, seizing on Marceline's avowal at the instant of recognition, I showed this woman humiliated, Bartholo's rejection of her and Figaro, son to them both, directing public vigilance to the true authors of those horrors into which the daughters of the common people, if they are fair of face, are so pitilessly dragged. This is how the scene proceeds:

BRID'OISON: (*speaking of* FIGARO *who has just recognised* MARCE-LINE *as his mother*) It's c-clear he will not marry her.

BARTHOLO: And nor will I!

MARCELINE: And nor will you? What of your son? You swore to me . . .

BARTHOLO: I was mad. If memories like that were binding, one would have to marry everybody.

BRID'OISON: And if you thought about it for as l-l-l-long as that, nobody would ever marry anyone.

BARTHOLO: Such notorious misdemeanours! Your lamentable youth!

MARCELINE: Yes, lamentable: and more so than you think. I don't deny I made mistakes! What has come to light today is more than proof enough of that. But it is very hard to have to expiate them after thirty years of leading a blameless life. From birth it was my nature to be virtuous, and I became so as soon as they permitted me to use my reason. . . . But at that age, when we have our illusions, our innocence and almost nothing else, when seducers are besieging us and we feel most keenly the cruel edge of poverty, what can a child do against so many enemies in league with one another? And yet some here condemn us most severely that may themselves have made a dozen women miserable.

FIGARO: Those that are the most guilty are least generous: that's always true.

MARCELINE: It's more than ingratitude in men: it's scorn, wanting to destroy the toys you played with in your lust: your victims! It's you that should be punished for the errors of our youth! You and your magistrates, so proud of being able to condemn us. . . . Even in the most exalted circles, women only receive the most contemptible treatment, trapped with the appearance of respect and love into a slavery that is all too real! Treated as children in property, punished as adults for our faults. However you consider it, your behaviour towards us can only inspire loathing, or else pity.

FIGARO: It's true.

COUNT: (*aside*) Too true.

BRID'OISON: My G-G-G-od, it's true!

MARCELINE: But what is it to us, my son, to be rejected by an unjust man? Do not consider where you came from, look where you are going. That is all that matters to any of us. In a few months your bride will be dependent on no one but herself. She'll marry you, I vouch for that. . . .

FIGARO: Everything you say is solid gold, mother, and I will follow your advice. What fools we are though! Thousands and thousands of years the earth's been turning, and in all that ocean of time, of which I happen to have scooped up thirty paltry years I'll never see again, I was torturing myself to find out who I owed them to! I pity anyone who lets it worry them. To spend a lifetime fretting, chafing endlessly against the yoke, like a poor old horse on the towpath, dragging against the stream, that can never rest even when they stop he goes on pulling although he has come to a standstill. We'll wait! Father, you have my apologies . . . and you, mother, embrace me . . . as maternally as you can.*

I much regretted having lost this scene and now the piece is known; if the players had the courage to restore it as I have besought them, I believe the public would thank them for it very heartily. They would no longer even be obliged to answer the accusation, as I was at the reading of it, made by certain critics in polite society, who reproached me for having aroused their interest in a loose woman. No, gentlemen, I do not speak of it here in order to excuse her morals but to make you blush at yours, on a point that is of all others most destructive to public decency: the corruption of the young. I was right to say you found my play too frivolous, for being sometimes too severe. It all depends how you choose to understand it.

'But your Figaro is a Catherine Wheel hurling out sparks and spilling fire and singeing everyone.' To say 'everyone' is to exaggerate. They should be grateful to me. It does not singe those that believe they recognise themselves depicted: the time might well be ripe to compose a stage play on the matter. Would they allow me to write like an author newly out of college, always to make children laugh without once making grown men think? Am I not to be permitted a little moralising for the sake of my having entertained you, as the French are allowed a little madness for the sake of their profound philosophy.

If I have only poured upon our follies a little gentle derision it is not for want of caustic I might douse them with: any man that has said all he knows in his work, has been more thorough than I have. But I keep a throng of ideas that press upon me one of the most moral subjects in the theatre, at present on my work bench. *A Mother's Guilt*: and if the deluge of public disgust ever allows me to complete it, my plan being to cause all women of feeling to shed tears, I shall make my language more elevated as befits the dignity of my dramatic situations, I shall squander strokes of the most dire morality, and pulverise those vices I have too much indulged. Make your preparations therefore, Gentlemen, to torment me once again: I have already grown in labour: I have blackened a great deal of paper in the service of your rage.

And you, honest men of no party, that take pleasure in everything without ever taking a side, you the young and virtuous and shy that find my *One Mad Day* entertains you – and I only undertake to defend it in order that your taste may be justified – when you see in Society one of those certain individuals vaguely criticise the play, condemning everything without citing any particular instance, finding it above all 'offends against decency', examine the man closely, inform yourself as to his office, his estate and character and you will know at once what line in the work it was that wounded him.

It is understood, I hope, that I am not talking of those literary parasites that sell their bulletins or their pamphlets for so many farthings a paragraph. These, like Father Bazile, may slander us: 'even if it was malicious gossip no one would believe him'.* Still less do I speak of those ignominious practitioners in libel that have found no other means to still their frenzy – assassination being too dangerous – than by hurling down iniquitous verses against the author from above the stage while his play was being performed. They are aware I know them: if it had been my purpose to name them it had been to those responsible for public order: their torment was to have lived in terror I would do so, and that is revenge enough for me. But no one will ever imagine the degree of public suspicion they were able to arouse with one craven epigram. Like those shifty street-traders on the Pont Neuf who try to lend lustre to their poisonous concoctions by hoisting a sign above their stalls with orders of merit, stars and coronets.

No, I mean our great men, who, wounded for reasons we are ignorant of by the criticism scattered through the work, take it upon themselves to malign it while continuing to be seen about the theatre.

It is a rare pleasure to watch them from below when they attend the play. Caught in the most diverting of predicaments, daring neither to seem entertained or angry: to see them lean forward at the edge of their box, ready to ridicule the author, then suddenly draw back to hide a snigger: carried away by one line from the stage, then all at once with a face like thunder at some piece of moralising: at the most trivial of jokes, gloomily affecting amazement, looking their wives straight in the eye with a kind of outraged innocence as if to reproach them for suffering anything so scandalous: then, when there is prolonged applause, staring at the audience with a withering contempt, as if wishing to reduce it to silence: always on the verge of shouting at them, like the courtier Molière speaks of, who, outraged at the success of *The School for Wives*, screamed down from his balcony 'Laugh, damn you, laugh!'* A pleasure indeed, and many is the time I have enjoyed it.

Which reminds me of another. At the first performance of *One Mad Day*, when the tempers were running high in the foyer – even among honest plebeians – at what they amusingly described as 'my audacity'. A little, dry, abrupt old man, irritated at all their shouting, struck the floor with his stick and said as he walked out, 'The people of this country are like children: they scream whenever anyone wipes their arse!' He had some sense that old man. What he said could have been more delicately expressed but I defy anyone to have improved the thought.

In this intention to find fault in everything it is inevitable the most judicious touches should have been wilfully misunderstood. Twenty times I must have heard a murmur coming down from the boxes on Figaro's line:

COUNT: A detestable reputation.
FIGARO: And if I am worth more than my reputation? Do you know many lords that you could say as much of?*

I, myself, would say there were none: that there could not be, save in very rare exceptions. A man that is obscure or little known may be worth more than his reputation, which is after all no more than the opinion of others. But though a fool in office seems twice the fool for being no longer able to conceal it, so a noble lord, a man raised up in honours, placed by birth and fortune upon the stage of public events, and who upon his entering into the world saw all things prejudiced in his favour, is still worth less than his reputation if he proceeds to squander it and render it forfeit. Is an assertion so simple and innocent of sarcasm to arouse a murmur of protest? If it seems offensive in its implications to great men that care little for their reputation, in what sense can it be taken as an epigram on those deserving of our respect; and what more valid maxim ever written for the stage can serve as a rein upon the powerful and teach a lesson to those that never receive any other?

Not that we should ever forget, as one stern writer observed,* and I take the liberty to quote him as he is of my own opinion – 'Not that we should ever forget', he said,

> how much we are beholden to the upper orders of society: far from it. It is right and proper that the advantages of birth should, of all others, be least open to dispute, because the gift freely bestowed by heredity, relating to the achievements, virtues and politics of the ancestors of whoever received it, cannot in any way offend the self-esteem of those to whom it was denied: because in a monarchy, were the intermediary ranks to be removed, there would be too great a distance between the monarch and his subjects: soon we should see only a despot and his slaves. The preservation of a graduated ladder from the ploughman to the potentate is of equal benefit to men of every rank, and is, in a monarchy, perhaps the most stable bulwark of its constitution.

But what author can have spoken so? Who made that profession of faith in the aristocracy I am supposed to be so far from ascribing to? It was Pierre-Augustin Caron de Beaumarchais, arguing in a written deposition to the Parlement of Aix in 1778 a case of great import and severity* that was soon to decide a matter of honour between a nobleman and himself. In the work I now defend there is no attack upon rank, but on the abuse of all rank: only those guilty of such abuse have reason to take against it: and so the murmurs are explained. But are we to believe that these abuses are become so sacred that a single one may not be attacked without us finding twenty supporters ready to defend it? Is a great advocate, a respected magistrate, to take as personal comment on himself Bartholo's defence or Brid'oison's judgement? Figaro's line on the undignified abuse of the privileges of the court in our own day – 'it is to degrade the noblest of institutions'* – has demonstrated well enough the case I make for the noble calling of attorney, and my respect for the magistrature can hardly remain in question when it is known in what school I studied when the following extract is read also from a moralist, who in talking of the magistrates, expresses himself in these formal terms.

> What man of leisure would be ready, for the most modest honorarium, to perform the harsh daily exercise of rising at four o'clock in the morning to go to the Palace of Justice, day after day, to concern himself, according to the rituals prescribed, with interests that are never his own, to suffer the ceaseless tedium of importunity, the nausea of solicitation, the attorneys' digressions, the monotony of hearings, the weariness of the deliberations and the concentration of mind

necessary to pronouncing judgement, if he did not believe himself rewarded for this toilsome life by the esteem and consideration of the public? And what is that esteem but a judgement that is only flattering to good magistrates by reason of its excessive rigour against the bad?

But what writer can be my teacher in these lessons? You will think that once again it was Pierre-Augustin: he, it is, in 1773, in his fourth 'Memorial',* defending to the death his miserable existence, then under attack by a so-called magistrate. I have therefore the highest regard for what all of us are obliged to respect, and condemn anything that can damage it.

'But in this *One Mad Day* you are not concerned with rooting out abuses! You take abominable liberties on the public stage: worst of all that monologue of yours about men fallen out of favour has things in it that go too far, Sir, far too far!' Ah! And do you imagine Gentlemen, I have some talisman to dangle that deceives, delights and captivates the senses when I come to submit my work? That I was not obliged to justify what I dared to write? What do I make Figaro say, talking as a man who has fallen out of favour. 'Insults in print are of no importance to anyone except to those who are trying to suppress them.' Is that revealing some truth that will have dangerous consequences? If, instead of the infantile and tiresome inquisitions that only lend dignity to what would otherwise have none, we were wise enough, as they are in England, to treat such insults with the contempt that shrivels them, instead of their being dragged out of the filthy midden that has spawned them, they would rot; never sprout and never propagate. What allows a libel to take hold and spread is the feebleness that fears its consequences: nothing sells petty fooleries like the foolery of suppressing.

And what was Figaro's conclusion? 'That without the liberty to criticise no praise has any value: that only little men are scared of little jokes'.* Are these strokes of criminal audacity or are they stairs to glory? Are they immoral and corrupting, or are they the fruit of sober thought: maxims both just and constructive?

Consider them rather to be born of memory and past experience. When, contented with the present, the author guards against future ills by a study of the past, who has the right to criticise him? And if, describing no specific time nor place nor person, he prepares the way in the theatre for desirable reforms is he not attaining his objective?

One Mad Day, then, explains how it is that in a time of prosperity under a just king and moderate ministers the writer can castigate oppression without fear of giving offence to any.

It is in the reigns of virtuous princes that the historian writes without peril of unrighteous kings: the wiser and more enlightened the government, the less freedom of speech will be restricted: each man doing his duty, no one fears innuendo: no man in office having cause to tremble before an institution he is obliged to esteem, there is then no reason to oppress our literature that is the glory of our nation abroad and gives us there a kind of primacy we may derive from no other source.

Indeed, to what title should we aspire? Every people stands by its faith and cherishes its form of government. We have not maintained greater courage than those we have conquered and then, in turn, have conquered us. Our manners are more polished but not more virtuous, and have no intrinsic merit that renders us superior. Our literature alone, held in the highest regard by every nation, extends the Empire of the French tongue and wins us from all Europe a confessed pre-eminence, so justifying the protection granted to it by our Government.

And as every man at all times desires whatever single advantage it is he lacks, we therefore see in our academies a courtier consorting with men of letters, individual talent and the dignity of ancient lineage arguing towards this noble end and the academic libraries filled in equal measure with the productions both of 'Town' and 'Gown'.

But to return to *One Mad Day*.

One gentleman of great understanding, though he is a little sparing in the use of it, said to me one evening 'Do explain to me, I beg of you, why it is your play contains so many slip-shod turns of speech that are not in your style?' 'In my style, Sir? If I was unfortunate enough to have one I would make very certain I had forgotten it when I was employed about a comedy. I know nothing so insipid in the theatre as those flat, pastel sketches where everything is blue or everything is pink and everything, whatever it is, is the author.'

The moment my subject takes hold of me, I summon up all my characters and plunge them into the crisis: 'Keep your wits about you, Figaro, your Master will find you out!' – 'Quick! Run, Chérubin! That is the Count you just touched!' – 'Oh Countess, how thoughtless of you, with a husband as violent as that!' What they will say I have no idea: it is what they will *do* that concerns me. Then, when they have all come to life, I write to their swift dictation, certain that they will not deceive me, that I shall recognise Bazile, who has not the wit of Figaro, who hasn't the aristocratic tone of voice of the Count, who hasn't the sensibility of the Countess, who hasn't the exuberance of Suzanne, who hasn't the mischievousness of the page, and surely none of them the exalted genius of Brid'oison. Each of them speaks in his own way: by all that is natural may they be preserved for ever speaking otherwise! So let us address ourselves solely to consider their ideas and not investigate whether I ought to have given them my style.

Some malicious spirits have sought to bring into disrepute another line of Figaro: 'Are we soldiers that kill and have themselves killed for causes they know nothing of? I want to know why I should be angry, I do!'* Through the mists of a confused perception they have pretended to understand that '*I cast a disparaging light on the arduous condition of the soldier and there are some things that ought to remain unsaid*'. There, in all its force is the case put forward by those same malicious spirits: it only remains to establish its stupidity.

If, comparing the harshness of military service with the pittance offered in reward, or arguing some other inconvenience of war and counting glory as nothing, I were to bring into disrepute that most noble of all horrific trades, I could with justice be asked to give account for letting slip the word unguardedly. But from the common soldier to the colonel, even the general himself – what imbecile clod of cannon fodder has ever given himself airs he ought to be made party to the secrets of the Ministry for whom he fights a campaign? That is all that is in question in what Figaro has to say. Let the lunatic show himself, if he exists we shall despatch him to study under the wise Babouc,* who discourses most eloquently on this point of military discipline.

Reasoning upon the use a man makes of his liberty in a moment of discomfiture, Figaro could equally compare his situation with any station in life that demands obedience be implicit: and the tonsured friar in his monastic zeal, whose duty it is to believe all unquestioning, is exactly like the valorous warrior, whose glory is to face all at a simple word of command, '*to kill and be killed for causes he knows nothing of*'. Figaro's line has therefore no meaning, save that a man whose liberty is unrestricted must act on other principles than those whose duty is blind obedience.

What uproar would have followed, may God preserve us, if I had used the saying attributed to the great Condé* and which I hear praised out of all reason by the same logical minds that fall into a frenzy at mine! If we are to believe them, the great Condé showed the most noble presence of mind when he restrained Louis XIV as he was about to spur his horse into the Rhine and said to the Monarch 'Sire, what can your Royal Highness need with a Marshal's baton?' Fortunately, it is nowhere proven that this great man was guilty of such great stupidity. It would have been tantamount to saying to the king in front of all his army 'You cannot be serious, Sire, to endanger your life in a skirmish!

To run risks of that kind you must either stand in grievous need of promotion or a pot of money!'

So the most valiant man, the greatest general of this century, would have counted as nothing honour, patriotism and glory? A base, calculating, self-interest would have been according to him the sole motive for gallantry. What an outrageous statement to have made! And if I had taken its sense to enclose it in some sally, I should deserve the reproaches gratuitously made me now.

Let us therefore leave these confused minds to praise or blame at random, without ever understanding what is going forward, to throw themselves into an ecstasy over some idiotic trifle no living soul could ever have said, and proscribe a just and simple saying that shows nothing but good sense.

One other very trenchant criticism, but one from which I was able to exonerate myself, is that I assigned as a retreat for the Countess a certain convent of *Ursulines*.* '*Ursulines!*' one member of the nobility cried out, bringing his hands together with a great clap – '*Ursulines!*' cried a lady, falling backwards in her surprise against a young Englishman in her box: '*Ursulines!* Ah, my Lord, if only you could understand French!' 'I can feel it, Madam, I can feel a great deal', said the young man, blushing. No one in a play has ever sent a woman to the *Ursulines*! 'Father, do explain! Father' – still leaning against the Englishman – 'What do you say to *Ursulines?*' 'Most improper', replies the priest, without ceasing to quiz Suzanne through his spy-glass. Fashionable society all repeated it: '*Ursulines* is most improper.' Poor author: you are deemed to have been judged and everyone returns to their own preoccupations. In vain I tried to argue but in the events depicted, the less the Countess intends to enter an enclosed order the more she must pretend and make her husband believe she has gone so far as to choose the place she will retire to and they would not have my *Ursulines*!

At the height of all this hubbub I, simple soul that I am, almost went so far as to beg one of the actresses that endow my play with whatever charm it has to ask these malcontents to what other convent they considered it was *proper* the Countess should be sent. For myself, it was of no matter, I would have sent her anywhere they wished: to the *Augustines*, the *Célestines*, the *Poor Clares*, the *Little Sisters of the Visitation*, even to the *Grey Ladies*,* so little was I bent upon the *Ursulines*. The people are so ruthless!

I am never, as you see, my enemy's enemy: in wishing me so much harm, they did none to my play, and if they felt as great a joy in tearing it to shreds as I had pleasure in putting it together then none has suffered. The tragedy is they do not laugh at it and they will not laugh at my play because no one laughs at theirs! I know a good few dilettantes that have even grown a great deal thinner since the success of the *Marriage*: let us therefore excuse the consequences of their rage.

In the face of moral points, both general and particular, cast upon the waves of irrepressible high spirits, a lively enough dialogue whose apparent facility conceals the work in it, if the author has provided a smoothly working plot where art conceals art, winding and unwinding through a throng of comic situations delightful and varied images that hold without wearing it the attention of the audience through the three and a half hours the spectacle lasts – something no man of letters had ever dared to attempt – what remained for the poor mischief-makers to do that all this only served to enrage? To attack and persecute the author by insults, verbal, scribbled or in print: that is what they have done relentlessly. They have even exhausted slander itself in their attempts to ruin me in the opinion of every man in France with any influence in the matter of the safety of the citizen. Fortunately my work lies open to inspection by my countrymen, who for ten long months have seen it, judged it and appreciated it. To allow it to be played for as long as it will give pleasure is the sole vengeance I have allowed myself. I do not write this for readers at this present time: to recount an injustice that is all too well known has little effect: but in eighty years it will bear its fruit. The writers of those times will compare their lot to ours, and our children will know how much it costs to entertain their fathers.

But let us come to the point: this is not all that has inflicted such wounds. True reason that remains concealed, that engenders in every fibre of the heart all the rest of the reproaches that have been made, is contained in the following quatrain:

> Why is this Figaro Gods adore
> Revil'd by Fools, that tear his flesh and rend?
> For 'take it, pocket it and ask for more'
> There is their wrath's Beginning and its End.

Indeed Figaro, speaking of the trade of courtier did define it in these stern terms. I cannot deny it: he said it. But am I to return to the point? If it is an evil the remedy will only be worse: I must needs spell out in full what I have done no more than indicate: go back and show that in French the words *Person at Court*, *Person of the Court* and *Courtier by trade* are not synonymous.

It will be necessary to repeat that *Person at Court* distinguishes only a member of the aristocracy: that it is understood to mean a person of quality living with the nobility and all the pomp his rank confers upon him: that if this *Person at Court* is inclined to love virtue and is without self-interest then, far from doing harm to any man, he earns the esteem of his masters, the love of his peers, the respect of all the world, and this meaning of the word gains a new lustre. I know more than one that I would name with pleasure should the occasion so demand.

It will be necessary to explain that *Person of the Court* is less the description of an estate than the indication of a character: adroit, amiable but with some reserve, squeezing every hand as he glides through a crowd, deftly managing his own schemes under colour of always serving others, never making enemies, always ready when there is a ditch near to set his shoulder to his best friend's back, should the opportunity present itself, if it will ensure the other's fall and his own advancement, abandoning any prejudice that might clog his progress, smiling at what he hates and finding fault with what he likes, always according to who it is is listening to him: in the matter of profitable liaisons formed by his wife and by his mistress seeing only what he needs to see, in other words:

> With hand outstretched, in every wile well-taught
> As doth befit a *Person of the Court.*
>
> > (La Fontaine)*

This sense of the word is not so derogatory as that of *Courtier by Trade,* and that is the man spoken of by Figaro.

But even were I to expound on how this last is best defined, if, exhausting all conceivable interpretations, I were to present him with his equivocating manner, at once haughty and base, arrogant in his crawling, promising everything and fulfilling nothing, affecting to be a patron of the arts solely in order to advance himself, denigrating any competitor who might discredit him, making a lucrative trade out of what should only be a source of honour, selling his mistresses to his master, making his master pay for his debauches, etc., etc., and four more pages of etceteras, I should still be obliged to come back in the end to Figaro's couplet:

> Take it, pocket it and ask for more
> That is the secret in a word.

This category I am entirely unacquainted with: such creatures did exist, we are told, in the reign of Henry III and under other kings as well, but they are of interest only to the historians: and, for myself, I am of the opinion that the great sinners of this century are like its saints: it will be a hundred years before they are canonised. But since I have promised a criticism of my play I must finally give it. In general its great fault is that *I did not draw from observation of society: that it depicts nothing of any reality as it exists, and never calls to mind our present way of life: and that the vile and corrupt morality it portrays does not even possess the merit of truth.* And that is what we were privileged to read recently in the fine, well-printed essay on the topic, written by a good and upright man* that, as a writer, needs but a little more wit to be very mediocre. He may be mediocre, he may not: but never having subscribed to that oblique and contorted style whereby a police spy who seems not even to be looking at you may slip a dagger in between your ribs, I am entirely of his opinion. I concede it may be true the last generation was very like my play, and that the next generation will be very like it also: but that as far as the present generation is concerned there is no resemblance whatsoever. I have never met a deceitful husband, or a lascivious landowner, or an acquisitive courtier, or a hotheaded and ignorant judge, or a truculent attorney, or mediocre men in power, or anyone who would stoop to the meanest act of betrayal out of jealousy. And if the pure souls that fail to recognise themselves portrayed fly into a rage against my play and never cease to attack it, it is solely out of respect for their grandsires' memory and their tender solicitude for generations yet unborn. I hope, having made that declaration, I will be left in peace: AND I HAVE FINISHED.

A WORD ON *A MOTHER'S GUILT*

During the long term of my exile, certain zealous friends had this play printed, solely in order to forestall the outrage of a pirated edition that would have been unfaithful to the text, underhand, and taken down in haste during performances.*

But these friends themselves, in order to avoid a brush with the agents of the Terror if they had allowed the Spanish characters to keep their rightful titles (for everything was dangerous in those days) believed themselves obliged to deface them, even to coarsen their language, and to mutilate several scenes.

Honourably recalled to my homeland after four years of distresses, and the play being asked for by the former actors of the Théâtre Français, well-known for their great abilities, I am restoring it in full to its original form. This is the edition I have authorised.

One of the intentions of these artists, of which I approve, is to present, on three consecutive evenings, the whole story of the Almaviva family, of which the first two eras do not seem, in their light-hearted gaiety, to offer any perceptible relation to the deep and moving moral lesson of the last; but they possess, in the author's plan, an intricate connection, and one that lends the most lively interest to performances of *A Mother's Guilt*.

I therefore thought, with the actors, that we could say to the public: 'After you have laughed heartily, on the first day, in *The Barber of Seville*, at the boisterous youth of Count Almaviva, which is as near as maybe that of all men . . .'

'After having, on the second day, light-heartedly considered, in *One Mad Day*, the faults of his hot-blooded manhood, that are too often our own . . .'

'By the picture of his old age, and seeing *A Mother's Guilt*, come and be convinced, with us, that every man that is not born an utter reprobate must in the end be good, when the age of passion passes, and above all when he has experienced the sweet happiness of being a father!

This is the moral object of the play. It contains several others that these more detailed observations will make apparent.'

And as the author I would add this: Come and judge *A Mother's Guilt* with the same generous spirit in which it was composed for you. If you find some pleasure in mingling your tears with the grief and the pious repentance of this unfortunate woman, if her weeping moves you to weep also, then weep tenderly and without restraint. Tears that are shed in the theatre, at imagined suffering, that does not wound as does the cruel reality, are sweet indeed. We are better when we feel ourselves crying. After such compassion we feel so good.

Besides this touching picture, I have presented for your scrutiny the machinator, the abominable man who today torments this unfortunate family: Oh, I swear to you I have seen him at work: I could not have invented him. Molière's *Tartuffe** was a *religious* hypocrite: also, of all Orgon's household, he deceived only its foolish head. This *Tartuffe* is more dangerous by far, a *moral* hypocrite, possessing the deep art of winning the respect and confidence of the entire family he is despoiling. This was the man to be unmasked. It is to preserve you from the snares of these monsters (and they exist everywhere) that I have been stern in transferring him to French soil. Forgive him for me, in view of his punishment, which makes the closing of my play. This Act V cost me dear: but I would have been wickeder than Bégearss if I had allowed him to enjoy the least advantage of his atrocities, if I had not calmed you after such violent alarms.

It may be that I have waited too long to complete this terrible work, that burned within my breast, and that it should have been written when I was younger and stronger.

My two Spanish comedies were done only as a preparation for it. Since then, as I have grown older, I have hesitated to take it up: I feared that I lacked the strength; and it may be that I had none left by the time I came to attempt it! But be that as it may, I composed it with the purest and the best intentions: with the cool head of a man, and the passionate heart of a woman, as it was thought of Rousseau. I have observed this combination: this moral hermaphroditism is less rare than is generally believed.

For the rest, without taking sides with any party or sect, *A Mother's Guilt* is a picture of the inner afflictions that divide many a family; afflictions for which divorce, good in itself, can be no remedy. Whatever we may do, these secret wounds are torn open rather than being healed.

Fatherly feelings, goodness of heart and forgiveness are the only remedies. That is what I wished to paint and to engrave on every soul.

Men of letters that are devoted to the theatre, in examining this play, will be able to discern in it the intrigue of a comedy, with its foundations in the pathos of a drama. This last form, too much despised by some prejudiced critics, did not seem to them strong enough to contain these two elements together. 'Intrigue', they said, 'is the property of light-hearted subjects, it is the very nerve of comedy: *pathos* is suited to the simple progress of the drama, to support its weakness.' But these arbitrary principles disappear when they are applied in practice, as anyone will be convinced who works in both forms. The execution, whether it be more or less good, will decide each writer's merit; the happy mixture of these two dramatic forms, used with skill, can produce a very great effect; and this is how I came to make the attempt.

Based upon past events already known (and this is a very great advantage) I made it so that an interesting dramatic situation should now exist between Count Almaviva, the Countess and the two children. If I had set the play earlier, in the years of inconstancy when the faults were committed, this is what would have happened:

First the drama would have had to be called not *A Mother's Guilt* but *A Wife's Inconstancy* or *A Husband's and a Wife's Guilt*: already there was not the same kind of dramatic tension. It would have been necessary to introduce lovers' intrigues, jealousies, confusion and who knows what other entirely different events: and the moral lesson that I wished to draw from so grave a dereliction of the duties of an honest wife, this moral would have been lost, shrouded in the hot passions of that age, would not have been perceived. But it is twenty years after the faults were committed, when passions are spent. When their objects no longer exist, at the moment when the consequences of disorders that have almost been forgotten come to weigh upon the household, on the fate of two unhappy children who were wholly ignorant of them, and who are nonetheless their victims: it is from these grave circumstances that the moral draws all its strength and so comes to the protection of young persons of good birth who, reading little of what the future holds, are in far greater danger of straying from the path of virtue than of being depraved. That is the subject of my drama.

Then, setting against the villain our clear-eyed Figaro, an old and very devoted servant, the only creature in the house the rogue has been unable to deceive, the intrigue in which they both become involved is established from another point of view.

The villain, anxious, says to himself, 'It is in vain I have discovered everybody's secret here, in vain that I am near to turn it to my profit: if I do not manage to have this valet sacked, no good will come to me.'

On the other side, I hear Figaro saying to himself, 'Unless I succeed in outwitting this monster, in making him drop his mask, the fortune, honour, the happiness of this house, all is lost.' Suzanne, thrown between these two embattled opponents, is here no more than a compliant instrument that each of them makes use of to hasten the downfall of the other.

In this way the *comedy of intrigue*, sustaining our curiosity, runs through the drama, strengthening the action without detracting from its interest, which is centred wholly upon the mother. The two children, in the audience's eyes, are in no real danger. It is clear that they will marry if the villain is put to flight, for what is established above all else in the work is that they are in no degree related, that they are strangers one to another, that this is well known, in their most secret hearts, by the Count, the Countess, the villain, Suzanne and Figaro, all aware of what has happened, not to mention the audience watching the play, from whom we have concealed nothing.

The whole art of the hypocrite, in tearing the hearts of father and mother, consists in terrifying the young people, in wrenching them apart by making them believe they are children of the same father. That is the basis of his intrigue. These are the workings of the double plot, which may indeed be called *complex*.

Such a dramatic action finds its application in any epoch, in any place where the great lineaments of Nature and all those that characterise the heart of man and his secrets can be seen by those who have eyes to see.

Diderot, comparing the works of Richardson to all those novels that we call 'historical', cries out in his enthusiasm for that true and profound author 'Painter of the human heart. You alone can never lie!'* What a sublime utterance! And I too, strive still to be a painter of the human heart: but my palette is dried by age and old hatreds. *A Mother's Guilt* must bear the marks of it!

But if my feeble execution may mar the interest of my plan, the principle I have advanced is nonetheless entirely right. Such an attempt may inspire other plays that are more powerfully orchestrated. Let a man of fire undertake it, mingling in it, with a bold pencil, intrigue with pathos. Let him cunningly grind and mix the vivid colours of each: let him paint for us in bold strokes man living in society, his estate, his passions, his vices, his virtues, his faults and his misfortunes, with the striking touch that exaggeration itself, that lends lustre to other forms of writing, does not always allow us to render so faithfully.

Moved, fascinated, instructed, we shall no longer say the drama is a colourless form,* born of the incapacity to produce a tragedy or a comedy. The art will have nobly sprung to life: it will have advanced another step.

Oh my fellow citizens! You to whom I dedicate this effort! If it seems feeble or wanting, criticise it, but do not insult me. When I wrote my other plays, I was long abused for having dared to present on the stage the young Figaro that you have since come to love. I was young too, and laughed with him. As one grows older, the soul becomes sadder, the turn of mind grows darker. There is nothing I can do: I no longer laugh when a malicious person or a rascal insults me for my works. I cannot help it.

Criticise the play, by all means. If the author is too old for you to find it fruitful, your words may be of value to others. Abuse is of value to no one, and is in bad taste. I may offer this observation to a nation famed for its old traditional politeness, for which it was once as much a model to others, as it is today for high valour.

NOTES

The Barber of Seville or All That Trouble For Nothing

p. 1 'I was a father and I could not die: Voltaire, *Zaïre*, Act II, 5. 580.

p. 3 Ferdinand and Isabella: Ferdinand II of Aragon (1479–1516) and Isabella of Castile (1474–1506).

p. 6 'When Green-eyed Envy spreads its grasping claws . . .': possibly a parody of verse by Voltaire in *La Henriade*, IX, 5. 45.

p. 6 actual harm: almost a literal quotation from Montaigne, 'De la vanité', *Essais*, III, 9.

p. 7 twenty-four hours: this refers probably to the time by which an appeal could be lodged.

p. 8 free-thinking, magnetism, electricity . . .: Bartholo inveighs against discoveries and ideas propounded in the years before and during the composition of the play. Newton was responsible for introducing the idea of **attraction** of one mass gravitationally to another. His work was popularised in France by Voltaire in the fifteenth of his *Lettres philosophiques* and in the *Eléments de la philosophie de Newton* (1738). Work was also conducted on magnetism. The Danish scientist, Hans Christian Oersted (1777–1851) later linked magnetism and electricity; knowledge of **electricity** was developed by the invention in 1745–6 of the Leyden jar (the first artificial device for producing large currents), Galvani's experiments with electrostatic stimuli and Franklin's experiments with his lightning rod, which for orthodoxy constituted a domestication or defiance of an unpredictable numinous power; **religious tolerance** was the subject of Monclar's memoir of 1755 pleading tolerance for the Protestants and Voltaire's *Traité sur la tolérance* (1763); **inoculation** was finally authorised in France in 1764 (Jenner would vaccinate with lymph from cows in 1796) after much disputing between the Church and philosophers. Voltaire had advocated inoculation in letter XI of his *Lettres philosophiques*; **quinine**, the chief alkaloid of cinchona and the first anti-malarial drug, seemed less controversial. La Fontaine had published a poem in its honour already in 1682; the **Encyclopædia**

of Diderot and d'Alembert was published in 1751; **dramas** were promoted as the æsthetic model of the age by Diderot and by Beaumarchais himself.

p. 10 Paseo del Prado: a place where the people of Madrid would stroll, on a site now occupied by the museum of that name.

p. 31 the right of whoever happens to be stronger: Bartholo invokes a 'right' or 'law' which had been discredited as fallacious and unjust in Rousseau's influential *Discours sur l'origine et les fondements de l'inégalité parmi les hommes* (1754).

One Mad Day or The Marriage of Figaro

Note When translating *The Marriage of Figaro*, with a modern audience in mind, John Wells made a number of very minor cuts to the original French. It is the only play in this collection to be slightly abridged.

p. 66 *droit de seigneur*: the alleged right of a lord to make love to his servant's bride on her wedding-night.

p. 67 'must hatred take its place?': Voltaire, *Nanine*, Act III, scene 6.

p. 84 *Vanloo*: Carle Vanloo (1707–71). For Diderot the 'tableau' became a crucial way of crystallising important moments in the theatre.

pp. 84–5 'I'll love until I die': Charles Péguy discusses this elegiac song in detail (*Oeuvres en prose complètes*, ed. Robert Burac, Paris: Gallimard, 1987; Bibliothèque de la Pléïade, III, 1085–6), arguing that we need to read *A Mother's Guilt* to appreciate fully its poignancy.

p. 93 Ursulines: see note to p. 258.

p. 106 as the good old king says in his song: Molière, *Le Misanthrope*, Act I, scene 2, 5. 411.

p. 111 Alonzo Calderon: a fictional author, not to be confused with Pedro Calderon.

p. 112 lovely Thalestris versus Alexander the Great: Quintus Curtius, *History of Alexander the Great*, Book V; Chapter 5.

p. 113 Gordian knot: Bartholo alludes again to Alexander the Great. The episode is related in Arrian, *The Anabasis of Alexander*, Book 2, 3.

p. 113 rhubarb . . . tamarind: these were commonly used as laxatives.

The New Tartuffe or A Mother's Guilt

p. 153 Léon's saint's day: the feast-day of Saint Leo the Great falls on 10 November.

p. 154 what's the use of telling me?: Beaumarchais allows himself a little joke early in the drama, uttering through Suzanne a muted apology for a particularly clumsy narrative device.

p. 156 when an orphan girl turns up . . .: a variant on this certainty is exploited in the reunion scene in *The Marriage of Figaro* when Figaro, a male orphan, finds his parents.

p. 157 divorce is now permitted: the 'glorious' laws permitting divorce were passed in 1792 (although the action takes place at the end of 1790), but they were restricted by Napoleon, abolished under the Restoration and only reintroduced in 1884 in specially severe cases.

p. 158 knight of Malta: the Knights Hospitaller of St John of Jerusalem (founded as an order to protect pilgrims to Jerusalem but established in Malta from 1550), were still active in the eighteenth century, particularly in engagements with African corsairs. They were sworn to chastity, poverty and obedience. The embodiment of ecclesiastical and aristocratic privilege, the order's entire property was confiscated in October 1792. In 1790 clerks were allowed to return to lay status and, after Napoleon's invasion of Malta in 1798, the order was in effect dissolved.

p. 160 Vera Cruz: a port in Mexico, then a colony of Spain.

p. 191 embodiment of evil that Milton writes about: *Paradise Lost*, Book I, 60–6.

p. 191 'My name is Legion': Luke 8.30: 'And Jesus asked him, saying, "What is thy name?" And he said, "Legion": because many devils were entered into him.'

p. 191 'O, que piacere!': O what a pleasure!

p. 192 'It's a long road that has no turning': 'Le soleil luit pour tout le monde': like the previous proverb, 'God helps those who help themselves', this platitude cannot actually be attributed to Solomon.

p. 213 Everyone's against duelling now: duelling was in fact banned by a series of edicts throughout the seventeenth and early eighteenth centuries but remained an important social symbol distinguishing the aristocracy from the other echelons of society. Duelling still occurred but was no longer the menace it had been. See Roland Mousnier, *The Institutions of France and the Absolute Monarchy 1598–1789*, 2 vols (Illinois: University of Chicago Press, 1979), I, 139–46 and, more generally, Robert Baldick, *The Duel: A History* (New York: Barnes & Noble, 1996).

p. 214 One day has changed our lives: like *One Mad Day*, the action is compressed into one day.

A Restrained Letter on the Failure of The Barber of Seville and Its Critics

p. 215 Tissot: Simon-André Tissot (1728–97) Swiss scientist who advocated inoculation and wrote *De la Santé des gens de lettres*.

p. 215 *Journal established in Bouillon*...: the *Journal encyclopédique par une société de gens de lettres* set up by Pierre Rousseau in 1756 in Bouillon, a small resort now in Belgium. Such writers as Voltaire, Prévost and Chamfort contributed.

p. 216 **Moses' Rod:** Numbers 20.11: 'And Moses lifted his hand, and with his rod he smote the rock twice, and the water came out abundantly, and the congregation drank, and their beasts also.'

p. 216 **Jacob's walking stick:** Genesis 22.10: 'And Jacob said ... with my staff I passed over Jordan, and now I am become two bands ....'

p. 216 **two poor miserable *Dramas*:** these dramas are *Eugénie* (1767) and *Les Deux amis* (1770).

p. 217 **between Tragedy and Comedy**...: the 'master' in question is Voltaire who, in a letter to Aleksandr Petrovich Sumaroikov of 26 February (D15488 in Voltaire's Correspondence edited by Besterman and published subsequently in the *Journal encyclopédique*, 1 May 1771, ii, 452–5), complained that no one had been capable of writing proper comedy or tragedy since Molière, and described drama as a sort of monstrous hybrid.

p. 217 **wretched legal *Memorials*:** the four memorials against Goëzman (1773–4).

p. 218 **Another**...: author of *La Correspondance littéraire secrète*, 25 February 1775.

p. 220 **Candide:** Voltaire, *Candide*, Chapter 6.

p. 220 **Sophocles and the ancient Dionysius died of joy:** Valerius Maximus, *Memorable Sayings and Actions*, IX.

p. 221 *ergotism*: arguing, wrangling, often of a pedantic kind.

p. 223 *redecilla*: the *redecilla*, or *rescille* as it is known in French, is a form of Spanish hair-net.

p. 223 **spatula, branded on his shaven scalp:** the recognition scene described here takes a different form in *The Marriage of Figaro*, Act III. A distinctive birthmark on Figaro's arm rather than a marking on his head gives him away. Perhaps more significantly, his mother Marceline, rather than Bartholo, recognises him, thereby lending the farce a more sentimental quality.

p. 223 **Bishop Gaurico:** Luca Gaurico (1476–1558), Bishop of Civita Ducale, an astrologer consulted by Catherine de Medici.

p. 224 **Thy son shall smite his cursèd father's head:** an echo of the Œdipus legend, which will be heard again when Marceline intends to marry Figaro.

p. 225 **Cardinal de Retz:** author of the *Memoirs* (*Oeuvres*, eds. Marie-Thérèse Hipp and Michel Pernet, Paris: Gallimard, 1984; Bibliothèque de la Pléiade, II, 293) from which this story is taken.

p. 225 **Henry the Great:** Henri IV (1558–1610), French king.

p. 230 Aubignac: author of *La Pratique du Théâtre* (1657).

p. 230 Moderns: opposed to the Ancients in the protracted and complicated quarrel from the mid-seventeenth century to 1715, the Moderns, led by Perrault and Fontenelle, were sceptical towards tradition and wished to foster a modern French culture less in awe of Antiquity.

p. 230 *They Can't Think of Everything*: *On ne s'avise jamais de tout*, a comic opera by Sedaine, with music by Monsigny.

p. 234 Vestris: a contemporary dancer from Florence (1729–1808) who joined the Paris opera in 1741.

p. 234 d'Auberval: a French dancer (1742–1806) who joined the Paris opera in 1761 and composed a 'ballet héroïque', *Le Page inconstant* (1805) based on *The Marriage of Figaro*.

p. 235 melodramas: experiments had been made in this genre earlier in the century, including one by Jean-Jacques Rousseau in 1761, *Pygmalion*. The word is introduced in the eighteenth century to denote a play in which certain scenes are accompanied by music. It is only later in the nineteenth century that it comes to mean a dramatic piece which involves intense emotions.

Preface to The Marriage of Figaro

p. 237 Racine's *The Attorneys*: *Les Plaideurs*, a comedy about the legal profession first performed in 1668.

p. 237 George Dandins: George Dandin is the eponymous protagonist in a Molière comdey first performed in 1668.

p. 237 *Turcaret*: a comedy by Lesage first performed in 1709 which echoes Molière's *Bourgeois gentilhomme*.

p. 238 Vendôme: the reference here is to Voltaire's play, *Adélaïde du Guesclin* (1734) in which Vendôme kills his brother.

p. 238 Mahomet: a tragedy by Voltaire (1742) which depicts the ill effects of fanaticism.

p. 239 Boileau in his epistle to the great Racine: Boileau's Epistle VII, *À Monsieur Racine*, 5. 23–32.

p. 239 a Memorial addressed by Molière to Louis XIV: Molière responded to a pamphlet of 1664 in which the Abbé Roullé attacked *Tartuffe*. See Molière, *Oeuvres complètes* (Bibliothèque de la Pléïade, I, 890).

p. 239 Heraclitus or Democritus: these are the archetypal responses to human foibles; the laughter of Democritus or the distress of Heraclitus.

p. 241 *Œuil de Boeuf*: a round or oval window, specifically that of the waiting-room in Versailles, adjacent to the king's room where the courtiers would watch the king's levee.

p. 242 the late Prince de Conti: this aristocrat (1717–76) had supported Beaumarchais in the Goëzman affair (1773–4).

p. 243 five or six: Coqueley de Chaussepierre, Suard, Gaillard, Guidi, Desfontaines and Bret were all censors of Beaumarchais.

p. 244 A brazen servant, in unseemly Strife: a quotation from Gudin de la Brenelleries, friend, editor and biographer of Beaumarchais.

p. 244 nation in despair: this is broadly the story of *Tarare* (1787) set to music by Salieri.

p. 245 obliged three times in the same day to kneel at his wife's feet: see *The Marriage of Figaro*, Act II, scene 9, Act IV, scenes 5 and 9.

p. 245 'The times you done it up and down the countryside!': *The Marriage of Figaro*, Act V, scene 14.

p. 247 A *Stroke of Luck*: the 'charming little play' to which Beaumarchais alludes is *Heureusement*, a play of one act by Rochon de Chabannes (1762).

p. 248 'the biggest little rip . . .': *The Marriage of Figaro*, Act I, scene 7.

p. 249 the trull or trollop in *The Misanthrope*: Molière, *Le Misanthrope*, Act V, scene 6.

pp. 250–1 '. . . as maternally as you can': *The Marriage of Figaro*, Act III, scene 16.

p. 252 'even if it was malicious gossip no one would believe him': *The Barber of Seville*, Act II, scene 9.

p. 253 'Laugh, damn you, laugh': Molière, *La Critique de l'école des femmes*, scene 5.

p. 253 Figaro's line: *The Marriage of Figaro*, Act III, scene 5. Not in this translation.

p. 253 'as one stern writer observed': this writer is Beaumarchais himself. This is a trick he plays repeatedly. The deception works here because he sounds just like Montesquieu *De l'esprit des lois*, II, 4.

p. 254 a case of great import and severity: an allusion to Beaumarchais' court case against La Blache which went before the Parlement of Aix-en-Provence.

p. 254 'the noblest of institutions': *The Marriage of Figaro*, Act III, scene 15.

p. 255 fourth 'Memorial': this is the Memorial against Goëzman.

p. 255 'only little men are scared of little jokes': this and the previous quotation are from *The Marriage of Figaro*, Act V, scene 3.

p. 257 'Are we soldiers that kill . . .?': *The Marriage of Figaro*, Act V, scene 12. Not in this translation.

p. 257 Babouc: a figure in a Voltaire story, *Le Monde comme il va* (*The World As It Is*), published in 1748, who is despatched by an angel to pass judgement on Persepolis (Paris). Babouc is particularly surprised and distressed by the use of mercenaries.

p. 257 Condé: Louis II de Bourbon, prince of Condé (1621–86). In fact Condé was injured crossing the Rhine with Louis XIV's army in 1672. See Pierre Coste, *Histoire de Louis de Bourbon, second de nom, Prince de Condé* (La Haye, 1748) Book V, 361 and Bernard Pujo, *Le Grand Condé* (Paris: Albin Michel, 1995), p. 335. Neither mentions any such anecdote, as Beaumarchais suggests.

p. 258 *Ursulines*: a nunnery in the order of St Ursula, probably that of the Faubourg St Jacques, Paris, founded in 1610 and mentioned in Act II (p. 92).

p. 258 the *Augustines*, the *Célestines* . . .: Augustines were in the order of St Augustine; the Célestines are nuns of the order of St Bernard; the poor Clares, known as Clairettes or Bernardines are Cistercian orders; while Visitantines are nuns of the Ordre de la Visitation founded by St François de Sales. The Grey Ladies were Cordelières in the order of St Francis of Assisi.

p. 260 La Fontaine: the lines quoted are from La Fontaine's poem, *Joconde*, in *Oeuvres diverses*, ed. Jean-Pierre Collinet (Paris: Gallimard, 1991; Bibliothèque de la Pléiade, I, 357).

p. 261 a good and upright man: Jean-Baptiste Suard who attacked Beaumarchais in a speech delivered to the Académie française (15 June 1784).

A Word on A Mother's Guilt

p. 262 exile . . . performances: Beaumarchais returned from exile in July 1796. This preface was written in 1797. The play was performed for the first time at the Théâtre du Marais on 26 June 1792.

p. 263 Tartuffe: Molière's *Le Tartuffe*, subtitled *L'Imposteur*, was first performed partially in 1664. It was thought by many to be a satire on the Jesuits and was banned from public performance until 1669. In Diderot's *Paradoxe sur le comédien* (1773) the play is agreed to be not only a satire but a comedy about the generic vice of hypocrisy. Indeed, the villain's name has passed into the French language to denote this.

p. 265 Diderot, comparing the works of Richardson . . .: Diderot, *Eloge de Richardson* (1762), *Œuvres* (Bibliothèque de la Pléiade), p. 1068. The quotation is slightly inaccurate.

p. 266 drama is a colourless form . . .: see note to the preface of *The Barber of Seville*, p. 217.

Note on the text John Wells' translation is based on the complete works of Beaumarchais (Garnier-Flammarion, 1965), which uses the 1775 text of *Le Barbier de Séville* (third edition), the 1785 Ruault edition of *Le mariage de Figaro*, and the 1797 text of *La mère coupable*.

BEAUMARCHAIS AND HIS CRITICS

Just as Beaumarchais was buffeted by the political vicissitudes of his day, so the reception of his plays has continued to be subject to the prejudices of the political agendas which have variously prevailed since his death. Contemporary evaluations of Beaumarchais' plays amounted to declarations of political allegiance. *The Barber of Seville* and *The Marriage of Figaro* were applauded by those who clamoured for change, deplored by those who opposed it. The assumption that Figaro was Beaumarchais and the scene of his theatre that of contemporary France soon determined in large part the reception of the plays. The authorities were fearful in particular of *The Marriage of Figaro* since its every detail seemed to carry some symbolical and satirical threat. The neglected Countess was obviously the Queen. The philandering, indecisive Count could only be the King. These were the first of innumerable interpretations which perceived the plays primarily as political satires.

Critical responses to Beaumarchais' plays have consistently aimed to disentangle the biographical strands which might lie behind them or to investigate their relationship to historical events, and the historical event which eclipsed all others was the French Revolution. It was increasingly with the Revolution in mind that the Figaro plays were evaluated. *The Marriage of Figaro* was therefore necessarily of the greatest interest.[1] Appreciations of the play have tended to be subordinate to investigations of its influences, whether those to which it is subject or its own revolutionary impact. The great historian Jules Michelet devoted some pages of his account of the Revolution to Figaro. Although an enthusiastic Republican he makes it clear that he does not like Figaro: he is not a man of the people, but, worse than those he attacks, he has the vices at once of the upper and lower classes. The sentence which closes Michelet's remarks on *The Marriage of Figaro* is ominously short: 'In this audience, Danton and Robespierre are twenty years old.'[2] The play's audiences and the circumstances of its production have continued to fascinate as much as the play itself. In his history of the French Revolution, Thomas Carlyle also devotes some words to *The Marriage of Figaro* and accounts for its success likewise only in terms of its political pertinence. Like Michelet, he is hard-pressed to find intrinsic merits in the play:

> Glance at Beaumarchais' *Mariage de Figaro*; which now [in 1784], after difficulty enough, has issued on the stage; and 'runs its hundred nights', to the admiration of all men. By what virtue or internal vigour it so ran, the reader of our day will rather wonder: – and indeed will know so much the better that it flattered some pruriency of the time; that it spoke what all were feeling, and longing to speak. Small substance in that *Figaro*: thin wire-drawn intrigues, thin wire-drawn sentiments and sarcasms; a thing lean, barren; yet which winds and whisks itself, as through a wholly mad universe, adroitly, with a high-sniffing air: wherein each, as was hinted, which is the grand secret, may see some image of himself, and of his own state and ways. So it runs its hundred nights, and all France runs with it; laughing applause.[3]

The Marriage of Figaro is considered the quintessential revolutionary text and has attracted historians and subsequent revolutionaries. In a famous production to celebrate the tenth anniversary of the Russian Revolution, *The Marriage of Figaro* was revived by Stanislavski in 1926–7. As a Soviet critic enthused in the 1980s: 'Beaumarchais' zestful romp, born just before the French Revolution of 1789, now marched in step with the people of Great October, the people who were building socialism.'[4]

Beaumarchais' plays have been revived, re-evaluated or repressed in accordance with the wars which have dominated this century. In the Second World War the Nazis banned *The Marriage of Figaro*. On the eve of the First World War, in which he was killed, Charles Péguy wrote the posthumously published text, *Clio, Dialogue de l'histoire et de l'âme païenne* (*Clio, Dialogue Between History and a Pagan Soul*). He is intrigued particularly by the figure of Chérubin, glimpsing perhaps in his fate that of the doomed youth of the war which was about to start. The song Chérubin sings as he goes to war is examined in particular detail, while the news of his death, embraced in the Count's laconic phrase, 'a certain Léon d'Astorga, who was once my page and was called Chérubin', is identified as the source of great sadness: 'Was there ever a more mortal, a more pious and more noble melancholy than that which flows from these simple words? Was there ever a greater or more austere melancholy? One which was more chaste, more simple or more classical?'[5] Only the full trilogy shows the poignant fragility of Beaumarchais' depiction of youth:

The more these characters are conceived as the very type of youth, and the more successfully they are presented as the very type of youth, the classical, traditional, successful, almost iconic representatives of youth, the more poignant it is to find them like everyone else, that is to say grown older, the men and women, like everyone else, at forty. Nothing is more poignant, said History, than the fate of these characters. The more clearly we are given to understand that they are young, the more poignant it is that there should be a play by Beaumarchais in which they are no longer young.[6]

This play is *A Mother's Guilt*, which momentarily becomes the rare object of attention. Indeed Péguy's chief reason for turning to it is to explain why so few others have done so, and to explore the circumstances which ensure the survival of a play into posterity. *A Mother's Guilt* is a play which has gone unnoticed. Although Péguy thought it 'a curious play, well and firmly written, and as silly as you like ... and above all thoroughly in tune with its time', it was bound not to become well-known because it was not well-known from the beginning.[7] Plays in particular, argues Péguy, only enjoy good fortune if they have a good birth. Fortune depends on birth, ironically just as in the *ancien régime* Figaro vilifies. The other plays lend *A Mother's Guilt* its right of birth, but the younger can never become the older. Péguy reminds us that even Napoleon was always conscious that he was not the oldest of eight. A play must explode upon its birth, in front of everyone. Péguy explains that *A Mother's Guilt* could not make its mark because quite simply there were other things to do in 1792. People did not have the time, as they did in 1775 or 1784.[8] Nevertheless, in conjunction all three plays unfold a history of these times. Once again the critical discourse insists on their historical importance:

If I were a teacher of French history, continued History, and perhaps if I were a teacher of world history, I should require my students to read this play.... I should first of all read them the two comedies, and then I should read them the drama. 1775, 1784, 1792: nothing could represent these three dates in the history of France and of the world as faithfully, as accurately, as profoundly, in a word nothing could date these three dates better than a reading of these three plays. Nothing could make it so easy to measure the difference of time, the difference of tone, in other words what really constitutes the context of an event in the history of a people and of the world. I should like to give my students the taste, the physical flavour, so to speak, of what 1775, 1784 and 1792 were like: I should simply read them these three plays.[9]

Victor Hugo, writing at the same time as Carlyle, was one of those who did notice *A Mother's Guilt*, as well as its partners. In the highly influential preface to his play *Cromwell* (1827), a great anti-classical credo which became the watchword of the Romantics, Beaumarchais' achievement is lifted from the political and historical context and is replaced in a wider dramatic tradition. Hugo ranks Beaumarchais alongside Corneille and Molière as the three great French geniuses of the stage, although Shakespeare alone embodies the attributes of all three in his opinion. Hugo validates a dynamic blend of the comic and the grotesque and recommends this admixture of registers as the model for French theatre. Quoting Napoleon's observation that there is but one step from the sublime to the ridiculous, Hugo observes that 'men of genius, howsoever great they may be, have always in their make-up a strain of the animal, which makes sport of their intelligence. In that respect they are akin to the generality of mankind, for in that they are dramatic.' It is Beaumarchais' recognition of the grotesque in all three plays that earns him a place in the most exalted company.

> By dint of meditating upon existence, of laying stress upon the bitter irony of it, of pouring forth sarcasm and mockery in floods upon our infirmities, these men who make us laugh so heartily become profoundly sad. This Democritus is a Heraclitus too, Beaumarchais was morose, Molière was dismal, Shakespeare melancholy.
>
> We insist then that the grotesque is one of the supreme beauties of the drama. It is not a convenience simply, it is oftentimes a necessity. Sometimes it appears in homogeneous masses, in characters which are grotesque and nothing else, as Dandin, Prusias, Trissotin, Brid'oison and Juliet's nurse; sometimes impregnated with terror, as Richard III, Bégearss, Tartuffe, Mephistopheles; sometimes, too, with a veil of charm and refinement, as Figaro, Osric, Mercutio, Don Juan.[10]

Sealed with Hugo's approval, Beaumarchais' place in the canon seemed henceforward secure within only thirty years of his death. But even if it was inspired by Hugo, the romantic appropriation of Beaumarchais' theatre tended to pare the grotesque edges. Unlike Hugo and Péguy, the composer Jules Massenet ignored the complications of *A Mother's Guilt*. In his rather saccharine opera *Chérubin* (first performed in 1905) he envisaged a neater, less challenging continuation of the adventures of Chérubin than the drama had proposed. Beaumarchais' influence was by now felt as keenly in the sphere of music as in that of criticism. By 1922 *The Barber of Seville* alone had spawned no fewer than eleven operas.[11] Critical and satirical perspectives tended to be sweetened in these musical responses. Beaumarchais' importance can be measured also by the number of theatrical adaptations and continuations his plays provoked – testimony to their suggestive, provisional qualities. Hugo enjoyed the amorphous and ambiguous aspects of the plays which left questions unanswered and caught the imagination. These qualities only enticed others eager to answer these questions to complete the trilogy in their own way. Both before and after Beaumarchais wrote *The Marriage of Figaro* and *A Mother's Guilt*, numerous sequels were offered.[12] A number of these projected Chérubin growing up and settling down. Among those tantalised or frustrated by Chérubin was Olympe de Gouges, a female author who in 1791 wrote a tract pleading for women's rights: *Déclaration des droits de la femme et de la citoyenne* (*The Rights of Woman and the Female Citizen*). She ventured her own optimistic conclusion in 1784 with *Le mariage inattendu de Chérubin* (*The Unexpected Marriage of Chérubin*), although within a few years she would also write a play on the necessity of divorce.

Gouges' desire to see Chérubin married is motivated possibly by a feminist indignation which has, in this century, produced scholarly articles rather than theatrical supplements. While Gouges is perhaps limited by the conventions of her time, Germaine Greer no longer envisages marriage as the only way to tame the philanderer. Far from representing a sentimental amusement in which Almaviva's *droit de seigneur* is a 'quaint antiquarian survival', opera and play, she argues, are still chillingly relevant.

> The truth is that determined and cold-blooded seducers like Count Almaviva are to be found wherever rich and powerful men are to be found. There is little point in a man being rich and powerful after all, if he cannot command more effective and more varied stimuli than lesser men. . . . Almaviva is moved by a predatory sexuality which is the older version of Cherubino's intense and unremitting interest in women. Cherubino's sneaking around the maid's room at daybreak and collecting ladies' ribbons will grow up to be the manly sports of voyeurism and stalking. The Count's bitter fury with Cherubino, his desire to kill him, is in part anger at his own insistent sexual need and in part envy of the boy's intense and incessant readiness for any and all sexual encounters. . . . Count Almaviva is rarely made to appear as dangerous on stage as such men are in reality . . . the temptation is to play him more *buffo* than the part actually is. . . . Even when Almaviva's vassals unpleasantly surprise him, he quickly regains his musical and mental balance, calculating their guilt and innocence and deciding all fates bar his own. He disdainfully recommends that his outraged dependants resort to *giudizia*, there being no question of *giustizia*. . . . Shift as they might, turning this way and that in their terror, the authority still remains with the persecutor. In the

fragility and unlikeliness of its happy ending, Le Nozze di Figaro reveals itself as a classic exploration of sexual Realpolitik.[13]

The operatic representation of sexual relations is from this perspective as critical and powerful as the play's portrayal. It is often, however, on the basis of Marceline's feminist tirade which was cut from the opera, that critics have chosen to affirm the particular place of the strong woman in the plays. In his article, 'Beaumarchais et l'autre revolution', Michel Delon signals the importance of women and their rights in the plays, describing Beaumarchais' affirmations as the 'other revolution' with which his plays engage.[14]

The discussion of the role of women in Beaumarchais' plays and in their musical adaptations raises more general questions about the respective emphases and merits of opera and play. When in 1989, again upon the anniversary of a revolution, The Marriage of Figaro was staged by the Comédie-Française, its director, Antoine Vitez (who had previously directed the opera) admitted to reservations which echo those of Carlyle:

> When I directed the Nozze di Figaro at Florence in 1979 . . . , I still thought Mozart's Marriage was superior to Beaumarchais'. In particular, Beaumarchais' text seemed flat and prosaic to me, too wordy and lacking in musical quality. I don't think that now, I even think the opposite. I was uncomfortable with the mots d'auteur in the play; I no longer am. I thought of Beaumarchais' theatre as a kind of theatre without hidden meaning, where everything is too transparent: a masterly framework for a work whose substance is rather slight. I thought all the depth had been provided by Mozart (and Da Ponte) by slimming down the dialogue, by condensing the last two acts and omitting one act, and above all by Mozart's mise en scène – not just a musical version – of The Marriage. Mozart has provided one approach to the interpretation of the characters (for after all, there are different ways of playing them). The Countess, for instance, full of nostalgia, sadness and regret: all of which are so well expressed in the 'Dové sono' of his Act II – whereas it is quite possible, just by reading Beaumarchais' text, to find something different.
>
> Mozart's version is in fact a way of directing the actors. In a play, one directs the actors by suggesting psychological attitudes and interpretations of the text; this is what Mozart does with his music. He dictates the intonation of the phrases – which is what a director does – and I thought to begin with that his was the only possible approach. Hence my difficulty in tackling The Marriage of Figaro; but I accepted the challenge, and discovered that there were indeed other ways of approaching the characters.[15]

With the development of critical theory detaching text from author, there has been a perceptible shift from the assumption that Figaro and Beaumarchais are essentially one and the same person and the notion that, in turn, Beaumarchais' plays are indissociable from narratives of his life. Productions like that of Vitez emphasise that the plays are susceptible to different interpretations and validate the indeterminacy of Beaumarchais' characterisation. If the old equation of Figaro and Beaumarchais simplified the texts it also diluted the biography of Beaumarchais. By liberating Figaro from Beaumarchais, Beaumarchais is also liberated from Figaro. René Pomeau's critical biography, *Beaumarchais ou la bizarre destinée* (Paris: Presses universitaires de France, 1987) is unusually cautious in trying to divorce author and character. A sense of the great complexity of Beaumarchais' simultaneous projects and ideas has been enhanced by Brian Morton's publication of the Correspondence, while recent research has shed light on some of Beaumarchais' many activities, whether his efforts to publish the Kehl edition of Voltaire's works or his smuggling of arms for the Americans.[16] Beaumarchais' biography continues to set challenges.

In their attention to its thematic aspects or in their emphasis that it represents critical moments in Beaumarchais' life or French history, many critics of Beaumarchais' work have neglected its status as theatre. A recent study of the plays, William D. Howarth's *Beaumarchais and the Theatre*, has aimed to restore a theatrical context to the plays, arguing that it is 'necessary to relate Beaumarchais' output as a dramatist as fully as possible to the history of the French theatre in the second half of the eighteenth century: not only the critical history of the works performed, but also the evolving relationship between dramatist, actors and their audiences, and changes in the composition of those audiences: what one might call the sociology of the theatre'.[17] While Howarth discusses all of Beaumarchais' plays in detail, he subscribes implicitly to Péguy's notion that the birth of a play ensures its posterity. Once again it is *The Marriage of Figaro*, the summation of the classical tradition, which looms largest, eclipsing his other plays as well as all those of the century:

> However abundant the titles of new plays [in the eighteenth century], it is a sad fact that almost none of these have been judged worthy by posterity of a permanent place in the active repertory. The present post-war period has seen the very occasional production of one or other of Regnard's comedies, and of Lesage's *Turcaret*; there has been a genuine vogue for Marivaux, both on stage and in the study; but towering above these lesser names ... is the author of *The Barber of Seville* and *The Marriage of*

Figaro. Without *The Marriage*, Beaumarchais would still have been reckoned a major comic author on the basis of his first Figaro play; but in the second, he took what had been most distinctive in the dramatic literature of the whole century, and brought it all together into a marvellous masterpiece.[18]

Howarth's panoramic view of eighteenth-century theatre not only confirms the importance of the play and the trilogy as a whole in its contemporary setting, but acknowledges its continuing vigour and inexhaustibility, even as the twentieth century draws to a close.

References

1. See, for a comprehensive study of the relations between play and revolution, Claude Petitfrère, *Le Scandale du Mariage de Figaro: Prélude à la Révolution française?* (Paris: Editions complexe, 1989).

2. Jules Michelet, *Histoire de France* (Paris: Abel Pilon, [n.d.]), 19 vols, XIX, 243.

3. Thomas Carlyle, *The French Revolution: A History* (Oxford: Oxford University Press, 1989), p. 62.

4. Elena Polyakova, *Stanislavsky*, trans. Liv Tudge (Moscow: Progress Publishers, 1982), p. 315.

5. Charles Péguy, *Clio, dialogue de l'histoire et de l'âme païenne* in *Oeuvres en prose complètes*, ed. Robert Burac, 3 vols to date (Paris: Gallimard, 1987–), III, 1080.

6. Péguy, p. 1073 (trans. William D. Howarth, *Beaumarchais and the Theatre* [London: Routledge, 1995], p. 215).

7. Ibid., p. 1061.

8. Ibid., pp. 1066–7.

9. Ibid., p. 1072 (trans. Howarth, pp. 214–15).

10. Victor Hugo, Preface to *Cromwell*, in *Dramas*, trans. I. G. Burnham, 4 vols (London: H. S. Nichols, 1895–6), IV, 21.

11. See the appendix to Georges Lemaître, *Beaumarchais* (New York: Alfred A. Knopf, 1949).

12. For a list of all these sequels, see Howarth, p. 190.

13. Germaine Greer, 'Danger Signals: The Sexuality of *Le Nozze di Figaro*', in *Glyndebourne Touring Opera 1996 Programme*, pp. 59–60.

14. Michel Delon, 'Beaumarchais et l'autre révolution', *Europe*, 528 (April 1973): 79–88.

15. Comédie-Française programme, 1989. Quoted in Howarth, p. 194.

16. For details, see Brian N. Morton and Donald C. Spinelli, *Beaumarchais: A Bibliography* (Ann Arbor: Olivia and Hill Press, 1988).

17. Howarth, p. 3.

18. Howarth, p. 223.

The Barber of Seville

ACT I

Count Almaviva, anxious to learn the identity of a beautiful girl he has seen in Madrid, has discovered that her name is Rosine, and that she is living in Seville with an elderly doctor, her guardian Bartholo. The Count is waiting under her window when Figaro appears, his former servant. After many vicissitudes he is now employed as a travelling barber, having been dismissed from his previous employment for writing plays. He declares his willingness to work for his old master again (scene 2).

Bartholo and Rosine appear at the window. He is angry with her for reading a play called *All That Trouble for Nothing*, the kind of modern work he disapproves of. She drops a paper into the street, a note asking the Count to identify himself in a song. Suspecting trouble, Bartholo resolves to marry Rosine as soon as possible, and sends her singing teacher, Don Bazile, to a notary with instructions to arrange their wedding for the next day (scene 5). Figaro must act quickly. He prompts the Count to sing, identifying himself as 'Lindor', and plots to get the Count into the house disguised as a soldier with orders to be billeted there.

ACT II

Having incapacitated the entire staff of the house, Figaro enters Rosine's room and confirms that 'Lindor' loves her. Alarmed that 'Lindor' may do something rash, Rosine hands Figaro a letter to him, explaining that she is motivated only by pure friendship (scene 2). Bartholo comes in, rails against Figaro, who has quickly withdrawn to the next room, and confronts Rosine with his suspicions. In a passionate outburst she admits that she has been talking to Figaro, and challenges Bartholo mockingly, as her gaoler, to brick up the windows (scene 4). Bazile, her singing teacher, arrives and tells Bartholo that the Count has arrived in Seville, looking for Rosine. They agree that the marriage must take place at once. Count Almaviva now appears, pretending to be a drunken soldier, and succeeds, despite Bartholo's watchfulness, in passing a letter to Rosine (scene 14). Bartholo sees it, and demands to read it. Rosine at first refuses, then manages to switch the letter for an innocent piece of paper which she surrenders.

ACT III

The Count now reappears in the house, this time disguised as 'Alonzo'. Bazile, he says, is ill, and he has come to give Rosine her singing lesson instead. Bartholo wants confirmation. In order to gain his trust, 'Alonzo' shows Bartholo Rosine's letter, written, he tells him, to a certain Count Almaviva. Bartholo determines to foil the Count's plans (scene 2). Figaro arrives, and with some difficulty persuades Bartholo to be shaved, leaving 'Alonzo' and Rosine to their singing lesson (scene 5). Bazile returns, but the conspirators contrive to keep him quiet: he leaves, bewildered (scene 11). Bartholo eventually unmasks 'Alonzo' and the Count and Figaro flee.

ACT IV

Bartholo orders Bazile to summon the notary immediately, and hands him the key of the house (scene 1). He then confronts Rosine with the letter she has written, claiming the Count has given it to some other woman he is in love with. Convinced she has been betrayed, Rosine agrees to marry Bartholo and completes her revenge by telling him that the Count and Figaro are planning to return to the house that night (scene 3). When they arrive, Rosine's wounded pride proves a temporary obstacle, but all is explained when the Count throws off his disguise. As they plan to leave, they find that the house is locked, and the ladder they came in by has been taken away (scene 6). Bartholo has gone to fetch a Justice of the Peace and Bazile now arrives with the notary. He is persuaded that there are two women of the same name, and that he should therefore marry this Rosine to the Count. Given money by Count Almaviva, Bazile overcomes his scruples and agrees to act as witness (scene 7). The Justice of the Peace brought by Bartholo to arrest the Count is surprised by the circumstances, but refuses to oppose what he sees as 'an eminently respectable marriage'. As Figaro concludes, when youth and love conspire against an old man, anything he does will be 'all that trouble for nothing'.

One Mad Day or The Marriage of Figaro

ACT I

The scene opens as Figaro, now major-domo to Count Almaviva at the Castle of Aguas Frescas, measures the new bedroom he will share with his bride, Suzanne, maid to the Countess. Suzanne tempers her fiancé's enthusiasm by pointing out that the room they have been given is conveniently close for the Count, who also intends to visit her there. The Count, she explains, wants to revive his old *droit de seigneur*, in exchange for which he has promised her a handsome dowry. Figaro is appalled, and realises he will have to use all his skill to deter the Count and ensure that he and Suzanne are married (scene 2). Another obstacle now appears in the shape of Marceline, the housekeeper, who claims Figaro has promised to marry her if he cannot repay some money he has borrowed from her. She is aided and abetted by Dr Bartholo, her former lover, and tries to stop Figaro's marriage by spreading scandal about the Count's interest in Suzanne (scene 5). Chérubin, the Count's pageboy, arrives and breathlessly confesses his love for the Countess, for Suzanne, and all women in general, managing to steal from Suzanne a ribbon belonging to the Countess. At that moment the Count appears, bent on continuing his pursuit of Suzanne, and Chérubin darts for cover behind an armchair. Then Bazile comes in and the Count runs behind the same armchair, while Chérubin scrambles into the chair, hidden by a dress. When the Count hears Bazile's gossip about Chérubin's passion for the Countess, he springs out, enraged, and describes how he found Chérubin hiding in the bedroom of little Fanchette, the gardener's daughter. As he demonstrates, he once again uncovers the page. Chérubin is dismissed (scene 9). Figaro arrives with a deputation from the household, come to celebrate the Count's renunciation of the old *droit de seigneur*. Seeing the Countess, he grudgingly assents to the celebration, forgives Chérubin, but insists he leave Aguas Frescas at once and take a commission in his regiment. Figaro discreetly tells him to pretend to leave and then come back.

ACT II

The act opens in the Countess's bedroom. As she listens to Suzanne's revelations about the Count's behaviour she reproaches herself that she has bored him by being too loving. Figaro appears and outlines his plans. He has given Bazile an anonymous note warning the Count that a stranger has made an assignation with the Countess while he is out hunting. Suzanne has also agreed to a rendezvous with the Count, meaning to send Chérubin instead, dressed in her clothes (scene 2). Chérubin comes in, and the two women dress him as a girl. They are charmed by his appearance, but he remains melancholy at having to leave the castle. The Count suddenly knocks at the door, and Chérubin scurries into a closet, locking the door (scene 10). The Count shows the Countess the anonymous letter, but as she argues her innocence Chérubin knocks over a chair inside the closet. The Count is enraged and demands the door be unlocked. The Countess, near to fainting, says it is Suzanne, who has in fact entered the bedroom and hidden herself, unseen by either of them. The Count now drags the Countess away to get the necessary implements to break down the closet door, locking the Countess's bedroom as they go. Suzanne pops out of hiding and persuades Chérubin to open the closet door. He jumps from the first floor window and she locks herself in the closet in his place.

   The Count and Countess return, both equally amazed to discover the person in the closet actually is Suzanne and not, as the Countess has desperately confessed, Chérubin. The Count is amazed by the Countess's 'performance' and begs her forgiveness. Thoughtlessly, the Countess admits that Figaro was responsible for the note about her meeting with the unknown stranger (scene 19). Figaro needs all his wits about him to answer the cross-questioning he is subjected to by the Count, particularly when Antonio comes in with news that someone has jumped out of the window and landed on his flowerbed. The

Count, foiled by Figaro's elaborate excuses, is happy to preside over the court assembling to pass judgement on Marceline's claim to Figaro's hand in marriage.

ACT III

The Count, still suspicious, sounds out Figaro about a scheme to take him to England, together with Suzanne, who will then be at the Count's mercy while Figaro is off running errands. Figaro assures the Count he'd have no trouble in England: all you need to manage there is the phrase 'God damn!' He is, however, perfectly happy at Aguas Frescas (scene 5). The Count is keen to favour Marceline's case, but Suzanne excites him by agreeing to their rendez-vous and saying that with the dowry she will receive for the exercise of his *droit de seigneur* Figaro will be able to repay his debt to Marceline (scene 9). This advantage is lost when the Count overhears Suzanne telling Figaro that he has won his case (scene 11). The Count determines that even if Figaro gets the money, his unknown parentage will tell against him in the trial. The court officials assemble, and the case is heard. They argue at length over the wording of the contract, but the problem of Figaro's parentage remains. He is, he claims, not only legitimate but of noble birth, stolen as a baby by gypsies. When he describes a birthmark there is a sensation in court: Marceline recognises him as her long-lost son. His father was Bartholo. The centre of attention and now supported by Figaro, Marceline makes a moving appeal for women to be better treated by men. Her love instantly turns maternal, and the Count is left fuming. Everyone is in league against him.

ACT IV

Figaro and Suzanne talk of their love for one another, relieved that chance has been on their side, and Suzanne promises she will play no more tricks on the Count. Then, as Figaro goes, the Countess arrives and persuades her to help her in a new plot to teach the Count a lesson: Suzanne is to write to him, making an assignation that night under the chestnut trees in the park, and the Countess will go there dressed in Suzanne's clothes. The note is sealed with a pin, which the Count is to send back (scene 3). Preparations for the double wedding of Suzanne to Figaro and Marceline to Bartholo continue, and a party of young girls (Chérubin among them in disguise) arrives to present flowers. Antonio the gardener spots Chérubin, but when Fanchette seems about to tell everyone about the Count's visits to her bedroom, the Count becomes more tolerant: Chérubin can stay for the wedding (scene 5). Amid the festivities Bazile declares his desire to marry Marceline, but is deterred by the thought of Figaro as a step-son (scene 10). Figaro then sees the Count receiving Suzanne's letter and pricking his finger on the pin: he determines to go to the chestnut grove and see what happens. Marceline, to whom he confides his doubts, sets off to warn Suzanne.

ACT V

The act is set at night in the chestnut grove in the park, equipped with two summerhouses or pavilions. Fanchette is waiting to meet Chérubin when Figaro arrives, desperately unhappy and convinced that all women are deceivers. He reflects on his remarkable life (scene 3). He hears someone coming and watches as the Countess appears, dressed as Suzanne. Chérubin leaps in and tries to kiss her, but at that moment the Count arrives and goes to strike him: in the semi-darkness he hits Figaro instead. As the Count flirts with his own wife, excited by the idea that she is Suzanne, Figaro recognises the deception, finds Suzanne herself disguised as the Countess and makes advances to her, suggesting they should take passionate revenge on their unfaithful companions. Suzanne is furious with him, proving her love, and Figaro collapses happily under a hail of blows. Seeing Figaro with (as he believes) the Countess, who runs to hide in one of the pavilions, the Count summons everyone to witness his wife's infidelity. One by one the characters are dragged out, and when the Countess appears from the other pavilion he realises he has been tricked. He again falls on his knees and asks for forgiveness. The play ends with a celebratory song and a dance. As Brid'oison sings in the final couplet, everything ends with a song, happily.

The New Tartuffe or A Mother's Guilt

ACT I

The play opens in a mood of mourning. It is the end of 1790, Aguas Frescas has been sold up, they have invested their capital in South American stock, and the Almaviva family have moved to Paris. Here they have been joined by Bégearss, a 'shifty Irishman' who served in the Count's regiment. Figaro, now the old family retainer, distrusts him as a hypocrite, a new Tartuffe.

It is San Léon's day, and the Countess is mysteriously wistful about a bereavement. The Count himself has been 'gloomy and desperate' since the death of their eldest son, a dissolute young man killed in a duel after an argument over cards. In order to encourage Bégearss to confide in Suzanne, she and Figaro stage a fierce argument in front of the Irishman (scene 3). Comforting her after Figaro's imagined cruelty, Bégearss confesses he means to turn Florestine, the Count's ward and godchild, against Léon, the Count and Countess's second son, who loves her, and to marry her himself. To make this easier, he plans to get both Léon and Figaro sent away. The advantage, he explains to Suzanne, is that Florestine will inherit all the Count's money.

The Count, we discover, suspects that Léon is not his son, but the child of Chérubin, Léon d'Astorga, who died twenty years before fighting with the Count's regiment in which Bégearss also served. Furious with his wife's deception, he now plans to substitute a picture of Chérubin for his own in a bracelet belonging to the Countess: when she sees it, he is convinced, her violent emotions will give her away (scene 9). Bégearss, helping him to replace the bracelet in the Countess's jewel case, makes sure that the Count also discovers a secret compartment containing letters. Léon appears, full of revolutionary idealism and affection for his father, who greets him coldly. He insists he calls him 'Sir' and not 'Father'.

ACT II

Left alone, the Count reads a letter he has found in the jewel case. Twenty years before, he reads, 'at night and without warning', Chérubin returned to Aguas Frescas and forced himself on the Countess. A child was born and christened Léon. Chérubin, in his remorse, had sought death in the most dangerous part of the battlefield, had been mortally wounded, and had written to the Countess in his dying moments on paper stained with his own blood, begging her forgiveness. Even the Count is moved as he reads it (scene 1). When he sees Florestine, however, (he insists she call him 'Father' and not 'Sir') he urges her to marry Bégearss. Moments later, Bégearss suggests to her that the Count may well be her real father (scene 3). While the family enthuses about a new bust of George Washingtron, Figaro begins to set the trap. Thanks to the stupidity of Wilhelm, a German servant employed by Bégearss, he is able to discover Bégearss's more detailed schemes for the Count's money (scene 9). Bégearss is also at work, persuading Florestine that as the Count is her father, Léon is her brother and marriage between them impossible. Florestine is shocked, but grateful to Bégearss for telling her (scene 13). Léon is at a loss to understand her sudden coolness and Figaro warns him that Bégearss must be behind it. But Bégearss also succeeds in alarming Léon with the threat of incest (scene 20). Léon is equally grateful to the Irishman for his warning. Behind the scenes, however, Figaro has succeeded in putting the Count's capital on deposit and the receipts out of Bégearss's reach. The act ends with the Count threatening to send Léon away to join the Knights of Malta, and Figaro with him.

ACT III

In her sitting room, the Countess is trying to understand Florestine's change of heart and the Count's own increasing hostility to Léon. She suspects he knows the truth. She confides her anxieties in Bégearss, who tells her that Florestine is the Count's natural daughter but that he suspects nothing of Léon's parentage. The Count's apparent hostility to Léon, Bégearss assures the Countess, is based only on his fear of an incestuous union (scene 2). The Countess is delighted: a reconciliation with her husband seems possible at last. She agrees to encourage Florestine to marry Bégearss, and looks forward to happiness for the first time in twenty years.

Bégearss, fearing that she may discover the missing letter, tells her she must destroy all her correspondence with Chérubin. She agrees reluctantly, Bégearss refusing to allow her even to re-read any of the letters (scene 6). Plans for the wedding of Florestine to Bégearss go forward. The Count gives Bégearss receipts enabling him to withdraw as much as he likes of the three million in gold that constitutes the family's capital.

ACT IV

In the Countess's sitting room Figaro reflects on the hypocrisy of Bégearss, and when the Irishman comes in there is a bitter quarrel between them. Left alone, Bégearss reveals that he also means to get rid of the Countess, who might thwart his plans by her influence on the Count. To this end he intends to engineer a confrontation in which the Count will antagonise her by his brutality (scene 3). He confides in Suzanne, exulting in his own skill at politics, his means of achieving domination of the household (scene 4). Florestine agrees to marry Bégearss, believing that it will please the Count and make him kinder to Léon, but both children are still distraught at the idea of the marriage. They beg the Countess to argue her son's case with the Count (scene 9). She sends for her husband, and prays for strength to move him (scene 12).

When the Count appears she reminds him of Léon's virtues, contrasting his behaviour with that of their eldest son, but the Count remains cold and furious, finally producing her letter to Chérubin. Mortified, she sees the substituted picture of Chérubin in the bracelet, and faints (scene 13). Having heard shouting from the next room, Léon rushes to help her, the Count now very upset at what he has done (scene 17). The Countess only wishes to die, and Léon promises he will die too. She confesses that she knows the truth about Florestine's birth, and it becomes clear that Bégearss was responsible for the Count finding her letter. The Count admits that Bégearss has the recepits. Figaro shows them another letter, exposing Bégearss's true intentions and runs off to find the clerk to prevent Bégearss from taking all the Count's money. As he goes the others gather round the Countess, supporting her.

ACT V

The scene opens in the great drawing-room we saw in Act I. Bégearss, it transpires, is a double-dyed villain with a wife in Ireland, who is using the Count's money to finance a gang of thieves. Florestine is told that she will never have to marry him, and she, Léon, the Count and Countess are all at last united (scene 3). Figaro comes back with the news that it is too late: Bégearss already has the money, and they will have to trick him out of it by staging a scene between the Count and Figaro (scene 4). Bégearss returns with no idea that anyone knows the truth, and the Count, as arranged, pretends to be about to dismiss Figaro for trying to obstruct Florestine's marriage to the Irishman. The clerk from the bank produces a clause in which the husband agrees to hand over his entire fortune to his new wife. Suspecting nothing, Bégearss admits that the three million is a marriage settlement and not, as he had claimed, a legacy from a relation. He also surrenders two thousand sovereigns for the wedding expenses. Once he has signed his name, the united family turn on him. Trapped, Bégearss challenges Léon to a duel: Léon wants to accept, but is dissuaded by the rest of the family in the name of the more enlightened age. Bégearss swears the Count's remaining estates will be confiscated, but Figaro has intercepted the royal warrant. When he threatens to expose the family for incest, Figaro confirms that the two children are in no way related (scene 7). As the household looks forward to a gentler time of forgiveness, Figaro declines the Count's reward of two thousand sovereigns, pledging loyalty to his master for the rest of his days. There is reward enough in any family in banishing a troublemaker.

SUGGESTIONS FOR FURTHER READING

Biographies

Jean-Pierre Beaumarchais, *Beaumarchais: Le voltigeur des Lumières* (Paris: Gallimard, 1996), published in the Découvertes/Littérature series, offers an informative introduction to Beaumarchais. It is full of reproductions in colour of documents, playbills, scripts and pictures from the family collection, many of which have never been published. The most accessible and recent biographies of Beaumarchais are those by F. Grendel, *Beaumarchais ou la Calomnie* (Paris: Flammarion, 1973), translated into English by R. Greaves as *Beaumarchais: The Man who was Figaro* (London: McDonald & Jane's, 1977), and Cynthia Cox, *The Real Figaro: The Extraordinary Career of Caron de Beaumarchais* (London: Longmans, 1962). These biographies cover both his life and work arguing, as their titles suggest, that the latter is a reflection of the former. For an English selection of Beaumarchais' correspondence see, *For the Good of Mankind: Pierre Augustin de Beaumarchais, Political Correspondence relative to the American Revolution*, ed. and trans. by Antoinette Shewmake (Lanham: University Press of America, 1987). Numerous works detail more specific episodes in Beaumarchais' life. Brian N. Morton and Donald C. Spinelli, *Beaumarchais: a Bibliography* (Ann Arbor: Olivia and Hill Press, 1988) contains information about these and all other aspects of Beaumarchais.

Studies of individual plays

For an introductory study of the *Barber of Seville* see John Dunkley, *Beaumarchais: Le Barbier de Seville* (London: Grant & Cutler, 1991). The *Marriage of Figaro* has attracted more critical attention. See A. R. Pugh, *Beaumarchais: Le Mariage de Figaro: An Interpretation* (London: Macmillan, 1970) and Robert Niklaus, *Beaumarchais: Le Mariage de Figaro* (London: Grant and Cutler, 1983). For *A Mother's Guilt* see Roseann Runte, 'Beaumarchais' *La Mère coupable*', *Kentucky Romance Quarterly*, 29, no. 2 (1982) 181–9 and R. A.

Francis, 'Figaro in changing times: Beaumarchais' *La Mère coupable*', *British Journal for Eighteenth-Century Studies*, 18, no. 1 (1995) 19–31.

General studies of Beaumarchais' theatre

The most recent general study, William D. Howarth, *Beaumarchais and the Theatre* (London: Routledge, 1995) outlines Beaumarchais' theatrical and political background before examining in detail all his plays. For the operatic adaptations of Beaumarchais see Nicholas Till, *Mozart and the Enlightenment: Truth, Virtue and Beauty in Mozart's Operas* (London: Faber & Faber, 1992), in particular the chapter on *Le Nozze di Figaro*: pp. 140–71, and Walter Rex, 'On the "storm music" of *The Barber of Seville*', in *Opera and Enlightenment*, eds. Thomas Bauman and Marita Petzoldt McClymonds (Cambridge: Cambridge University Press, 1995): pp. 243–59. See also Richard Osborne, *Rossini* (London: J. M. Dent, 1993) in particular his chapter, '*Il Barbiere di Siviglia* and the transformation of a tradition': pp. 184–91.